Full Stack Development with JHipster

Build modern web applications and microservices with Spring and Angular

Deepu K Sasidharan
Sendil Kumar N

BIRMINGHAM - MUMBAI

Full Stack Development with JHipster

Commissioning Editor: Merint Mathew
Acquisition Editor: Alok Dhuri
Content Development Editor: Akshada Iyer
Technical Editor: Mehul Singh
Copy Editor: Safis Editing
Project Coordinator: Prajakta Naik
Proofreader: Safis Editing
Indexer: Rekha Nair
Graphics: Jisha Chirayil
Production Coordinator: Arvindkumar Gupta

First published: March 2018

Production reference: 1200318

Published by Packt Publishing Ltd.
Livery Place
35 Livery Street
Birmingham
B3 2PB, UK.

ISBN 978-1-78847-631-7

www.packtpub.com

To my mother, Latha Kumari, and my father, K Sasidharan, for making me who I am.
To my loving wife, Sabitha, for being supportive and patient throughout our journey
together.To my family, friends, colleagues, and the JHipster community.

– Deepu K Sasidharan

To Nellaiyapen, Amutha, Sakthi, and Sahana for their advice, patience, and faith.
To my amigos and all the awesome full-stack developers out there.

– Sendil Kumar N

`mapt.io`

Mapt is an online digital library that gives you full access to over 5,000 books and videos, as well as industry leading tools to help you plan your personal development and advance your career. For more information, please visit our website.

Why subscribe?

- Spend less time learning and more time coding with practical eBooks and Videos from over 4,000 industry professionals

- Improve your learning with Skill Plans built especially for you

- Get a free eBook or video every month

- Mapt is fully searchable

- Copy and paste, print, and bookmark content

PacktPub.com

Did you know that Packt offers eBook versions of every book published, with PDF and ePub files available? You can upgrade to the eBook version at `www.PacktPub.com` and as a print book customer, you are entitled to a discount on the eBook copy. Get in touch with us at `service@packtpub.com` for more details.

At `www.PacktPub.com`, you can also read a collection of free technical articles, sign up for a range of free newsletters, and receive exclusive discounts and offers on Packt books and eBooks.

Foreword

The first time I used JHipster was in 2013. I was an independent consultant at the time, and I used JHipster to demonstrate to my client that you could quickly generate an AngularJS and Spring Boot application. I liked the project so much that I decided to write a mini-book about JHipster for InfoQ. As part of my writing process, I developed a sample application and found bugs in JHipster. I reported these bugs to the project, sometimes with fixes.

JHipster is an incredible project. It gives Java developers the opportunity to generate applications that use modern JavaScript frameworks for their UI, while also using the Spring frameworks they know and love on the backend. The project started as an application generator and has gradually morphed into a development platform that makes it possible to create, build, and deploy both monoliths and microservices. Not only that, but it follows many of its dependent project's best practices. Simply put, it creates code for you, allows you to concentrate on your business logic, and makes your development experience fantastic.

Deepu has been a joy to work with ever since I started reporting issues to JHipster. Not only does he know Angular and React exceptionally well, but he also knows the internals of Yeoman and Node, which helps the project keep its momentum. Whenever there's a new major version of JHipster, Deepu is the one who seems to work the hardest and commit the most code.

I met Sendil Kumar N through the JHipster project as well. Sendil was an instrumental figure in migrating from AngularJS to Angular (initially called Angular 2) in 2016 and optimizing our webpack configuration. He's also been crucial to JHipster's React support and is also a fun guy to be around. I recall fondly meeting him for the first time at Devoxx Belgium 2017.

Deepu and Sendil are staples in the JHipster community, and I'm sure this book will not disappoint you. Both of them always go the extra mile to deliver exceptional code, and I expect the same from their writing.

Become a hip Java Developer and build awesome apps with JHipster!

Matt Raible

Web Developer, Java Champion, and Developer Advocate at Okta
Denver, Colorado, USA

Contributors

About the authors

Deepu K Sasidharan is the co-lead of JHipster. He has been part of the core JHipster team from its inception and is an active contributor to the project. He currently works for XebiaLabs, a DevOps software company, as a senior full-stack product developer. Before that, he worked at TCS as a technical consultant, focusing on innovative solutions for Airlines. He has over 8 years of experience in the architecture, design, and implementation of enterprise web applications and pre-sales. He is also a JavaScript and Web technology expert. When not coding, he likes to read about astronomy and science.

First and foremost, I would like to thank my, wife Sabitha, for her patience and support. I would also like to thank Sendil Kumar N, Julien Dubois, Antonio Goncalves, and the JHipster team for their support. Last but not the least, I would like to thank the entire Packt editorial team for supporting me in this endeavor.

Sendil Kumar N is a part of the JHipster and Webpack team. He is a vivid open source enthusiast and a contributor to many open source projects. He loves to explore and experiment new technologies and frameworks. He is passionate about (re)learning. He currently works at XebiaLabs as a senior full-stack product developer, where he develops the solution for enterprises to design and orchestrate their releases. Before that, he developed ideas for enterprise products and successfully set up a complete DevOps, agile, and cloud team in a more traditional environment.

Thanks to my wife, Sakthi, and daughter, Sahana, for their love and support. I would also like to thank Deepu K Sasidharan, Julien Dubois, Antonio Goncalves, and the entire JHipster team for their support and for this awesome product. Finally, thanks to the Packt team, who were helpful and encouraging.

About the reviewers

Julien Dubois is the creator and lead developer of JHipster. He has more than 20 years of experience as a software developer, mainly in Java and Web technologies. He has a strong knowledge of the Spring Framework, having coauthored a best-selling book on the subject, and has managed SpringSource's France subsidiary.

Today, Julien works as the Chief Innovation Officer at Ippon Technologies, an IT consulting company that has delivered many JHipster-based applications to its clients worldwide.

I would like to thank my wife, Aurélie, and our children, Gabrielle, Adrien, and Alice, for their patience during the reviewing of this book and the development of JHipster.

Antonio Goncalves is a senior Java developer expert on distributed systems. Despite being a consultant, he loves to build bonds with the community, so he created the Paris Java User Group and Devoxx France. As a JCP expert member on various JSRs, Antonio uses this expertise to write books on Java EE and to talk at international conferences. For his expertise and all of his work for the Java community, Antonio has been elected Java Champion. Follow him on Twitter at `@agoncal`.

Packt is searching for authors like you

If you're interested in becoming an author for Packt, please visit `authors.packtpub.com` and apply today. We have worked with thousands of developers and tech professionals, just like you, to help them share their insight with the global tech community. You can make a general application, apply for a specific hot topic that we are recruiting an author for, or submit your own idea.

Table of Contents

Preface

This book, *Full Stack development with JHipster*, aims to address the following challenges faced by full-stack developers today:

- There are multitudes of technologies and options out there to learn
- Customer demands have increased and hence time to market has become more stringent
- Client-side frameworks have become complicated and difficult to integrate
- There is so much integration between technologies and concepts that it overwhelms most novice and even proficient developers

JHipster provides a platform for developers to easily create web applications and microservices from scratch, without having to spend a lot of time wiring everything together and integrating technologies together. This frees up time immensely for developers to actually focus on their solution rather than spending time learning and writing boilerplate code. JHipster will help novice and experienced developers to be more productive from day one. It's like pair programming with an entire community.

This book will take you on a journey from zero to hero in full stack development. You will learn to create complex production-ready Spring Boot and Angular web applications from scratch using JHipster and will go on to develop and deploy features and business logic on cloud services. You will also learn about microservices and how to convert a monolithic application into the microservice architecture as it evolves using JHipster. Additionally, you will learn how to make use of the new React support being introduced in JHipster and about various best practices and suggestions from the JHipster community and the core development team.

Who this book is for

Anyone with a basic understanding of building Java web applications and basic exposure to Spring and Angular/React can benefit from using this book to learn how to use JHipster for cutting-edge full-stack development or to improve their productivity by cutting down boilerplate and learning new techniques. The audience can be broadly classified as follows:

- Full stack web app developers who want to reduce the amount of boilerplate they write and save time, especially for greenfield projects.
- Backend developers who want to learn full stack development with Angular or React
- Full-stack developers who want to learn microservice development
- Developers who want to jump-start their full stack web application or microservice development
- Developers who want to quickly prototype web applications or microservices

What this book covers

Chapter 1, *Introduction to Modern Web Application Development*, introduces two widely used full-stack web application development architectures. It also lays out commonly faced challenges in full stack web application development.

Chapter 2, *Getting Started with JHipster*, introduces the JHipster platform. It will also give the reader a brief overview of different server-side, client-side, and DB technology options offered by JHipster. This chapter will also provide instructions to install and use JHipster and various tools and options supported by it.

Chapter 3, *Building Monolithic Web Applications with JHipster*, guides the user through the creation of a production-ready Spring boot and Angular web applications from scratch using JHipster and will take the reader through the generated code, screens, and concepts.

Chapter 4, *Entity Modeling with JHipster Domain Language*, introduces the reader to JHipster domain language (JDL) and will teach build business logic with entity modeling and entity creation using JDL and JDL studio.

Chapter 5, *Customization and Further Development*, guides the reader through further development of the generated application. It will also teach how to the reader more about using technologies such as Angular, Bootstrap, Spring Security, Spring MVC REST, and Spring Data.

Chapter 6, *Testing and Continuous Integration*, guides the reader through testing and setting up a continuous integration pipeline using Jenkins.

Chapter 7, *Going into Production*, shows the reader how to use Docker and how to build and package the app for production. It will also introduce the reader to some of the production cloud deployment options supported by JHipster.

Chapter 8, *Introduction to Microservice Server-Side Technologies*, gives an overview of different options available in the JHipster microservice stack.

Chapter 9, *Building Microservices with JHipster*, guides the reader through converting a JHipster monolith web application into a full-fledged microservice architecture with a Gateway, Registry, monitoring console, and multiple microservices. It will also guide the reader through the generated code and components such as JHipster registry, JHipster console, API gateway, and JWT.

Chapter 10, *Working with Microservices*, guides the reader through running the generated applications locally and creating domain entities for the microservice architecture using JHipster domain language.

Chapter 11, *Deploying with Docker Compose*, introduces the reader to advanced local and cloud deployment options for microservices. It will also guide the user through local deployment and testing of the generated microservice stack using Docker Compose and JHipster.

Chapter 12, *Deploying to the Cloud with Kubernetes*, guides the user through the Google cloud deployment of the generated microservice stack using Kubernetes and JHipster.

Chapter 13, *Using React for the Client-Side*, takes the user through generating an application with React on the client side instead of Angular using JHipster.

Chapter 14, *Best Practices with JHipster*, summarizes what the reader has learned so far and will suggest best practices and next steps to utilize the skills learned.

To get the most out of this book

To get the most out of this book, you will need to know basics of the following technologies:

- Web technologies (HTML, JavaScript, and CSS)
- Java 8
- Basics of the Spring Framework
- Basic understanding of SQL databases
- Build tools (Maven or Gradle)
- npm or Yarn

It will also be easier if you are familiar with using technologies such as Docker and Kubernetes, as it will help you grasp some of the chapters easily.

You will also need JDK8, Git, Docker, and NodeJS installed; your favorite web browser; a terminal application; and your favorite code editor/IDE.

Download the example code files

You can download the example code files for this book from your account at www.packtpub.com. If you purchased this book elsewhere, you can visit www.packtpub.com/support and register to have the files emailed directly to you.

You can download the code files by following these steps:

1. Log in or register at www.packtpub.com.
2. Select the **SUPPORT** tab.
3. Click on **Code Downloads & Errata**.
4. Enter the name of the book in the **Search** box and follow the onscreen instructions.

Once the file is downloaded, please make sure that you unzip or extract the folder using the latest version of:

- WinRAR/7-Zip for Windows
- Zipeg/iZip/UnRarX for Mac
- 7-Zip/PeaZip for Linux

The code bundle for the book is also hosted on GitHub at `https://github.com/PacktPublishing/Full-Stack-Development-with-JHipster`. In case there's an update to the code, it will be updated on the existing GitHub repository.

We also have other code bundles from our rich catalog of books and videos available at `https://github.com/PacktPublishing/`. Check them out!

Conventions used

There are a number of text conventions used throughout this book.

`CodeInText`: Indicates code words in text, database table names, folder names, filenames, file extensions, pathnames, dummy URLs, user input, and Twitter handles. Here is an example: "At the backend, modify the `save` method of `ProductOrderService.java` to create an Invoice and Shipment for the `ProductOrder` and save them all."

A block of code is set as follows:

```
entity Product {
    name String required
    description String
    price BigDecimal required min(0)
    size Size required
    image ImageBlob
}

enum Size {
    S, M, L, XL, XXL
}

entity ProductCategory {
    name String required
    description String
}
```

When we wish to draw your attention to a particular part of a code block, the relevant lines or items are set in bold:

```
entity ProductOrder {
    placedDate Instant required
    status OrderStatus required
    invoiceId Long
    code String required
}
```

Any command-line input or output is written as follows:

```
> cd invoice
> ./gradlew
```

Bold: Indicates a new term, an important word, or words that you see onscreen. For example, words in menus or dialog boxes appear in the text like this. Here is an example: "You can alternatively test this via your **Gateway** application. Log in to our **Gateway** application and then navigate to **Administration | Gateway**."

Warnings or important notes appear like this.

Tips and tricks appear like this.

Get in touch

Feedback from our readers is always welcome.

General feedback: Email feedback@packtpub.com and mention the book title in the subject of your message. If you have questions about any aspect of this book, please email us at questions@packtpub.com.

Errata: Although we have taken every care to ensure the accuracy of our content, mistakes do happen. If you have found a mistake in this book, we would be grateful if you would report this to us. Please visit www.packtpub.com/submit-errata, selecting your book, clicking on the Errata Submission Form link, and entering the details.

Piracy: If you come across any illegal copies of our works in any form on the Internet, we would be grateful if you would provide us with the location address or website name. Please contact us at copyright@packtpub.com with a link to the material.

If you are interested in becoming an author: If there is a topic that you have expertise in and you are interested in either writing or contributing to a book, please visit authors.packtpub.com.

Reviews

Please leave a review. Once you have read and used this book, why not leave a review on the site that you purchased it from? Potential readers can then see and use your unbiased opinion to make purchase decisions, we at Packt can understand what you think about our products, and our authors can see your feedback on their book. Thank you!

For more information about Packt, please visit packtpub.com.

1
Introduction to Modern Web Application Development

According to the Stack Overflow developer survey 2017 (`https://insights.` `stackoverflow.com/survey/2017#developer-profile-specific-developer-types`), *full-stack web developer* is the most popular developer title. The software industry defines a full-stack developer as someone who can work on different areas of an application stack. The term stack refers to different components and tools that make up an application.

In terms of web application development, the stack can be broadly classified into two areas—**frontend** and **backend** stack or **client-side** and **server-side** stack. Frontend generally refers to the part that is responsible for rendering the user interface, and backend refers to the part that is responsible for the business logic, database interactions, user authentication, server configuration, and so on. A full-stack Java web application developer is expected to work on both frontend and backend technologies, ranging from writing HTML/JavaScript for the user interface to writing Java class files for business logic and SQL queries for database operations as required.

With an ever-evolving software architecture landscape, the scope of technologies that a full-stack web developer is expected to work has increased tremendously. It is no longer enough that we can write HTML and JavaScript to build a user interface, we are expected to know client-side frameworks such as Angular, React, VueJS, and so on. It is also not enough that we are proficient in enterprise Java and SQL, we are expected to know server-side frameworks such as Spring, Hibernate, Play, and so on.

In this chapter, we will introduce the following topics:

- Modern full-stack web development
- Web architecture patterns
- Choosing the right pattern

Modern full-stack web development

If we were to even begin discussing the life of a full-stack developer, it would be worthy of a whole book by itself – so let's leave that for another day.

Let's look at a user story about a full-stack Java web application and see what is involved.

Let's use an example of developing a user management module for a typical Java web application. Let's assume that you would be writing unit test cases for the all the code hence we won't detail them out here:

- You would start by designing the architecture for the feature. You would decide on the plugins and frameworks to use, patterns to follow, and so on.
- You will be modeling the domain model for the feature depending on the database technology used.
- Then, you would create server-side code and database queries to persist and fetch data from the database.
- Once the data is ready you would implement server-side code for any business logic.
- Then, you would implement an API that can be used to provide data for the presentation over an HTTP connection.
- You would write integration tests for the API.
- Now, since the backend is ready, you would start writing frontend code in JavaScript or a similar technology.
- You would write client-side services to fetch data from the backend API.
- You would write client-side components to display the data on a web page.
- You would build the page and style it as per the design provided.
- You would write automated end to end tests for the web page.
- It is not done yet. Once you have tested everything works locally you would create pull requests or check-in the code to the version control system used.
- You would wait for the continuous integration process to verify everything, and fix anything that is broken.

- Once everything is green and the code is accepted, typically you would start the deployment of this feature to a staging or acceptance environment, either on-premises or to a cloud provider. If it is the latter you would be expected to be familiar with the cloud technologies used as well. You would also be upgrading the database schema as necessary and writing migration scripts when required.

- Once the feature is accepted you might be responsible for deploying it into the production environment in a similar way, and troubleshoot issues where necessary. In some teams, you might swap the steps with other team members so that you would be deploying a feature developed by your co-worker while s/he deploys yours.

- You might also be responsible, along with your co-workers, to make sure the production environment is up and running including the database, virtual machines, and so on.

As you can see it is no easy task. The range of responsibilities spawns across making stylesheet updates on the client side to running database migration scripts on a virtual machine in the production cloud service. If you are not familiar enough, this would be a herculean task and you would soon be lost in the vast ocean of frameworks, technologies, and design patterns out there.

Full stack development is not for the faint-hearted. It takes a lot of time and effort in keeping yourself up to date with various technologies and patterns in multiple disciplines of software development. Following are some of the common problems you might face as a full-stack Java developer:

- Client-side development is not just about writing plain HTML and JavaScript anymore. It is becoming as complex as server-side development with build tools, transpilers, frameworks, and patterns.

- There is a new framework almost every week in the JavaScript world and if you are coming from a Java background it could be very overwhelming for you.

- Container technologies such as Docker revolutionalized the software industry but they also introduced a lot of new stuff to learn and keep track of, such as orchestration tools, container management tools, and so on.

- Cloud services are growing day by day. To stay on track you would have to familiarize yourself with their API and related orchestration tools.

- Java server-side technologies have also undergone a major shift in recent times with the introduction of JVM languages such as Scala, Groovy, Kotlin, and so on, forcing you to keep yourself up to date with them. On the other side, server-side frameworks are becoming more feature rich and hence more complex.

The most important thing of all is the pain of making sure all of these work together well when required. It will need a lot of configuration, some glue code, and endless cups of coffee.

 Transpilers are source-to-source compilers. Whereas a traditional compiler compiles from source to binary, a transpiler compiles from one type of source code to another type of source code. TypeScript and CoffeeScript are excellent examples of this, both compile down to JavaScript.

It's very easy to get lost here and this is where technologies such as JHipster and Spring Boot step in to help. We will see the details in later chapters but in short, they help by providing the wiring between moving parts so that you only need to concentrate on writing business code. JHipster also helps by providing the abstractions to deploy and manage the application to various cloud providers.

Web architecture patterns

The full-stack landscape is further complicated by the different web architecture patterns commonly used these days. The widely used web application architecture patterns today can be broadly classified into two—**monolithic architecture** and **microservice architecture**, the latter being the new kid on the block.

Let's take a look at the following in detail:

- Monolithic architecture
- Microservice architecture

Monolithic web architecture

A monolithic architecture is the most used pattern for web applications due to its simplicity in development and deployment. Though the actual moving parts will differ from application to application, the general pattern remains the same. In general, a monolithic web application may do the following:

- It can support different clients such as desktop/mobile browsers and native desktop/mobile applications
- It can expose APIs for third-party consumption
- It can integrate with other applications over REST/SOAP web services or message queues
- It can handle HTTP requests, execute business logic, access a database, and can exchange data with other systems
- It can run on web application containers such as Tomcat, JBoss, and so on
- It can be scaled vertically by increasing the power of the machines it runs on or scaled horizontally by adding additional instances behind load balancers

 REST (Representational State Transfer) relies on a stateless, client-server, cacheable communications protocol. HTTP is the most commonly used protocol for REST. It is a lightweight architectural style in which RESTful HTTP communication is used to transfer data between a client and server or between two systems.

SOAP (Simple Object Access Protocol) is a messaging protocol using HTTP and XML. It is widely used in SOAP web services to transfer data between two different systems.

An example of a typical monolithic web application architecture would be as follows:

Let's imagine an online hotel reservation system that takes reservation orders online from customers, verifies the room availability, verifies the payment option, makes the reservation, and notifies the hotel. The application consists of several layers and components including a client-side app, which builds a nice rich user interface, and several other backend components responsible for managing the reservations, verifying payment, notifying customers/hotels, and so on.

The application will be deployed as a single monolithic **Web Application Archive (WAR)** file that runs on a web application container such as Tomcat and will be scaled horizontally by adding multiple instances behind an Apache web server acting as a load balancer. Take a look at the following diagram:

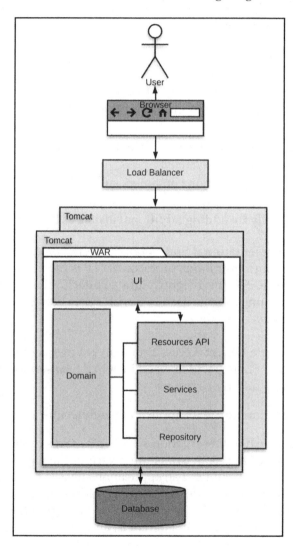

The advantages of a monolithic web application architecture are as detailed here:

- Simpler to develop as the technology stack is uniform throughout all layers.
- Simpler to test as the entire application is bundled in a single package making it easier to run integration and end-to-end tests.
- Simpler and faster to deploy, as you only have one package to worry about.
- Simpler to scale as you can multiply the number of instances behind a load balancer to scale out.
- Requires a smaller team to maintain the application.
- Team members share more or less the same skill set.
- The technical stack is simpler and most of the times easier to learn.
- Initial development is faster hence making time to market faster.
- Requires simpler infrastructure. Even a simple application container or JVM will be sufficient to run the application.

The disadvantages of a monolithic web application architecture are as detailed here:

- Components are tightly coupled together resulting in unwanted side effects such as changes to one component causing a regression in another and so on.
- Becomes complex and huge over time resulting in slow development turnaround. New features will take more time to develop and refactoring of existing features will be more difficult due to tight coupling.
- The entire application needs to be redeployed for any changes.
- Is less reliable due to tightly coupled modules. A small issue in a service might break the entire application.
- Newer technology adoption is difficult as entire application needs to be migrated. Incremental migration is not possible most of the time. Hence many monolithic applications end up having an outdated technology stack.
- Critical services cannot be scaled individually resulting in increased resource usage as the entire application will need to be scaled.
- Huge monolith applications will have a higher start-up time and high resource usage in terms of CPU and memory.
- Teams will be more interdependent and it will be challenging to scale the teams.

Microservice architecture

The microservice architecture has gained momentum in recent years, and is gaining popularity in web application development due to its modularity and scalability. Microservice architecture can offer almost all the features of a monolith that we saw in the earlier section. Additionally, it offers many more features and flexibility, and hence is often considered a superior choice for complex applications. Unlike the monolithic architecture, it's quite difficult to generalize the microservice architecture as it could vary heavily depending on the use case and implementation. But they do share some common traits and they are, in general, the following:

- Microservice components are loosely coupled. Components can be developed, tested, deployed, and scaled independently without disrupting other components.
- Components need not be developed using the same technology stack. This means a single component can choose its own technology stack and programming language.
- They often utilize advanced features such as service discovery, circuit breaking, load balancing, and so on.
- Microservice components are mostly lightweight and they do a specific functionality. For example, an authentication service will only care about authenticating a user into the system.
- Often has an extensive monitoring and troubleshooting setup.

An example of a microservice web application architecture would be as follows:

Let's imagine a huge online e-commerce system where customers can go through categories of merchandise, maintain favorites, add items to a shopping cart, make and track orders, and so on. The system has inventory management, customer management, multiple payment modes, order management, and so on. The application consists of several modules and components including a UI gateway application, which builds a nice rich user interface and also handles user authentication and load balancing, and several other backend applications responsible for managing the inventory, verifying payment, and managing orders. It also has performance monitoring and automatic failover for services.

The application will be deployed as multiple executable WAR files in Docker containers hosted by a cloud provider. Take a look at the following diagram:

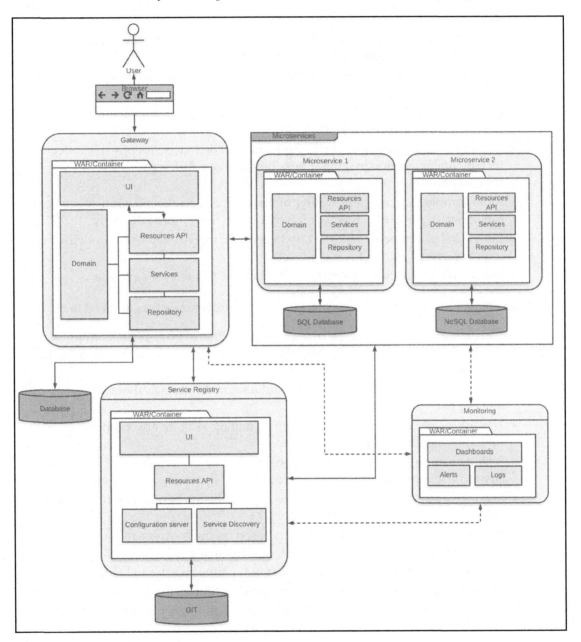

The advantages of a microservice web application architecture are as detailed here:

- Loosely coupled components resulting in better isolation, easier to test and faster to startup.
- Faster development turnaround and better time to market. New features can be built faster and existing features can be easily refactored.
- Services can be deployed independently making the application more reliable and make patching easier.
- Issues, such as a memory leak in one of the services, are isolated and hence will not bring down the entire application.
- Technology adoption is easier, components can be independently upgraded in incremental migration making it possible to have a different stack for each component.
- More complex and efficient scaling models can be established. Critical services can be scaled more effectively. Infrastructure is used more efficiently.
- Individual components will start up faster making it possible to parallelize and improve overall start-up.
- Teams will be less dependent on each other. Best suited for agile teams.

The disadvantages of a microservice web application architecture are as detailed here:

- More complex in terms of the overall stack as different components might have different technology stacks forcing the team to invest more time in keeping up with them.
- Difficult to perform end-to-end tests and integration tests as there are more moving parts in the stack.
- The entire application is more complex to deploy as there are complexities with containers and virtualization involved.
- Scaling is more efficient but setting upscaling is more complex as it would require advanced features such as service discovery, DNS routing, and so on.
- Requires a larger team to maintain the application as there are more components and more technologies involved.
- Team members share varying skill sets based on the component they work on, making replacements and knowledge sharing harder.
- The technical stack is complex and most of the times harder to learn.
- Initial development time will be higher making time to market slower.
- Requires a complex infrastructure. Most often will require containers (Docker) and multiple JVM or app containers to run on.

Choosing the right pattern

When starting a new project, it is always difficult to choose an architecture pattern these days. There are so many factors to take into account and it is easy to get confused with all the **hype** around different patterns and technologies (see **Hype Driven Development** (`https://blog.daftcode.pl/hype-driven-development-3469fc2e9b22`)). Following are some general guidelines on when to choose a monolithic web application architecture over a microservice architecture and vice versa.

When to choose a monolithic architecture

The following list can be used as a general guide when choosing a monolithic architecture. This is not a definitive list but gives an idea of when to go with a monolithic architecture over microservices:

- When the **application scope** is small and well defined, and you are sure that the application will not grow tremendously in terms of features. For example, a blog, a simple online shopping website, a simple CRUD application, and so on.
- When the **team size** is small, say less than eight people (it's not a hard limit but rather practical).
- When the **average skill set** of the team is either novice or intermediate.
- When **time to market** is critical.
- When you do not want to spend too much on **infrastructure**, monitoring, and so on.
- When your **user base** is rather small and you do not expect them to grow. For example, an enterprise app targeting a specific set of users.

In most practical use cases, a monolithic architecture would suffice. Read on to the next section to see when you should consider a microservice architecture over monolithic.

When to choose a microservice architecture

The following list can be used as a general guide when choosing a microservice architecture. This is not a definitive list but gives an idea of when to go with microservices architecture over a monolith. Please note that unlike choosing a monolithic architecture, the decision here is more complex and may involve cross consideration among many of the following points:

- When the **application scope** is large and well defined and you are sure that the application will grow tremendously in terms of features. For example, an online e-commerce store, a social media service, a video streaming service with a large user base, an API provider, and so on.
- When the **team size** is large, there must be enough members to effectively develop individual components independently.
- When the **average skill set** of the team is good and team members are confident about advanced microservice patterns.
- When **time to market** is not critical. The microservice architecture will take more time to get right up front.
- When you are ready to spend more on **infrastructure**, monitoring, and so on, in order to improve the product quality.
- When your **user base** is huge and you expect them to grow. For example, a social media application targeting users all over the world.

Though a monolithic architecture would suffice in most cases, investing up front in a microservice architecture will reap long-term benefits when the application grows huge.

 For more on these architecture patterns, you can refer to `https://articles.microservices.com/monolithic-vs-microservices-architecture-5c4848858f59`.

Summary

So far, we've seen what full stack development is and compared two of the most prominent architecture patterns. We also learned advantages and disadvantages of monolithic and microservice architecture, which helps us to choose the right pattern for our use cases at hand.

In the next chapter, we will take a deep dive into the JHipster platform and look at all the options it provides. We will also learn how to install JHipster and set up our tools and development environment.

2
Getting Started with JHipster

JHipster is a development platform that helps you go from zero to hero! JHipster can help you to create beautiful web applications and complex microservice architectures in a jiffy. JHipster also offers various tools to develop the application further using business entities, and deploy it to various cloud services and platforms. At its core, JHipster is a Yeoman generator that creates Spring Boot and Angular/React based applications. It can create monolithic architecture as well as microservice architecture with every feature working out-of-the-box.

In this chapter, we will cover the following topics:

- Why use JHipster and how it helps compared to traditional development approaches
- What is the goal of JHipster?
- The various server-side and client-side technology options available in JHipster
- Preparation of a development environment
- Installation of JHipster and required dependencies

 Yeoman (`http://yeoman.io`) is a scaffolding tool that helps you to create code generators. You can use it to create any kind of application generator with the help of the built-in template engine and tools.

Why JHipster?

If you are wondering why you should be using JHipster, then just imagine the following scenario. You are tasked to build a web application, let us say a blog with an Angular frontend and a Java backend, with features for users to create blog posts and be able to display blog posts based on user permissions. You are also asked to build administrative modules such as user management, monitoring, and so on. Finally, you have to test and deploy the application to a cloud service.

If you are approaching this challenge the traditional way you will most probably be doing the following steps. Let's skip the details for simplicity. So, the steps would be as follows:

1. Design an architecture stack and decide on various libraries to use (let's say you choose Spring Framework for the backend, with Spring Security and Spring MVC)
2. Create an application base with all the technologies wired together (for example, you will have to make sure the authentication flow between the Angular client side and Spring Security is wired properly)
3. Write a build system for the application (let's say you used webpack to build the Angular client side and Gradle to build the server side)
4. Write integration tests and unit tests for the base
5. Create administrative modules
6. Design business entities and create them with the Angular client side and Java server side with test coverage
7. Write all the business logic, test the application, and deploy it

While this approach definitely works, for this simple application you would have spent anywhere between four to six weeks depending on the team size. Now, more than 70% of the effort would have been spent on writing boilerplate code and making sure all the libraries work well together. Now, would you believe me if I say that you could develop, test, and deploy this application in less than 30 minutes using JHipster? Yes, you can, while still getting high-quality production grade code with lots of extra bells and whistles. We will see this in action in our next chapter where we will build a real-world application using JHipster.

Goal and adoption of JHipster

The goal of JHipster is to provide developers a platform where you can focus on your business logic rather than worrying about wiring different technologies together, and also that provides a great developer experience. Of course, you can use available boilerplate within your organization or from the internet and try to wire them up together, but then you will be wasting a lot of time re-inventing the wheel. With JHipster, you will create a modern web application or microservice architecture with all the required technologies wired together and working out-of-the-box, such as the following:

- A robust and high-performance Spring Framework-based Java stack on the backend
- A rich mobile-first frontend with Angular or React supported by Bootstrap
- A battle-tested microservice architecture unifying Netflix OSS, Elastic stack, and Docker
- A great tooling and development workflow using Maven/Gradle, webpack, and Yarn/NPM
- Out-of-the-box continuous integration using Jenkins, Travis, or GitLab
- Excellent Docker support and support for orchestration tools such as Kubernetes, Rancher, and Openshift out-of-the-box
- Out-of-the-box support for various cloud deployments
- Above all, great code with lots of best practices and industry standards at your fingertips

 Netflix OSS (`https://netflix.github.io`) is a collection of open source tools and software produced by the NETFLIX, INC team geared toward microservice architecture. Elastic stack (`https://www.elastic.co/products`) (formerly known as **ELK stack**) is a collection of software tools, which help in monitoring and analytics of microservices developed by the Elasticsearch (`https://www.elastic.co`) team.

JHipster has been steadily increasing in popularity as Spring Boot and Angular gained momentum, and lots of developers have started to adopt them as the de facto frameworks for web development. As per official statistics at the time of writing (beginning of 2018), there are more than 5,000 applications generated per month and JHipster was installed around 1 million times. It has more than 400 contributors with official contributions from Google, RedHat, Heroku, and so on.

Introduction to technologies available

JHipster supports an incredible number of modern web application technologies out of the box. Some of them are used as the base or core of the generated application while some technologies are opt-in via choices made during application generation. Let us see the different technologies supported mainly for monolithic applications in brief:

- Client-side technologies
- Server-side technologies
- Database options

There are many more technologies supported and we will look at them in later chapters when we touch upon microservices.

Client-side technologies

The role of client-side technologies in full-stack development has grown from just using JavaScript for client-side validations, to writing full-blown, single page applications using client-side MVVM frameworks. The frameworks and toolchains used have become complex and overwhelming for developers who are new to the client-side landscape. Fortunately for us, JHipster provides support for most of the following, widely used, client-side technologies. Let us take a brief look and get familiar with the important tools and technologies that we will use. No need to worry if it is overwhelming, we will take a deeper look at some of the more important ones during the course of the book.

HTML5 and CSS3

Web technologies, especially HTML and CSS, have undergone major updates and are becoming better day by day due to excellent support in modern browsers.

HTML5

HTML5 (https://developer.mozilla.org/en-US/docs/Web/Guide/HTML/HTML5) is the latest of the **HTML (HyperText Markup Language)** standard, which introduces new elements, attributes, and behaviors. The term is used to collectively refer to all the HTML technologies used to build modern web applications. This iteration introduced support for features such as offline storage, WebSockets, web workers, WebGL, and more. JHipster also uses best practices from the HTML5 Boilerplate (https://html5boilerplate.com).

HTML5 Boilerplate is a collection of modern technologies, default settings, and best practices that kick-start modern web development faster.

CSS3

CSS3 (https://developer.mozilla.org/en-US/docs/Web/CSS/CSS3) is the latest of the **Cascading Style Sheets** (CSS) specification. It adds support for media query, animations, flexbox, round corners, and a lot more. CSS3 makes it possible to natively animate elements, apply special effects, apply filters, and so on to get rid of the many JavaScript hacks that were used earlier.

Flexible Box, or flexbox, is a layout mode (https://developer.mozilla.org/en-US/docs/Web/CSS/Layout_mode) that can be used instead of the box model used traditionally. This allows having a flexible box model making responsive layouts easier to handle without floats and margin collapse issues.

Sass

Syntactically awesome style sheets (**Sass**) (http://sass-lang.com) is a CSS extension language. It is preprocessed and converted to CSS during compile time. It has similar semantics to CSS and is 100% compatible with all versions of CSS. It additionally supports advanced features such as nested syntax, variables, mixins, inheritance, partials, and so on. Sass makes it possible to reuse CSS and to write maintainable style sheets.

Bootstrap

Bootstrap (https://getbootstrap.com) is a responsive UI framework for modern web development. It offers a mobile-first approach for web development with utilities and UI components that are fully responsive. Bootstrap 4 is the latest version, uses flexbox for layout, and is completely written in Sass, which makes it easier to customize. Bootstrap supports a 12-column grid framework, which lets you build responsive web pages with ease. JHipster uses ng-bootstrap (https://ng-bootstrap.github.io) so that pure Angular components are used instead of the ones provided by Bootstrap, which are built using JQuery, and Bootstrap is used only for styling.

Mobile first web development is an approach where the UX/UI is designed for smaller screen sizes first thus forcing you to focus on the most important data/elements to be presented. This design is then gradually enhanced for bigger screen sizes making the end result responsive and efficient.

MVVM framework

Model-View-View-Model (**MVVM**) is an architectural pattern originally developed by Microsoft. It helps to abstract or separate the client side (GUI) development from the server side (data model). The view model is an abstraction of the View and represents the state of data in the Model. With JHipster, you can choose between Angular and React as the client-side framework.

Angular

AngularJS (`https://angularjs.org`) (version 1.x) is a client-side MVVM framework, maintained by Google, which helps to develop **Single Page Applications** (**SPA**). It is based on a declarative programming model and it extends standard HTML with the ability to add additional behavior, elements, and attributes through directives.

Angular (`https://angular.io`)(version 2 and above) is a complete rewrite of the framework and hence is not backward compatible with AngularJS. Angular is written in TypeScript and recommends the use of TypeScript to write Angular applications as well. Angular removed some of the concepts that were used in AngularJS such as scope, controller, factory, and so on. It also has a different syntax for binding attributes and events. Another major difference is that the Angular library is modular and hence you can choose the modules that you need, to reduce bundle size. Angular also introduced advanced concepts such as **AOT** (**Ahead of Time Compilation**), lazy loading, reactive programming, and so on.

TypeScript is a superset of ECMAScript 6 (ES6 - version 6 of JavaScript) and is backward compatible with ES5. It has additional features such as static typing, generics, class attribute visibility modifiers, and so on. Since TypeScript is a superset of ES6, we can also use ES6 features (`http://es6-features.org`) such as modules, lambdas (arrow functions), generators, iterators, string templates, reflection, spread operators, and so on.

React

React (`https://reactjs.org`) is not a full-fledged MVVM framework. It is a JavaScript library for building client-side views or user interfaces. It is developed and backed by Facebook and has a vibrant community and ecosystem behind it. React follows an HTML in JS approach and has a special format called **JSX** to help us write React components. Unlike Angular, React doesn't have too many concepts or APIs to learn and hence is easier to start with, but React only cares about rendering the UI and hence to get similar functionality offered by Angular, we would have to pair React with other libraries like React Router (`https://reacttraining.com/react-router`), Redux (`https://redux.js.org`), MobX (`https://mobx.js.org`), and so on. JHipster uses React along with Redux and React Router and similar to Angular, JHipster uses TypeScript for React as well. But this is optional as React can be written using JavaScript as well, preferably ES6 (`http://es6-features.org`). React is fast to render due to its use of a virtual DOM (`https://reactjs.org/docs/faq-internals.html`) to manipulate a view instead of using the actual browser DOM.

 If you are starting a new project, it is best to choose either Angular or React as they are well maintained. However, with older versions of JHipster, AngularJS 1.x was also offered as an option but it is becoming legacy and will soon be discontinued in JHipster 5.x. JHipster will provide an official blueprint for those who are still interested in using AngularJS 1.x. Just run the command `jhipster --blueprint generator-jhipster-angularjs` to use it.

Build tools

The client side has evolved a lot and become as complex as the server side, hence it requires a lot more tools in your toolbelt to produce optimized results. You would need a build tool to transpile, minimize, and optimize your HTML, JavaScript, and CSS code. One of the most popular is Webpack. JHipster uses Webpack for Angular and React.

Webpack

Webpack (`https://webpack.js.org`) is a module bundler with a very flexible loader/plugin system. Webpack walks through the dependency graph and passes it through the configured loaders and plugins. With Webpack, you can transpile TypeScript to JavaScript, minimize, and optimize CSS and JS, compile Sass, revision, hash your assets, and so on. Webpack can remove dead code in a process called **tree shaking**, thus reducing bundle size. Webpack is configured using a configuration file and can be run from the command line or via NPM/YARN scripts.

BrowserSync

BrowserSync (`https://browsersync.io`) is a NodeJS tool that helps in browser testing by synchronizing file changes and interactions of the web page across multiple browsers and devices. It provides features such as auto-reload on file changes, synchronized UI interactions, scrolling, and so on. It integrates with Webpack/GulpJS to provide a productive development setup. It makes testing a web page on multiple browsers and devices super easy.

Testing tools

Gone are the days when the client-side code didn't require unit testing. With the evolution of client-side frameworks, the testing possibilities also improved. There are many frameworks and tools available for unit testing, end-to-end testing, and so on. JHipster creates unit tests for client-side code using Karma and Jasmine out-of-the-box and also supports creating end-to-end tests using Protractor.

Karma

Karma (`https://karma-runner.github.io/2.0/index.html`) is a test runner that can execute JavaScript code in real browsers. It creates a web server and executes the test code against the source code. Karma supports multiple testing frameworks such as Jasmine, Mocha, and Qunit, and integrates well with continuous integration tools.

Protractor

Protractor (`http://www.protractortest.org`) is an end-to-end testing framework developed by the Angular team. It was originally intended for Angular and AngularJS applications but it is flexible enough to be used with any framework, such as React, JQuery, VueJS, and so on. Protractor runs e2e tests against real browsers using the Selenium web driver API.

Internationalization

Internationalization (i18n) is a very important feature these days and JHipster supports this out-of-the-box. Multiple languages can be chosen during application creation. On the client side, this is achieved by storing GUI text in JSON files per language and using an Angular/React library to dynamically load this based on the language selected at runtime.

Do you know why internationalization is abbreviated as **i18n**? Because there are 18 characters between **I** and **N**. There are other similarly named abbreviations in web technology, for example, **Accessibility(a11y)**, **Localization (l10n)**, **Globalization (g11n)**, and **Localizability (l12y)**.

Server-side technologies

Server-side technologies in web development have evolved a lot, and with the rise of frameworks such as Spring and Play, the need for Java EE has reduced and opened doors for more feature-rich alternatives, such as Spring Boot, for example. Some of the core technologies such as Hibernate are here to stay, while newer concepts such as JWT, Liquibase, Swagger, Kafka, and WebSockets bring a lot of additional opportunities. Let us take a quick look at some of the important technologies supported by JHipster; we will encounter these later on in the book and will take a deeper look at some of these technologies.

Spring Framework

The Spring Framework (`https://spring.io`) might be the best thing since sliced bread in the Java world. It changed the Java web application landscape for the good. The landscape was monopolized by JavaEE vendors before the rise of Spring and soon after Spring, it became the number one choice for Java web developers, giving JavaEE a run for its money. At its core, Spring is an **Inversion of Control (IoC)** (`https://docs.spring.io/spring/docs/current/spring-framework-reference/core.html#beans`) container providing dependency injection and application context. The main features of Spring or the Spring triangle, combine IoC, **Aspect-Oriented Programming (AOP)** (`https://docs.spring.io/spring/docs/current/spring-framework-reference/core.html#aop`), and technology abstractions together in a consistent way. The framework has numerous modules aimed at different tasks, such as data management, security, REST, web services, and so on. Spring Framework and its modules are free and open source. Let us see some of the important modules in a bit more detail.

IoC is a software design pattern where custom or task-specific code is invoked by a library, rather than the traditional procedural programming approach where custom code calls libraries when required. IoC helps to make the code more modular and extendable. AOP provides another way of thinking about program structure. The unit of modularity is the aspect that enables the modularization of concerns such as transaction management that cut across multiple types and objects.

Spring Boot

Spring Boot (`https://projects.spring.io/spring-boot`) is a widely used solution these days for Java web application development. It has an opinionated convention over configuration approach. It is completely configuration driven and makes using Spring Framework and many other third-party libraries a pleasure. Spring Boot applications are production grade and can just *run* in any environment that has a JVM installed. It uses an embedded servlet container such as Tomcat, Jetty, or Undertow to run the application. It auto-configures Spring wherever possible and has starter POM for many modules and third-party libraries. It does not require any XML configuration and lets you customize autoconfigured beans using Java configuration.

JHipster by default uses Undertow as the embedded server in the applications generated. **Undertow** is very lightweight and faster to start, and is ideal for the development and production of lightweight applications.

Spring Security

Spring Security (`https://projects.spring.io/spring-security`) is the de facto solution for security in a Spring Framework-based application. It provides API and utilities to manage all aspects of security, such as authentication and authorization. It supports a wide range of authentication mechanism such as OAuth2, JWT, Session (Web form), LDAP, **SSO (Single Sign-On)** servers, **JAAS (Java Authentication and Authorization Service)**, Kerberos, and so on. It also has features such as remember me, concurrent session, and so on.

Spring MVC

Spring MVC (`https://docs.spring.io/spring/docs/current/spring-framework-reference/web.html`) is the default solution to work with the Servlet API within Spring applications. It is a request-based system and abstracts the Servlet API to make it easier to design controllers to serve HTTP requests. REST is the de facto standard for designing API endpoints these days and Spring MVC REST is a specific subset that makes it easier to design and implement RESTful services.

Spring data

Spring data (`http://projects.spring.io/spring-data`) is a module that abstracts data access operations for many different data access technologies and databases. It provides a consistent API to work seamlessly with different underlying implementations. This frees us from worrying about the underlying database and data access technology. It has powerful features such as dynamic query generation from method names, custom object mapping abstractions, and so on. Spring data supports working with JPA, MongoDB, Redis, and Elasticsearch to name a few. It also lets you export Spring data repositories as RESTful resources.

Security

In modern web applications, there are multiple ways to implement authentication and authorization. Spring security supports a wide range of mechanisms, as we saw earlier, and JHipster provides support for the following standards.

JWT

JSON Web Token (JWT) (`https://jwt.io`) is an open industry standard for security tokens. JWT authentication works by a server and client passing and verifying claims. A server generates a JWT token and passes it back to the client when user credentials are successfully validated. The client will store this token locally and use it to request protect resources from the server later by passing the token in the request header. This is a stateless authentication mechanism. This is explained in detail in Chapter 9, *Building Microservices with JHipster*.

Session

Session-based authentication is the traditional web form-based authentication mechanism where the server creates and maintains a session for the validated user credentials. This is stateful and normally is not very scalable unless you use a distributed HTTP session, which is possible using a distributed cache such as Hazelcast or using the session replication features of a dedicated web server or load balancer. JHipster adds a lot of features on top of the standard mechanism, such as secured tokens that are stored in DB, and can be invalidated, used in remember me mechanisms, and so on.

OAuth2

OAuth2 (`https://developer.okta.com/blog/2017/06/21/what-the-heck-is-oauth`) is a protocol for stateless authentication and authorization. The protocol allows applications to obtain limited access to user accounts on services. User authentication is delegated to a service, typically an OAuth2 server. OAuth2 is more complicated to set up when compared to the previously mentioned mechanisms. JHipster supports setting up OAuth with **OpenID Connect** (OIDC) and can use Keycloak (`https://keycloak.org`) or Okta (`https://developer.okta.com/blog/2017/10/20/oidc-with-jhipster`) out of the box.

Build tools

JHipster supports using either Maven or Gradle as the build tool for the server-side code. Both are free and open source.

Maven

Maven (`https://maven.apache.org`) is a build automation tool that uses an XML document called `pom.xml` to specify how an application is built and its dependencies. Plugins and dependencies are downloaded from a central server and cached locally. The Maven build file is called a **Project Object Model** (POM) and it describes the build process itself. Maven has a long history and is much more stable and reliable compared to Gradle. It also has a huge ecosystem of plugins.

Gradle

Gradle (`https://gradle.org`) is a build automation tool which uses a Groovy DSL to specify the build plan and dependencies. It is a strong contender rapidly gaining popularity and adoption. Gradle is much more flexible and feature-rich than Maven, making it an ideal choice for very complex build setups. The latest version of Gradle easily surpasses Maven in terms of speed and features. Another unique advantage of Gradle is the ability to write standard Groovy code in the build script, making it possible to do pretty much everything programmatically. It has great plugin support as well.

Hibernate

Hibernate (`http://hibernate.org`) is the most popular **ORM (Object Relational Mapping)** tool for Java. It helps to map an object-oriented domain model to a relational database scheme using Java annotations. It implements **JPA (Java Persistence API)** and is the go-to provider for a JPA implementation. Hibernate also offers many additional features such as entity auditing, bean validation, and so on. Hibernate automatically generates SQL queries depending on the underlying database semantics and makes it possible to switch the databases of an application very easily. It also makes the application database independent without any vendor lock-in. Hibernate is free and open source software.

Liquibase

Liquibase (`http://www.liquibase.org`) is a free and open source version control tool for the database. It lets you track, manage, and apply database schema changes using configuration files without having to fiddle with SQL. It is database independent and goes well with JPA, making the application database independent. Liquibase can be run from within the application, making database setup and management seamless, and eliminate the need for a DBA for most DB management. Liquibase can also add/remove data to/from a database, making it good for migrations as well.

Caching

Caching is a good practice in software development and it improves the performance of read operations considerably. Caching can be enabled for Hibernate 2nd level cache, and also with Spring Cache abstraction to enable caching at the method level. JHipster supports JCache-compatible Hibernate 2nd level cache provided by EhCache, Hazelcast, and Infinispan.

Ehcache

Ehcache (http://www.ehcache.org) is an open source JCache provider and is one of the most widely used Java caching solutions. It is JCache compatible and is a good choice for applications that are not clustered. For clustered environments, additional Terracotta servers are required. It is stable, fast, and simple to set up.

Hazelcast

Hazelcast (https://hazelcast.org) is an open source distributed in-memory data grid solution. It has excellent support for clustered applications and distributed environments and hence becomes a good choice for caching. While Hazelcast has numerous other features and use-cases, caching remains one of the important ones. It is highly scalable and a good option for microservices due to its distributed nature.

Infinispan

Infinispan (http://infinispan.org) is a distributed cache and key-value store from Red Hat. It is free and open source. It supports clustered environments and is hence a good choice for microservices. It has more features such as in-memory data grids, MapReduce support, and so on.

Swagger

OpenAPI specification (previously known as **Swagger specification**) is an open standard for designing and consuming RESTful web services and API. The OpenAPI specification is a standard founded by a variety of companies including Google, Microsoft, and IBM. The Swagger (https://swagger.io) name is now used for the associated tooling. JHipster supports API-first development model with Swagger code-gen and also supports API visualization with Swagger UI.

Thymeleaf

Thymeleaf (http://www.thymeleaf.org) is an open source Java server-side templating engine with very good integration with Spring. Thymeleaf can be used to generated web pages on the server side, for templating email messages and so on. Although server-side web page templates are slowly losing out to client-side MVVM frameworks, it is still a useful tool if one wants to have something more than a single page application using Angular.

Dropwizard metrics

Dropwizard metrics (http://metrics.dropwizard.io/4.0.0/) is an excellent open source library for measuring the performance of your Java web application. Paired with Spring Boot, this can bring a lot of value by measuring the performance of the REST API, measuring the performance of cache layer and database, and so on. Dropwizard provides handy annotations to mark methods to be monitored. It supports counters, timers, and so on.

WebSocket

WebSocket (https://developer.mozilla.org/en-US/docs/Web/API/WebSockets_API) is a communication protocol that works on top of TCP. It provides a full-duplex communication channel over a single TCP connection. It was standardized by W3C (https://www.w3.org). It is lightweight and enables real-time communication between a client and server. In terms of web applications, this enables the server to communicate with the client app in the browser without a request from the client. This opens the door to pushing data from server to client in real-time and for implementations such as real time chat, notifications, and so on. On the server side, JHipster relies on Spring, which provides the necessary support (https://spring.io/guides/gs/messaging-stomp-websocket/) to work with WebSocket.

Kafka

Kafka (https://kafka.apache.org) is an open source stream processing system. It has a distributed pub/sub-based message queue for storage. Its fault tolerance and scale has helped it to replace JMS and AMQP as the preferred messaging queue. Spring provides an abstraction on top of Kafka to make it easier to configure and work with Kafka.

JMS (Java Message Service) (https://en.wikipedia.org/wiki/Java_Message_Service) is a messaging standard developed for Java EE and enables sending and receiving asynchronous messages between components using topics and queues. **AMQP (Advanced Message Queuing Protocol)** (https://www.amqp.org/) is an open standard protocol for message-oriented middleware, providing features such as queuing, routing, and publish-subscribe mechanisms.

Testing frameworks

Server-side testing can be mainly categorized into unit testing, integration testing, performance testing, and behavior testing. JHipster supports all of these with the following tools out of which JUnit comes out-of-the-box, and others are opt-in.

JUnit

JUnit (https://junit.org/junit5/) is the most widely used Java testing framework. It is a free and open source software. It was originally intended for unit testing but combined with Spring Test Framework (https://docs.spring.io/spring/docs/current/spring-framework-reference/testing.html#testing-introduction) it can also be used for Integration testing. JHipster creates unit tests and REST API integration tests using JUnit and Spring Test Framework.

Gatling

Gatling (https://gatling.io/) is a free and open source performance and load testing tool. It is based on Scala and uses a Scala DSL to write test spec. It creates detailed reports of the load testing and it can be used to simulate all kinds of load on a system. It is a required tool for performance critical applications.

Cucumber

Cucumber (https://cucumber.io/) is a **Behavior-Driven Development (BDD)** testing framework used mainly for acceptance testing. It uses a language parser called **Gherkin**, which is very human readable as looks similar to plain English.

Introduction to database options

Today, there are a wide variety of database options out there. These can be broadly classified into the following:

- SQL databases
- NoSQL databases

 You can visit; https://db-engines.com/en/ranking to see the popularity of different databases.

JHipster supports some of the most widely used databases, as detailed here.

SQL databases

SQL databases or **Relational Database Management Systems (RDBMS)** are those that support a relational table-oriented data model. They support table schema defined by the fixed name and number of columns/attributes with a fixed data type. Each row in a table contains a value for every column. Tables can be related to each other.

H2

H2 (`http://www.h2database.com/html/main.html`) is a free embedded RDBMS commonly used for development and testing. It normally can run in file system mode for persistence or in-memory mode. It has a very small footprint and is extremely easy to configure and use. It doesn't have many of the enterprise features offered by other mainstream database engines and hence normally is not preferred for production usage.

MySQL

MySQL (`https://www.mysql.com/`) is one of the most popular database engines and is free and open source software. It is from Oracle but also has a very vibrant community. It has enterprise-ready features such as sharding, replication, partitioning, and so on. It is one of the most preferred SQL databases these days.

MariaDB

MariaDB (`https://mariadb.org/`) is a MySQL compliant database engine with an additional focus on security, performance, and high availability. It is gaining popularity and is sought as a good alternative for MySQL. It is free and open source software.

PostgreSQL

PostgreSQL (`https://www.postgresql.org/`) is another free and open source database system that is very much in demand. It is actively maintained by a community. One of the unique features of PostgreSQL is the advanced JSON object storage with the capability to index and query within the JSON. This makes it possible to use it as a NoSQL database or in Hybrid mode. It also has enterprise-ready features such as replication, high availability, and so on.

MS SQL

MS SQL server (https://www.microsoft.com/nl-nl/sql-server/sql-server-2017) is an enterprise database system developed and supported by Microsoft. It is commercial software and requires a paid license to use. It has enterprise-ready features and premium support from Microsoft. It is one of the popular choices for mission-critical systems.

Oracle

Oracle (https://www.oracle.com/database/index.html) is the most used database due to its legacy and enterprise features. It is commercial software and requires a paid license to use. It has enterprise-ready features such as sharding, replication, high availability, and so on.

NoSQL databases

This is a wide umbrella that encompasses any database that is not an RDBMS. This includes document stores, wide column stores, search engines, key-value stores, graph DBMS, content stores, and so on. A general trait of such databases is that they can be schema-less and do not rely on relational data.

MongoDB

MongoDB (https://www.mongodb.com/) is a cross-platform document store and is one of the most popular choices for NoSQL databases. It has a proprietary JSON-based API and query language. It supports MapReduce and enterprise features such as sharding, replication, and so on. It is free and open source software.

 MapReduce is a data processing paradigm where a job is split into multiple parallel map tasks, with the produced output sorted and reduced into the result. This makes processing large datasets efficient and faster.

Cassandra

Apache Cassandra (http://cassandra.apache.org/) is distributed column store with a focus on high availability, scalability, and performance. Due to its distributed nature, it doesn't have a single point of failure making it is the most popular choice for critical high availability systems. It was originally developed and open sourced by Facebook.

Did you know that Cassandra can have up to 2 billion columns per row?

Elasticsearch

Elasticsearch (`https://www.elastic.co/products/elasticsearch`) is a search and analytics engine based on Apache Lucene (`http://lucene.apache.org/`). It is technically a NoSQL database but it is primarily used as a search engine due to its indexing capability and high performance. It can be distributed and multi-tenant with full-text search capability. It has a web interface and JSON documents. It is one of the most used search engines.

Installation and setup

To get started with JHipster, you will have to install the JHipster CLI tool. The JHipster CLI comes with commands required to use all of the features offered by the platform.

JHipster Online: If you would like to create an application without installing anything, you can do so by visiting `https://start.jhipster.tech`. You can authorize the application to generate a project directly in your GitHub account or you can download the source as a ZIP file.

Prerequisites

Before we install the JHipster CLI, let's take a look at the prerequisites. We will need to install some dependencies and configure our favorite IDE to work best with generated code. You can visit `http://www.jhipster.tech/installation/` to get up to date information about this.

Tools required

The following are the tools required to install JHipster and to work with the generated applications. If you do not have them installed already follow, these steps and install them.

You will need to use a command-line interface (Command Prompt or Terminal application) throughout this section and hence it is better to have one open. Since the installation of some of the following tools will alter the environment variables, you might have to close and reopen the Terminal after the installation of a tool:

- On Windows, use the default **Command Prompt (CMD)** or Powershell
- On Linux, use Bash or your favorite Terminal emulator
- On macOS, use iTerm or your favorite Terminal application

Installation procedure

Let us see the installation procedure for each of the tools.

Java 8

Java 9 is the latest Java release introducing features like modules, reactive streams and so on. While JHipster applications will work with Java 9 it is recommended to stick to the more stable Java 8 until Java 9 support is stable in all the dependencies used.

The generated applications use Java 8 and hence it is required to compile the applications:

1. Check for your installed Java version by running the command `java -version` in the Terminal. It should display `java version "1.8.x"` where x could be any patch version.
2. If you do not have the correct version installed, you can visit the Oracle website (`http://www.oracle.com/technetwork/java/javase/downloads/index.html`) and follow the instructions to install the JDK for Java 8.
3. Once installed, check the command in step 1 again to make sure. As the JDK alters the environment variable to set `JAVA_HOME` you would have to open a new Terminal here.

Git

Git is the most used version control system for source code management. It promotes distributed revision control and is an integral part of development these days.

JHipster uses Git for upgrading applications and Git is also recommended for the smooth working of NodeJS and NPM ecosystems:

1. Check for Git by running `git --version` in the Terminal. It should display `git version x.x.x`; the version number can be anything.
2. If the command is not found, you can visit git-scm (`https://git-scm.com/downloads`) and follow the instructions to install Git on your operating system.
3. Once installed, check the command in step 1 again to make sure.

Node.js

Node.js is a JavaScript runtime environment. It revolutionized the JavaScript world and made JavaScript the most popular development language among developers today (according to `https://insights.stackoverflow.com/survey/2017#technology-programming-languages`). The Node ecosystem is the largest in the world with over 600,000 packages and is managed by NPM, the default package manager.

The JHipster CLI is a NodeJS application and hence requires NodeJS, to run, and many of the tools used in the generated application will also require NodeJS:

1. Check for NodeJS by typing `node -v` in the Terminal. It should display a version number. Make sure that the version number is greater than 8.9 and corresponds to the latest LTS version of NodeJS.
2. If the command is not found or if you have a lower version of NodeJS then you can visit the Node.js website (`https://nodejs.org/en/download/`) and follow the instructions to install the latest LTS version available. Please note that non-LTS versions (current) might not be stable and it is advised not to use them.
3. Once installed, check the command in step 1 again to make sure. As NodeJS alters the environment variables, you would have to open a new Terminal here.
4. NPM is automatically installed when you install NodeJS. You can check this by running `npm -v` in the Terminal.

 You can install multiple NPM packages by running the command `npm -g install bower gulp-cli` CLI or using Yarn, `yarn global add bower gulp-cli`.

Yarn

Yarn is a package manager for NodeJS. It is API and feature compatible with NPM and provides better performance and a flat package tree.

JHipster, by default, uses Yarn instead of NPM as Yarn is much faster at the time of writing. If you prefer to use NPM, then you can skip this step:

1. You can visit the Yarn website (`https://yarnpkg.com/en/docs/install`) and follow the instructions to install Yarn.
2. Once installed, check by running `yarn --version` to make sure.

Docker

Docker is the defacto standard for container management and it made using containers a breeze. It provides tools to create, share and deploy containers.

You will need Docker and `docker-compose` to run the generated database images and for the development of microservices:

1. Check for Docker by running `docker -v` in a terminal. It should display a version number.
2. Check for `docker-compose` by running `docker-compose -v` in a Terminal. It should display a version number. If you are on Mac or Linux you could just run `docker -v && docker-compose -v` together.
3. If the command is not found, you can visit the Docker website (`https://docs.docker.com/install/`) and follow the instructions to install it. Also, install Docker Compose (`https://docs.docker.com/compose/install/`) by following the instructions.
4. Once installed, check the command in step 1 again to make sure.

Optionally Install a Java build tool: Normally JHipster will automatically install the Maven Wrapper (`https://github.com/takari/maven-wrapper`) or the Gradle Wrapper (`https://docs.gradle.org/current/userguide/gradle_wrapper.html`) for you, based on your choice of build tool. If you don't want to use those wrappers, go to the official Maven website (`http://maven.apache.org/`) or Gradle website (`https://gradle.org/`) to do your own installation.

IDE configuration

JHipster applications can be created by using a command-line interface and JHipster CLI. Technically speaking, an IDE is not a requirement but when you continue development of a generated application it is highly recommended that you use a proper Java IDE such as IntelliJ, Eclipse, or Netbeans. Sometimes you could also use advanced text editors such as Visual Studio Code or Atom with appropriate plugins to get the work done. Depending on the IDE/text editor you choose, it is recommended to use the following plugins to make development more productive:

- Angular/React: Tslint, TypeScript, editor config
- Java: Spring, Gradle/Maven, Java Language support (VS Code)

Regardless of IDE/text Editor, always exclude the folders `node_modules`, `git`, `build`, and `target` to speed up indexing. Some IDEs will do this automatically based on the `.gitignore` file.

 Visit `http://www.jhipster.tech/configuring-ide/` in your favorite browser to read more about this.

System setup

Before installing and diving into JHipster, here are a few pointers to prepare you for some of the common issues that one might encounter:

- When using Yarn on macOS or Linux, you need to have `$HOME/.config/yarn/global/node_modules/.bin` in the path. This will normally be automatically done when you install Yarn but if not, you can run the command `export PATH="$PATH:`yarn global bin`:$HOME/.config/yarn/global/node_modules/.bin"` in a Terminal to do this.
- If you are behind a corporate proxy, you will have to bypass it for NPM, Bower, and Maven/Gradle to work properly. Visit `http://www.jhipster.tech/configuring-a-corporate-proxy/` to see what proxy options can be set for different tools used.

If you are on Mac or Linux and if you are using Oh-My-Zsh or the Fisherman shell then you could use the specific plugins from JHipster for that. Visit http://www.jhipster.tech/shell-plugins/ for details.

Installation of JHipster

OK, now let's get started for real. JHipster can be used from a local installation with NPM or Yarn, from a Vagrant image provided by the team, or using a Docker image. Alternatively, there is also the JHipster online application we saw earlier.

Among all the options, the best way to utilize the full power of JHipster would be by installing the JHipster CLI using Yarn or NPM. Open a Terminal and run:

```
> yarn add global generator-jhipster
```

If you would prefer NPM, then just run:

```
> npm install -g generator-jhipster
```

Wait for the installation to finish and in the Terminal run jhipster --version. You should see the version info as shown here:

```
$ jhipster --version
Using JHipster version installed globally
4.13.3
```

That's it; we are ready to roll.

If you are someone who cannot wait for new versions to arrive, you can always use the current development code by following these steps after installing the JHipster CLI following the preceding steps:

1. In a Terminal, navigate to a directory you would like to use. For example, if you have a folder called `project` in your home directory, run `cd ~/projects/` and for Windows run `cd c:\Users\<username>\Desktop\projects`

2. Run, `git clone https://github.com/jhipster/generator-jhipster.git`

3. Now, navigate to the folder by running `cd generator-jhipster`

4. Run `npm link` to create a symbolic link from this folder into the globally installed application in `global node_modules`

5. Now when you run the JHipster commands you will be using the version you cloned instead of the version you installed

Please note that you should be doing this only if you are absolutely sure of what you are doing. Also please note that development versions of the software will always be unstable and might contain bugs.

If you prefer to isolate the installation in a virtual environment, then you can use the Vagrant development box or the Docker image from the JHipster team. Visit `https://github.com/jhipster/jhipster-devbox` for instructions to use the Vagrant box or visit `http://www.jhipster.tech/installation` and scroll down to the Docker installation (for advanced users only) section for instructions to use a Docker image.

Summary

In this chapter, we discovered JHipster and the different technology options provided by it. We had a brief introduction of the important pieces of the client-side and server-side stack. We had a quick overview of Spring technologies, Angular, Bootstrap, and so on. We also had an overview of different database options supported by JHipster. We learned about the tools required to work with JHipster and we have successfully set up our environment to work with JHipster and installed JHipster CLI. In the next chapter, we will see how JHipster can be used to build a production-grade monolithic web application.

3

Building Monolithic Web Applications with JHipster

Let's get into action and build a production-grade web application using JHipster. Before we start, we need a use case. We will be building an e-commerce web application that manages products, customers, and their orders and invoices. The web application will use a MySQL database for production and will have an Angular front end. The UI for the actual shopping website will be different from the back office features, which will only be available for employees who have an administrator role. For this exercise, we will only be building a simple UI for the client-facing part. We will talk about other option as we go through this chapter.

In this chapter, we will:

- See how to create a monolithic web application using JHipster
- Walk through important aspects of the generated code
- See the security aspects of the generated application
- See how to run the application and tests
- See the generated frontend screens
- See the tools included that will ease further development

 This chapter will require the use of a terminal (command prompt on windows) app throughout. You can the see previous chapter for more info about that.

Application generation

Before we start generating the application, we need to prepare our workspace as this workspace will be used throughout this book, and you will be creating many Git branches on this workspace as we proceed.

Visit `http://rogerdudler.github.io/git-guide/` for a quick reference guide on Git commands.

Step 1 – preparing the workspace

Let's create a new folder for the workspace. Create a folder called `e-commerce-app` and from the terminal, navigate to the folder:

```
> mkdir e-commerce-app
> cd e-commerce-app
```

Now, create a new folder for our application; let's call it `online-store` and navigate to it:

```
> mkdir online-store
> cd online-store
```

Now, we are ready to invoke JHipster. Let's first make sure everything is ready by running the `jhipster --version` command. It should print a globally installed JHipster version, otherwise you'll need to follow the instructions from the previous chapter to set it up.

It is always better to use the latest versions of the tools as they might include important bug fixes. You can upgrade JHipster anytime using the command `yarn global upgrade generator-jhipster`

Step 2 – generating code using JHipster

Initialize JHipster by running the `jhipster` command into the terminal, which will produce the following output:

```
$ jhipster
Using JHipster version installed globally
Running default command
Executing jhipster:app
Options:

         JHIPSTER

            http://www.jhipster.tech

Welcome to the JHipster Generator v4.13.3
─────────────────────────────────────────────────────────────────────────────
  If you find JHipster useful consider supporting our collective https://opencollective.com/generator-jhipster
  Documentation for creating an application: http://www.jhipster.tech/creating-an-app/
─────────────────────────────────────────────────────────────────────────────
Application files will be generated in folder: /home/deepu/workspace/temp/online-store
? Which *type* of application would you like to create? (Use arrow keys)
❯ Monolithic application (recommended for simple projects)
  Microservice application
  Microservice gateway
  JHipster UAA server (for microservice OAuth2 authentication)
```

JHipster will ask a number questions to get input about different options which are required. The first question is about the application type that we want, and we are presented with the following four options:

- **Monolithic application**: As the name suggests, it creates a monolithic web application with a Spring Boot-based backend and an SPA frontend.
- **Microservice application**: This creates a Spring Boot microservice without any frontend, and is designed to work with a JHipster microservice architecture.
- **Microservice gateway**: This creates a Spring Boot application very similar to the monolithic application but geared towards a microservice architecture with additional configurations. It features an SPA frontend.
- **JHipster UAA server**: This creates an OAuth2 User authentication and Authorization service. This will not feature any frontend code and is designed to be used in a JHipster microservice architecture.

We will choose the **monolithic application** for our use case. We will talk and look at the other options in detail in `Chapter 8`, *Introduction to Microservice Server-Side Technologies*, of this book.

Run `jhipster --help` to see all available commands. Run `jhipster <command> --help` to see help information for a specific command; for example, `jhipster app --help` will display help information for the main app generation process.

Server-side options

The generator will now start asking us about the server side options that we need. Let's go through them one by one:

- **Question 1**: This prompt asks for a base name for the application, which is used for creating the main class file names, database names, and so on. By default, JHipster will suggest the current directory name if it doesn't contain any special characters in the name. Let's name our application as `store`. Please note that the files will be created in the current directory you are in:

```
Application files will be generated in folder: /home/deepu/workspace/temp/online-store
? Which *type* of application would you like to create? Monolithic application (recommended for simple projects)
? What is the base name of your application? (jhipster) store
```

- **Question 2**: This prompt asks for a Java package name. Let's choose `com.mycompany.store`:

```
? Which *type* of application would you like to create? Monolithic application (recommended for simple projects)
? What is the base name of your application? store
? What is your default Java package name? (com.mycompany.myapp) com.mycompany.store
```

- **Question 3**. This prompt asks whether we need to configure JHipster registry for this instance. JHipster registry provides a service discovery and config server implementation which is very useful for centralized configuration management and scaling of the application. For this use case, we will not need it, so let's choose **No**. We will learn more about the JHipster Registry in `Chapter 8`, *Introduction to Microservice Server-Side Technologies*, of this book:

```
? Which *type* of application would you like to create? Monolithic application (recommended for simple projects)
? What is the base name of your application? store
? What is your default Java package name? com.mycompany.store
? Do you want to use the JHipster Registry to configure, monitor and scale your application? (Use arrow keys)
> No
  Yes
```

- **Question 4**: This prompt asks us to select an authentication mechanism. We are presented with three options:
  - **JWT authentication**
  - **HTTP Session Authentication**
  - **OAuth 2.0/OIDC Authentication**

  We already saw how these defer in the previous chapter, and for our use case, let's choose **JWT authentication**:

```
? Which *type* of application would you like to create? Monolithic application (recommended for simple projects)
? What is the base name of your application? store
? What is your default Java package name? com.mycompany.store
? Do you want to use the JHipster Registry to configure, monitor and scale your application? No
? Which *type* of authentication would you like to use? (Use arrow keys)
> JWT authentication (stateless, with a token)
  OAuth 2.0 / OIDC Authentication (stateful, works with Keycloak and Okta)
  HTTP Session Authentication (stateful, default Spring Security mechanism)
```

- **Question 5**: This prompt asks us to select a database type; the options provided are **SQL**, **MongoDB**, **Couchbase**, and **Cassandra**. We already learned about the different database options in the previous chapter. For our application, let's choose an **SQL** database:

```
? Which *type* of application would you like to create? Monolithic application (recommended for simple projects)
? What is the base name of your application? store
? What is your default Java package name? com.mycompany.store
? Do you want to use the JHipster Registry to configure, monitor and scale your application? No
? Which *type* of authentication would you like to use? JWT authentication (stateless, with a token)
? Which *type* of database would you like to use? (Use arrow keys)
> SQL (H2, MySQL, MariaDB, PostgreSQL, Oracle, MSSQL)
  MongoDB
  Cassandra
  [BETA] Couchbase
```

- **Question 6**: This prompt asks us to choose a specific SQL database that we would like to use in production; the available options are **MySQL**, **MariaDB**, **PostgreSQL**, **Oracle**, and **Microsoft SQL Server**. Let's choose **MySQL** here:

```
? Which *type* of application would you like to create? Monolithic application (recommended for simple projects)
? What is the base name of your application? store
? What is your default Java package name? com.mycompany.store
? Do you want to use the JHipster Registry to configure, monitor and scale your application? No
? Which *type* of authentication would you like to use? JWT authentication (stateless, with a token)
? Which *type* of database would you like to use? SQL (H2, MySQL, MariaDB, PostgreSQL, Oracle, MSSQL)
? Which *production* database would you like to use? (Use arrow keys)
> MySQL
  MariaDB
  PostgreSQL
  Oracle (Please follow our documentation to use the Oracle proprietary driver)
  Microsoft SQL Server
```

- **Question 7**: This prompt asks us to choose between our chosen SQL database and H2 embedded database for development. H2 embedded DB is especially useful as it makes development faster and self-contained, without the need to have a MySQL instance running. So, let's choose the **H2 disk-based persistence** here as it is lightweight and easier in development compared to having a full-fledged DB service running:

```
? Which *type* of application would you like to create? Monolithic application (recommended for simple projects)
? What is the base name of your application? store
? What is your default Java package name? com.mycompany.store
? Do you want to use the JHipster Registry to configure, monitor and scale your application? No
? Which *type* of authentication would you like to use? JWT authentication (stateless, with a token)
? Which *type* of database would you like to use? SQL (H2, MySQL, MariaDB, PostgreSQL, Oracle, MSSQL)
? Which *production* database would you like to use? MySQL
? Which *development* database would you like to use? (Use arrow keys)
> H2 with disk-based persistence
  H2 with in-memory persistence
  MySQL
```

 If your use case requires working with persisted data in development and if the model is not going to change often, then you could also choose MySQL for development as it would give you a faster startup time. This is because the embedded H2 DB doesn't need to be initialized, but the downside is each time you make schema changes or recreate entities, you would have to update the DB using generated liquibase diff changelogs manually, or wipe the DB manually and start over again. With an embedded H2 DB, you could run `./gradlew clean` to wipe it.

- **Question 8**: This prompt asks us to choose a Spring cache implementation. We have the option to choose between no cache, **EHCache**, **Hazelcast**, and **Infinispan**. Since we learned about these in the previous chapter, let's go ahead and choose **Hazelcast** here:

```
? Which *type* of application would you like to create? Monolithic application (recommended for simple projects)
? What is the base name of your application? store
? What is your default Java package name? com.mycompany.store
? Do you want to use the JHipster Registry to configure, monitor and scale your application? No
? Which *type* of authentication would you like to use? JWT authentication (stateless, with a token)
? Which *type* of database would you like to use? SQL (H2, MySQL, MariaDB, PostgreSQL, Oracle, MSSQL)
? Which *production* database would you like to use? MySQL
? Which *development* database would you like to use? H2 with disk-based persistence
? Do you want to use the Spring cache abstraction?
  Yes, with the Ehcache implementation (local cache, for a single node)
> Yes, with the Hazelcast implementation (distributed cache, for multiple nodes)
  [BETA] Yes, with the Infinispan (hybrid cache, for multiple nodes)
  No (when using an SQL database, this will also disable the Hibernate L2 cache)
```

- **Question 9**. This prompt asks us to choose if we need a 2nd level cache for Hibernate. Let's choose **Yes**. It will use the same cache implementation we chose for the previous question:

```
? Which *type* of application would you like to create? Monolithic application (recommended for simple projects)
? What is the base name of your application? store
? What is your default Java package name? com.mycompany.store
? Do you want to use the JHipster Registry to configure, monitor and scale your application? No
? Which *type* of authentication would you like to use? JWT authentication (stateless, with a token)
? Which *type* of database would you like to use? SQL (H2, MySQL, MariaDB, PostgreSQL, Oracle, MSSQL)
? Which *production* database would you like to use? MySQL
? Which *development* database would you like to use? H2 with disk-based persistence
? Do you want to use the Spring cache abstraction? Yes, with the Hazelcast implementation (distributed cache, for multiple nodes)
? Do you want to use Hibernate 2nd level cache? (Y/n) y
```

- **Question 10**: This prompt gives us the choice of the build tool to use for the project; the options are **Maven** and **Gradle**. Let's choose **Gradle** here as it is more modern and powerful:

```
? Which *type* of application would you like to create? Monolithic application (recommended for simple projects)
? What is the base name of your application? store
? What is your default Java package name? com.mycompany.store
? Do you want to use the JHipster Registry to configure, monitor and scale your application? No
? Which *type* of authentication would you like to use? JWT authentication (stateless, with a token)
? Which *type* of database would you like to use? SQL (H2, MySQL, MariaDB, PostgreSQL, Oracle, MSSQL)
? Which *production* database would you like to use? MySQL
? Which *development* database would you like to use? H2 with disk-based persistence
? Do you want to use the Spring cache abstraction? Yes, with the Hazelcast implementation (distributed cache, for multiple nodes)
? Do you want to use Hibernate 2nd level cache? Yes
? Would you like to use Maven or Gradle for building the backend?
  Maven
> Gradle
```

- **Question 11**: This prompt is interesting as it presents various additional options supported by JHipster. The options are:
  - **Social login**: Adds support for using a Social login provider like Facebook, Twitter, and so on for login(Social login option is removed in JHipster 5 and you need to choose OAuth 2.0/OIDC Authentication instead to use **Social login** provided by the OIDC provider)
  - **Elasticsearch**: Adds Elasticsearch support for the generated entities
  - **WebSockets**: Adds WebSocket support using Spring WebSocket, SocketJS, and Stomp protocol
  - **API first development with swagger-codegen**: Adds Swagger codegen support for API first development
  - **Apache Kafka**: Adds support for asynchronous queue using Kafka

Let's keep it simple and choose **WebSockets using Spring WebSocket**:

```
? Which *type* of application would you like to create? Monolithic application (recommended for simple projects)
? What is the base name of your application? store
? What is your default Java package name? com.mycompany.store
? Do you want to use the JHipster Registry to configure, monitor and scale your application? No
? Which *type* of authentication would you like to use? JWT authentication (stateless, with a token)
? Which *type* of database would you like to use? SQL (H2, MySQL, MariaDB, PostgreSQL, Oracle, MSSQL)
? Which *production* database would you like to use? MySQL
? Which *development* database would you like to use? H2 with disk-based persistence
? Do you want to use the Spring cache abstraction? Yes, with the Hazelcast implementation (distributed cache, for multiple nodes)
? Do you want to use Hibernate 2nd level cache? Yes
? Would you like to use Maven or Gradle for building the backend? Gradle
? Which other technologies would you like to use?
 ◯ Social login (Google, Facebook, Twitter)
 ◯ Search engine using Elasticsearch
 ◉ WebSockets using Spring Websocket
 ◯ API first development using swagger-codegen
 ◯ Asynchronous messages using Apache Kafka
```

Client-side options

Now, the generator will ask us about the client side option, including the client-side framework we wish to use:

- **Question 1**: This prompt asks us to select a client-side MVVM framework; the options include **Angular 5** and **React**. Let's choose **Angular 5** here:

```
? Which *type* of application would you like to create? Monolithic application (recommended for simple projects)
? What is the base name of your application? store
? What is your default Java package name? com.mycompany.store
? Do you want to use the JHipster Registry to configure, monitor and scale your application? No
? Which *type* of authentication would you like to use? JWT authentication (stateless, with a token)
? Which *type* of database would you like to use? SQL (H2, MySQL, MariaDB, PostgreSQL, Oracle, MSSQL)
? Which *production* database would you like to use? MySQL
? Which *development* database would you like to use? H2 with disk-based persistence
? Do you want to use the Spring cache abstraction? Yes, with the Hazelcast implementation (distributed cache, for multiple nodes)
? Do you want to use Hibernate 2nd level cache? Yes
? Would you like to use Maven or Gradle for building the backend? Gradle
? Which other technologies would you like to use? WebSockets using Spring Websocket
? Which *Framework* would you like to use for the client? (Use arrow keys)
❯ Angular 5
  [BETA] React
```

- **Question 2**. This prompt lets us enable SASS support for our CSS, and since SASS is awesome, let's enable it by selecting **Yes**:

```
? Which *type* of application would you like to create? Monolithic application (recommended for simple projects)
? What is the base name of your application? store
? What is your default Java package name? com.mycompany.store
? Do you want to use the JHipster Registry to configure, monitor and scale your application? No
? Which *type* of authentication would you like to use? JWT authentication (stateless, with a token)
? Which *type* of database would you like to use? SQL (H2, MySQL, MariaDB, PostgreSQL, Oracle, MSSQL)
? Which *production* database would you like to use? MySQL
? Which *development* database would you like to use? H2 with disk-based persistence
? Do you want to use the Spring cache abstraction? Yes, with the Hazelcast implementation (distributed cache, for multiple nodes)
? Do you want to use Hibernate 2nd level cache? Yes
? Would you like to use Maven or Gradle for building the backend? Gradle
? Which other technologies would you like to use? WebSockets using Spring Websocket
? Which *Framework* would you like to use for the client? Angular 5
? Would you like to enable *SASS* support using the LibSass stylesheet preprocessor? (y/N) y
```

Internationalization options

We will now have the opportunity to enable internationalization and select the languages we would like:

- **Question 1**. This prompt lets us enable **internationalization (i18n)**. Let's choose **Yes** here:

```
? Which *type* of application would you like to create? Monolithic application (recommended for simple projects)
? What is the base name of your application? store
? What is your default Java package name? com.mycompany.store
? Do you want to use the JHipster Registry to configure, monitor and scale your application? No
? Which *type* of authentication would you like to use? JWT authentication (stateless, with a token)
? Which *type* of database would you like to use? SQL (H2, MySQL, MariaDB, PostgreSQL, Oracle, MSSQL)
? Which *production* database would you like to use? MySQL
? Which *development* database would you like to use? H2 with disk-based persistence
? Do you want to use the Spring cache abstraction? Yes, with the Hazelcast implementation (distributed cache, for multiple nodes)
? Do you want to use Hibernate 2nd level cache? Yes
? Would you like to use Maven or Gradle for building the backend? Gradle
? Which other technologies would you like to use? WebSockets using Spring Websocket
? Which *Framework* would you like to use for the client? Angular 5
? Would you like to enable *SASS* support using the LibSass stylesheet preprocessor? Yes
? Would you like to enable internationalization support? (Y/n) y
```

- **Question 2**: Since we enabled i18n, we will be given the option to choose a primary language and additional i18n languages. At the time of writing, there are 36 supported languages including 2 **RTL (Right to Left)** languages. Let's choose **English** as the primary language and **Simplified Chinese** as the additional language:

```
? Which *type* of application would you like to create? Monolithic application (recommended for simple projects)
? What is the base name of your application? store
? What is your default Java package name? com.mycompany.store
? Do you want to use the JHipster Registry to configure, monitor and scale your application? No
? Which *type* of authentication would you like to use? JWT authentication (stateless, with a token)
? Which *type* of database would you like to use? SQL (H2, MySQL, MariaDB, PostgreSQL, Oracle, MSSQL)
? Which *production* database would you like to use? MySQL
? Which *development* database would you like to use? H2 with disk-based persistence
? Do you want to use the Spring cache abstraction? Yes, with the Hazelcast implementation (distributed cache, for multiple nodes)
? Do you want to use Hibernate 2nd level cache? Yes
? Would you like to use Maven or Gradle for building the backend? Gradle
? Which other technologies would you like to use? WebSockets using Spring Websocket
? Which *Framework* would you like to use for the client? Angular 5
? Would you like to enable *SASS* support using the LibSass stylesheet preprocessor? Yes
? Would you like to enable internationalization support? Yes
? Please choose the native language of the application English
? Please choose additional languages to install
○ Arabic (Libya)
○ Armenian
○ Catalan
❯● Chinese (Simplified)
○ Chinese (Traditional)
○ Czech
○ Danish
(Move up and down to reveal more choices)
```

Testing

Now, we can choose testing options for our application.

This prompt lets us choose testing frameworks for our application, which will also create sample tests for the application and entities. The options are **Gatling**, **Cucumber**, and **Protractor**. Let's choose **Protractor** here:

```
? Which *type* of application would you like to create? Monolithic application (recommended for simple projects)
? What is the base name of your application? store
? What is your default Java package name? com.mycompany.store
? Do you want to use the JHipster Registry to configure, monitor and scale your application? No
? Which *type* of authentication would you like to use? JWT authentication (stateless, with a token)
? Which *type* of database would you like to use? SQL (H2, MySQL, MariaDB, PostgreSQL, Oracle, MSSQL)
? Which *production* database would you like to use? MySQL
? Which *development* database would you like to use? H2 with disk-based persistence
? Do you want to use the Spring cache abstraction? Yes, with the Hazelcast implementation (distributed cache, for multiple nodes)
? Do you want to use Hibernate 2nd level cache? Yes
? Would you like to use Maven or Gradle for building the backend? Gradle
? Which other technologies would you like to use? WebSockets using Spring Websocket
? Which *Framework* would you like to use for the client? Angular 5
? Would you like to enable *SASS* support using the LibSass stylesheet preprocessor? Yes
? Would you like to enable internationalization support? Yes
? Please choose the native language of the application English
? Please choose additional languages to install Chinese (Simplified)
? Besides JUnit and Karma, which testing frameworks would you like to use?
○ Gatling
○ Cucumber
❯● Protractor
```

Modules

This prompt lets us choose additional third-party modules from the JHipster marketplace (https://www.jhipster.tech/modules/marketplace). This can be helpful if we want to use additional features not supported directly by JHipster. We will look at this in later chapters. For now, let's choose **No**. Don't worry about this, as these modules can be added to the application later when required as well:

```
? Which *type* of application would you like to create? Monolithic application (recommended for simple projects)
? What is the base name of your application? store
? What is your default Java package name? com.mycompany.store
? Do you want to use the JHipster Registry to configure, monitor and scale your application? No
? Which *type* of authentication would you like to use? JWT authentication (stateless, with a token)
? Which *type* of database would you like to use? SQL (H2, MySQL, MariaDB, PostgreSQL, Oracle, MSSQL)
? Which *production* database would you like to use? MySQL
? Which *development* database would you like to use? H2 with disk-based persistence
? Do you want to use the Spring cache abstraction? Yes, with the Hazelcast implementation (distributed cache, for multiple nodes)
? Do you want to use Hibernate 2nd level cache? Yes
? Would you like to use Maven or Gradle for building the backend? Gradle
? Which other technologies would you like to use? WebSockets using Spring Websocket
? Which *Framework* would you like to use for the client? Angular 5
? Would you like to enable *SASS* support using the LibSass stylesheet preprocessor? Yes
? Would you like to enable internationalization support? Yes
? Please choose the native language of the application English
? Please choose additional languages to install Chinese (Simplified)
? Besides JUnit and Karma, which testing frameworks would you like to use? Protractor
? Would you like to install other generators from the JHipster Marketplace? (y/N) n
```

Once all the questions are answered, the code generation will start and you will see an output like following, listing the files created, and then running yarn installation to get all the frontend dependencies installed.

 If you do not want the Yarn install and Webpack build steps to run, you could use the `--skip-install` flag while running JHipster to skip this. Just run `jhipster --skip-install`

Once the installation is complete, the generator will trigger a webpack build for the client side so that when we start the application, we have everything ready:

```
create src/main/webapp/i18n/zh-cn/global.json
create src/main/webapp/i18n/zh-cn/health.json
create src/main/webapp/i18n/zh-cn/reset.json
create src/main/resources/i18n/messages_zh_cn.properties

I'm all done. Running yarn install for you to install the required dependencies. If this fails, try running the command yourself.

yarn install v1.0.2
info No lockfile found.
[1/5] Validating package.json...
[2/5] Resolving packages...
```

 JHipster will check your environment to see if all the required dependencies like Java8, NodeJS, Git, and NPM/Yarn are installed. If not, it will show friendly warning messages before code generation starts.

Once the process is complete, you will see successful messages as follows, and instructions to start the application:

```
Server application generated successfully.

Run your Spring Boot application:
 ./gradlew

Client application generated successfully.

Start your Webpack development server with:
 yarn start

Execution complete
```

 There are command-line flags that can be passed while executing the jhipster command. Running jhipster app --help will list all of the available command-line flags. One of the interesting flags, for example, is npm, which lets you use NPM instead of Yarn for dependency management.

JHipster will automatically initialize a Git repository for the folder and commit the generated file. If you wish to do this step yourself, you can do so by passing the `skip-git` flag during executing `jhipster --skip-git` and execute the steps manually as follows:

```
> git init
> git add --all
> git commit -am "generated online store application"
```

> You could also use a GUI tool like Sourcetree or GitKraken if you wish to do so to work with Git.

Code walkthrough

Now that we have generated our application with JHipster, let's go through important pieces of the source code which have been created. Let's open our application in our favorite IDE or Editor.

> If you are using IntelliJ IDEA, you can execute `idea .` in a terminal from the application folder to launch it. Otherwise, you can import the application as a new Gradle project using the menu option **File** | **New** | **Project** from existing sources and select the project folder before selecting **Gradle** from the options and click **Next** and then **Finish**. If you are using Eclipse, open the **File** | **Import...** dialog and select **Gradle Project** in the list and follow the instructions.

File structure

The created application will have the following file structure:

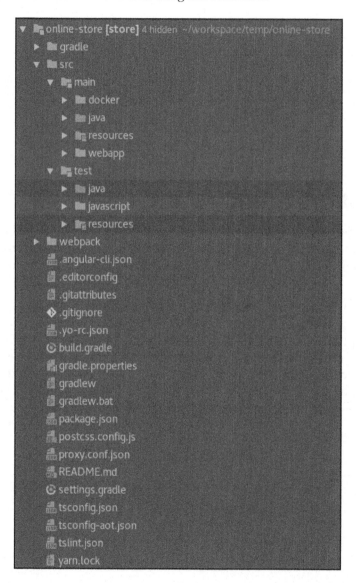

As you can see, the root folder is quite busy with a few folders but a lot of configuration files. The most interesting among them is:

- `src`: This is the source folder which holds the main application source and the test source files.
- `webpack`: This folder holds all the Webpack client-side build configurations for development, production, and testing.
- `gradle`: This folder has Gradle wrapper and additional Gradle build scripts which will be used by the main Gradle build file (JHipster provides a similar wrapper if Maven is chosen as well).
- `build.gradle`: This is our Gradle build file which specifies our applications build lifecycle. It also has the server side dependencies specified. The build uses properties defined in the `gradle.properties` file alongside it. You can also find an executable named `gradlew` (`gradlew.bat` for Windows), which lets you use Gradle without having to install it.
- `.yo-rc.json`: This is the configuration file for JHipster. This file stores the options we selected during app creation, and it is used for app regeneration and upgrades.
- `package.json`: This is the NPM configuration file which specifies all your client-side dependencies, client-side build dependencies, and tasks.
- `tsconfig.json`: This is the configuration for Typescript. There is also `tsconfig-aot.json` for Angular **AOT** (**Ahead-of-Time**) compilation.
- `tslint.json`: This is the lint configuration for Typescript.

Install and configure Typescript and the Tslint plugin for your IDE or editor to make the most out of Typescript.

Now, let's take a look at the source folder. It has a main folder and a test folder, which holds the main app source code and tests the source code accordingly. The folder structure is as follows:

- `main`:
  - `docker`: Holds the Dockerfile for the application and Docker configurations for the selected options
  - `java`: Holds the main Java source code for the application
  - `resources`: Holds Spring Boot configuration files, Liquibase changelogs, and static resources like server-side i18n files and email templates used by the application
  - `webapp`: Holds the Angular application source code and the client side static content like images, stylesheets, i18n files, and so on
- `test`:
  - `java`: Holds the unit and integration test source for the server side
  - `javascript`: Holds the Karma unit test specs and Protractor end-to-end specs for the client side application
  - `resources`: Holds Spring configuration files and static resources like server-side i18n files and email templates used by the application for test

Server-side source code

The server-side code is situated in the Java and resources folder under `src/main`, as seen in the preceding screenshot. The folder structure is as follows:

You may notice that the Spring components do not use the traditional `@Autowired` or `@Inject` annotations for dependency injection in the generated code. This is because we use constructor injection instead of field injection, and Spring Boot doesn't need explicit annotations for constructor injection. Constructor injection is considered better as it enables us to write better unit tests and avoids design issues, whereas field injection is more elegant but easily makes a class monolithic. Constructor injection is a suggested best practice by the Spring team. Constructor injection also makes unit testing components easier.

Java source

The important parts of the Java source code are:

- `StoreApp.java`: This is the main entry class for the application. Since this is a Spring Boot application, the main class is executable and you can start the application by just running this class from an IDE. Let's take a look at this class:
    - The class is annotated with a bunch of Spring JavaConfig annotations:

        ```
        @ComponentScan
        @EnableAutoConfiguration(exclude =
        {MetricFilterAutoConfiguration.class,
        MetricRepositoryAutoConfiguration.class})
        @EnableConfigurationProperties({LiquibaseProperties.cla
        ss, ApplicationProperties.class})
        ```

    - The first one, `@ComponentScan`, tells the Spring application to scan the source files and auto detect Spring components (Services, Repository, Resource, Configuration classes that define Spring beans, and so on).
    - The second one is `@EnableAutoConfiguration`, which tells Spring Boot to try to guess and auto-configure beans that the application might need based on the classes found on the classpath and the configurations we have provided. The exclude settings specifically tells Spring Boot not to auto-configure the specified beans.
    - The third one, `@EnableConfigurationProperties`, helps register additional configurations for the application via property files.

- The main method of the class bootstraps the Spring Boot application and runs it:

```
public static void main(String[] args) throws
UnknownHostException {
    SpringApplication app = new
SpringApplication(StoreApp.class);
    DefaultProfileUtil.addDefaultProfile(app);
    Environment env = app.run(args).getEnvironment();
    ...
}
```

- `config`: This package contains Spring bean configurations for the database, cache, WebSocket, and so on. This is where we will configure various options for the application. Some of the important ones are:
    - `CacheConfiguration.java`: This class configures the Hibernate second level cache for the application. Since we chose Hazelcast as the cache provider, this class configures the same way.
    - `DatabaseConfiguration.java`: This class configures the database for the application and enables transaction management, JPA auditing, and JPA repositories for the application. It also configures Liquibase to manage DB migrations and the H2 database for development.
    - `SecurityConfiguration.java`: This is a very important part of the application as it configures security for the application. Let's take a look at important parts of the class:
        - The annotations enable web security and method level security so that we can use `@Secured` and `@Pre/PostAuthorize` annotations on individual methods:

```
@EnableWebSecurity
@EnableGlobalMethodSecurity(prePostEnabled =
true, securedEnabled = true)
```

- The following configuration tells the application to
  ignore static content and certain APIs from Spring
  security configuration:

```
@Override
public void configure(WebSecurity web) throws
Exception {
    web.ignoring()
        .antMatchers(HttpMethod.OPTIONS,
"/**")
        .antMatchers("/app/**/*.{js,html}")
        .antMatchers("/i18n/**")
        .antMatchers("/content/**")
        .antMatchers("/swagger-ui/index.html")
        .antMatchers("/api/register")
        .antMatchers("/api/activate")
        .antMatchers("/api/account/reset-
          password/init")
        .antMatchers("/api/account/reset-
          password/finish")
        .antMatchers("/test/**")
        .antMatchers("/h2-console/**");
}
```

- The following configuration tells Spring security
  which endpoints are permitted for all users, which
  endpoints should be authenticated, and which
  endpoints require a specific role (ADMIN, in this case):

```
@Override
protected void configure(HttpSecurity http)
throws Exception {
    http
        ...
    .and()
        .authorizeRequests()
.antMatchers("/api/register").permitAll()
        ...
.antMatchers("/api/**").authenticated()
        .antMatchers("/websocket/tracker")
.hasAuthority(AuthoritiesConstants.ADMIN)
.antMatchers("/websocket/**").permitAll()
.antMatchers("/management/health").permitAll()
        .antMatchers("/management/**")
.hasAuthority(AuthoritiesConstants.ADMIN)
        .antMatchers("/v2/api-
```

```
docs/**").permitAll()
        .antMatchers("/swagger-
resources/configuration/ui").permitAll()
        .antMatchers("/swagger-ui/index.html")
.hasAuthority(AuthoritiesConstants.ADMIN)
    .and()
        .apply(securityConfigurerAdapter());
}
```

- `WebConfigurer.java`: This is where we set up HTTP cache headers, MIME mappings, static assets location, and **CORS (Cross-Origin Resource Sharing)**.

JHipster provides great CORS support out of the box:

- CORS can be configured using the `jhipster.cors` property, as defined in the JHipster common application properties (`http://www.jhipster.tech/common-application-properties/`).
- It is enabled by default in `dev` mode for monoliths and gateways. It is disabled by default for microservices as you are supposed to access them through a gateway.
- It is disabled by default in `prod` mode for both monoliths and microservices, for security reasons.

- `domain`: The domain model classes for the application are in this package. These are simple POJOs which have JPA annotations mapping it to a Hibernate entity. When the Elasticsearch option is selected, these also act as the Document object. Let's take a look at the `User.java` class:
  - An entity class is characterized by the following annotations. The `@Entity` annotation marks the class as a JPA entity. The `@Table` annotation maps the entity to a database table. The `@Cache` annotation enables second level caching of the entity, and it also specifies a caching strategy:

    ```
    @Entity
    @Table(name = "jhi_user")
    @Cache(usage =
    CacheConcurrencyStrategy.NONSTRICT_READ_WRITE)
    ```

- There are various annotations used at field level in these classes. `@Id` marks the primary key for the entity. `@Column` maps a field to a database table column by the same name when no override is provided. `@NotNull`, `@Pattern`, and `@Size` are annotations that are used for validation. `@JsonIgnore` is used by Jackson to ignore fields when converting the objects into JSON which are to be returned in the REST API requests. This is especially useful with Hibernate as it avoids circular references between relationships, which create tons of SQL DB requests and fail:

```
@Id
@GeneratedValue(strategy = GenerationType.IDENTITY)
private Long id;

@NotNull
@Pattern(regexp = Constants.LOGIN_REGEX)
@Size(min = 1, max = 50)
@Column(length = 50, unique = true, nullable = false)
private String login;

@JsonIgnore
@NotNull
@Size(min = 60, max = 60)
@Column(name = "password_hash",length = 60)
private String password;
```

- The relationships between the database tables are also mapped to the entities using JPA annotations. Here, for example, it maps a many-to-many relationship between a user and user authorities. It also specifies a join table to be used for the mapping:

```
@JsonIgnore
@ManyToMany
@JoinTable(
    name = "jhi_user_authority",
    joinColumns = {@JoinColumn(name = "user_id",
referencedColumnName = "id")},
    inverseJoinColumns = {@JoinColumn(name =
"authority_name", referencedColumnName = "name")})
@Cache(usage =
CacheConcurrencyStrategy.NONSTRICT_READ_WRITE)
@BatchSize(size = 20)
private Set<Authority> authorities = new HashSet<>();
```

- repository: This package holds the Spring Data repositories for the entities. These typically interface definitions which are automatically implemented by Spring Data. This removes the need for us to write any boilerplate implementations for the data access layer. Let's look at the UserRepository.java example:

```
@Repository
public interface UserRepository extends JpaRepository<User, Long> {

    Optional<User> findOneByActivationKey(String activationKey);

    List<User>
findAllByActivatedIsFalseAndCreatedDateBefore(Instant
    dateTime);

    Optional<User> findOneByResetKey(String resetKey);

    Optional<User> findOneByEmailIgnoreCase(String email);
    ...
}
```

- The @Repository annotation marks this as a Spring data repository component.
- The interface extends JpaRepository, which lets it inherit all the default CRUD operations like findOne, findAll, save, count, and delete.
- Custom methods are written as simple method definitions following the Spring data naming conventions so that the method name specifies the query to be generated. For example, findOneByEmailIgnoreCase generates a query equivalent of SELECT * FROM user WHERE LOWER(email) = LOWER(:email).

- security: This package holds Spring security-related components and utils, and since we chose JWT as our authentication mechanism, it holds JWT-related classes such as TokenProvider, JWTFilter, and JWTConfigurer as well.
- service: This package holds the service layer consisting of Spring service beans, DTOs, Mapstruct DTO mappers, and service utilities.

- web: This package holds the web resource classes, view models classes and utility classes.
  - rest: This package holds Spring resource classes for the REST API. It also holds view model objects and utilities. Let's take a look at UserResource.java:
    - The resource classes are marked with the @RestController and @RequestMapping("/api") annotations from Spring. The latter specifies the base URL path for the controller so that all <applicationContext>/api/* requests are forwarded to this class.
    - Request methods are annotated with annotations according to their purpose, for example, the below marks the createUser method as a PostMapping for "/users", which means all POST requests to <applicationContext>/api/users will be served by this method. The @Timed annotation is used to measure the performance of the method. The @Secured annotation restricts the method access to the specified role:

```
@PostMapping("/users")
@Timed
@Secured(AuthoritiesConstants.ADMIN)
public ResponseEntity createUser(@Valid
@RequestBody ManagedUserVM managedUserVM)
throws URISyntaxException {
    ...
}
```

  - WebSocket: This package holds the Websocket controllers and view models.

 JHipster uses **DTO (Data Transfer Object)** and **VM (View Model)** on the server side. DTOs are for transferring data from the service layer to and from the resource layer. They **break** the Hibernate transactions and avoids further lazy loading from being triggered by the resource layer. VMs are only used for displaying data on the web frontend and don't interact with the service layer.

Resources

The important parts of resources are:

- `config`: This holds the application property YAML files and Liquibase changelogs. The `application.yml` file holds configurable Spring Boot, JHipster, and application-specific properties while the `application.(dev|prod).yml` files hold properties that should be applied when the specific dev or prod profile is active. The test configurations are under `src/test/resource/application.yml`.
- `i18n`: This holds the server-side i18n resource files.
- `mails`: This holds Thymeleaf templates for emails.
- `templates`: This holds Thymeleaf templates for the client side.

client-side source code

The client-side source code is under the `src/main/webapp` folder, as we saw earlier. The structure is as follows:

The most noteworthy among these are:

- app: This folder holds the Angular application's Typescript source code, which is organized with a folder per feature:
  - app.main.ts: This is the main file for the Angular app. This bootstraps the Angular application. Notice that it uses platformBrowserDynamic, which lets the application work with **JIT (Just-in-time)** compilation in the browser. This is ideal for development:

```
platformBrowserDynamic().bootstrapModule(StoreAppModule
)
.then((success) => console.log(`Application started`))
.catch((err) => console.error(err));
```

- app.module.ts: This is the main module for the Angular app. It declares app level components and providers, and imports other modules for the application. It also bootstraps the main application component:

```
@NgModule({
    imports: [
        BrowserModule,
        ...
        StoreEntityModule,
        // jhipster-needle-angular-add-module JHipster
        will add new module here
    ],
    declarations: [
        JhiMainComponent,
        ...
        FooterComponent
    ],
    providers: [
        ProfileService,
        ...
        UserRouteAccessService
    ],
    bootstrap: [ JhiMainComponent ]
})
export class StoreAppModule {}
```

- `account`: This module consists of account-related features such as activate, password, password-reset, register, and settings. Each typical component consists of `component.html`, `component.ts`, `route.ts`, and `service.ts` files.
- `admin`: This module consists of admin-related features such as audits, configuration, docs, health, logs, metrics, tracker, and user-management. Each typical component consists of `component.html`, `component.ts`, `route.ts`, and `service.ts` files.
  - `blocks`: This folder consists of HTTP interceptors and other configs used by the application.
  - `entities`: This is where entity modules will be created.
  - `home`: The homepage module.
  - `layouts`: This folder has layout components like the navbar, footer, error pages, and so on.
  - `shared`: This module contains all the shared services (auth, tracker, user), components (login, alert), entity models, and utilities required for the application.
- `content`: This folder contains static content like images, CSS, and SASS files.
- `i18n`: This is where the i18n JSON files live. Each language has a folder with numerous JSON files organized by modules.
- `swagger-ui`: This folder has the Swagger UI client used in development for API documentation.
- `index.html`: This is the web application's index file. This contains very minimal code for loading the angular application's main component. It is a single page Angular application. You will also find some commented out utility code like Google analytics script and Service worker scripts on this file. These can be enabled if required:

```html
<!doctype html>
<html class="no-js" lang="en" dir="ltr">
<head>
    ...
</head>
<body>
    ...
    <jhi-main></jhi-main>
    <noscript>
        <h1>You must enable javascript to view this page.</h1>
    </noscript>
    ...
```

```
</body>
</html>
```

 To enable PWA mode using service workers, just uncomment the corresponding code in `src/main/webapp/index.html` to register the service worker. JHipster uses workbox (`https://developers.google.com/web/tools/workbox/`), which creates the respective service worker and dynamically generates the `sw.js`.

Starting the application

Now, let's start the application and see the output. There are multiple ways to run the application:

- By using the Spring Boot Gradle task from the terminal/command line
- By executing the main Java class `src/main/java/com/mycompany/store/StoreApp.java` from an IDE
- By executing the packaged application file using the `java -jar` command

Let's start the application using the Gradle task. If you want to run the application directly in the IDE, just open the main app file `StoreApp.java` mentioned earlier, right-click, and choose **Run 'StoreApp'**.

To start the application via Gradle, open a terminal/command line and navigate to the application folder. Then, execute the Gradle command as follows (if you are on windows, execute `gradlew.bat`). This will trigger the default task `bootRun`:

```
> cd online-store
> ./gradlew
```

Running `./gradlew` is equivalent to running `./gradlew bootRun -Pdev`. For the client side, the webpack build needs to be run before starting the server for the first time, otherwise you will see a blank page. This task is run automatically during the app generation, but if it fails for some reason, it can be triggered manually by running `yarn run webpack:build`. The task can be triggered directly by the Gradle command as well by running `./gradlew webpackBuildDev bootRun -Pdev`.

Gradle will start downloading the wrapper and dependencies, and you should see the console output similar to the following screenshot after some time (anywhere from a few seconds to a few minutes depending on network speed):

```
2017-10-15 22:23:53.512  INFO 7713 --- [  restartedMain] com.mycompany.store.StoreApp            : Started StoreApp in 15.134 seconds (JVM running for 16.284)
2017-10-15 22:23:53.513  INFO 7713 --- [  restartedMain] com.mycompany.store.StoreApp            :
----------------------------------------------------------
    Application 'store' is running! Access URLs:
    Local:          http://localhost:8080
    External:       http://192.168.2.4:8080
    Profile(s):     [swagger, dev]
----------------------------------------------------------
<=========----> 90% EXECUTING [1m 49s]
```

The app has started successfully and is available on `http://localhost:8080`. Open your favorite browser and navigate to the URL.

Note that the build preceding will stay at 90% as the process is running continuously.

Application modules

Let's see the different modules available out of the box. The modules can be grouped into:

- Home and Login
- Account
- Admin

Home and Login modules

Once you open the URL, you will see a cool-looking hipster drinking coffee on the homepage as follows:

This is the home page. Let's log in to the application using the default credentials.

1. Click on the **Sign in** link on the page, or **Account** | **Sign in**. You will see the following login screen. Enter the default credentials—**Username**—admin, **Password**—admin, and click **Sign in**:

Once signed in, you will see the authenticated home page with all the authenticated menu items in the navbar:

2. Since we enabled internationalization, we get a **Language** menu. Let's try to switch to a different language. Click on the **Language** menu and choose the next available language:

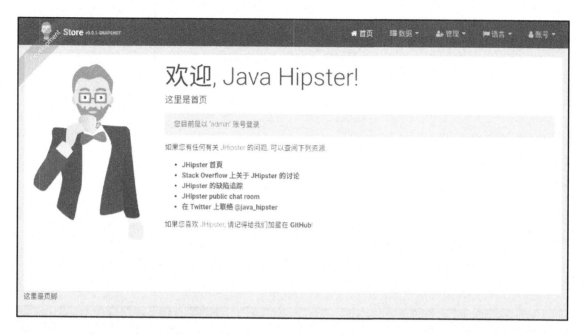

Account modules

Now, let's look at the account modules that are created out of the box. Under **Account** menu, you will see a **Sign out** option and following modules:

- Settings
- Password
- Registration

Settings

This module lets you change user settings such as name, email, and language:

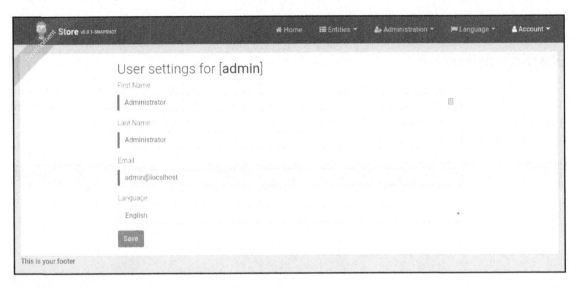

Password

This module lets you change the password for the current user. There is also a forgot password flow with email verification out of the box:

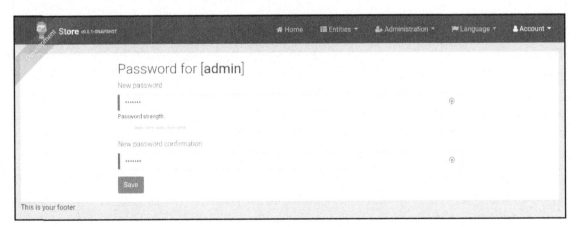

To use the email features, you will have to configure an SMTP server in the application properties. We will look at this in a later chapter.

Registration

This module is available only when you are not logged in. This lets you signup/register as a new user for the application. This will trigger a user activation flow with an activation email and verification. This module will not be available when choosing **Oauth2** as your authentication:

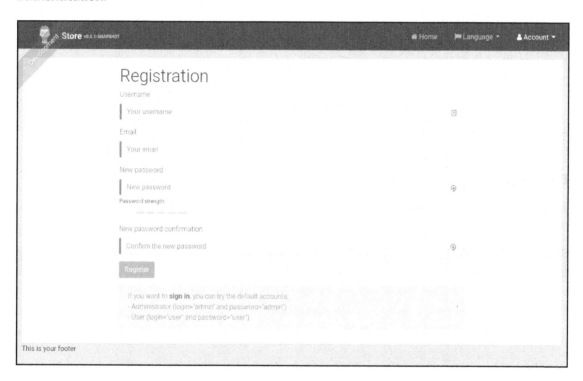

Admin module

Now, let's look at the generated admin module screens. These are very useful for development and monitoring of the application. Under the **Admin** menu, you will find the following modules:

- User management
- Metrics
- Health
- Configuration
- Audits
- Logs
- API

User management

This module provides you with CRUD functionality to manage users. The results are paginated by default. By default, users who register using the registration module will be deactivated unless they complete the registration process:

Metrics

This module visualizes data provided by the Spring Boot actuator and Dropwizard metrics. This is very useful for monitoring application performance as it gives method level performance information along with JVM, HTTP, database, and cache metrics. The eye icon near **Threads** will let you see the thread dump as well:

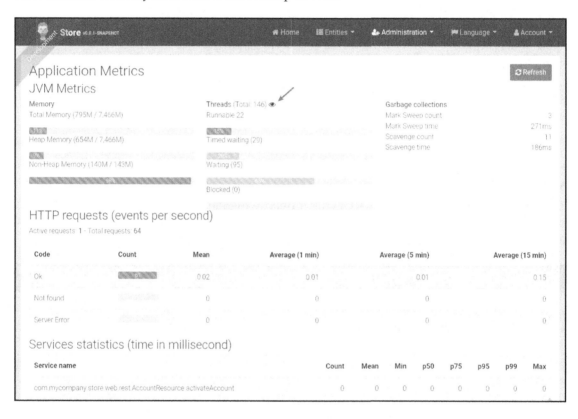

Health

This module provides the health status of application components like **Database** and other info like **Disk space**:

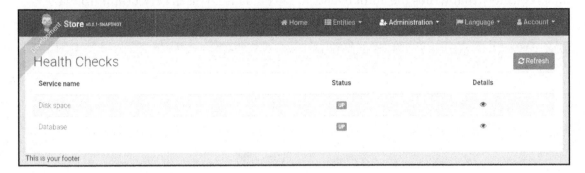

Configuration

This module helps to visualize the current application configuration in effect. This is very useful for troubleshooting configuration issues:

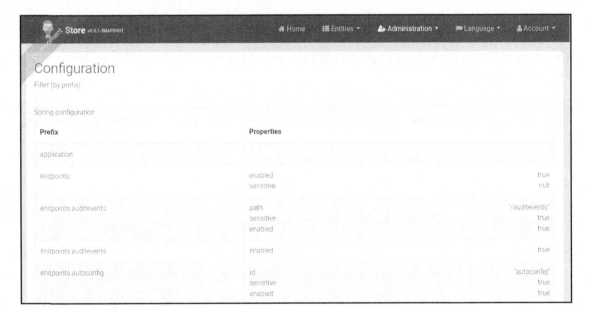

Audits

This module lists all the user authentication audit logs since JHipster enables audits for Spring security, and hence all the security events are captured. There is a special Spring data repository that writes the audit events to the database. This is very useful from a security standpoint:

Logs

This module helps to view and update application log levels at runtime. This is very useful for troubleshooting:

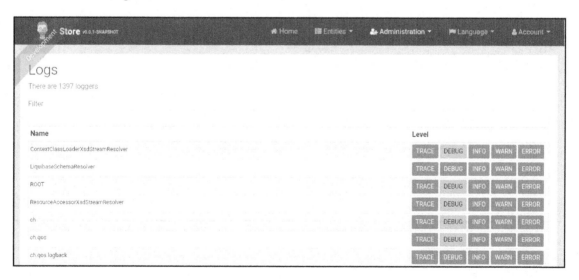

API

This module provides the Swagger API documentation for the application's REST API. It also provides a **Try it out** editor for the endpoints:

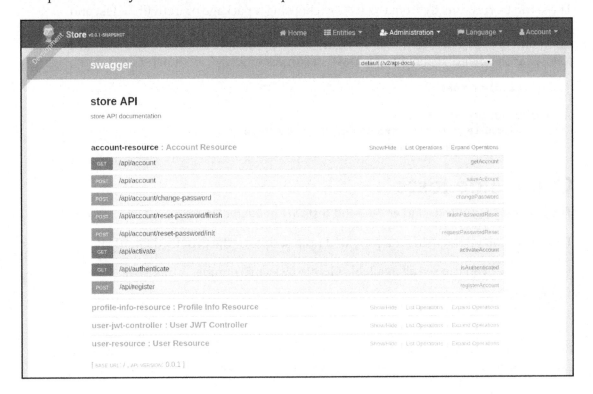

Running generated tests

Good software development is never complete without good testing. JHipster generates quite a lot of automated tests out of the box, and there are options to choose even more. Let's run the generated server side and client side tests for the application to make sure everything is working as expected.

First, open a terminal/command line and navigate to the project folder.

Server-side tests

The server-side integration tests and unit tests are present in the `src/test/java` folder.

These can be run directly from the IDE by choosing a package or individual test and running it, or via the command line by running a Gradle `test` task. Let's run it using the command line. In a new terminal, navigate to the application source folder and execute the following command. It should finish with a success message, as shown here:

```
> ./gradlew test
...
BUILD SUCCESSFUL in 45s
8 actionable tasks: 6 executed, 2 up-to-date
```

Client-side tests

The client-side unit tests and end-to-end tests are available under `src/test/javascript`.

These tests can be run using the provided npm scripts or the provided Gradle tasks.

 You can see all available Gradle tasks by running `./gradlew tasks`.

Let's run them using the npm scripts. First, let's run the Karma unit tests. In the terminal, execute the following code. You can also use `npm` instead of `yarn` if you prefer:

```
> yarn test
```

It should produce a similar output in the end:

```
PhantomJS 2.1.1 (Linux 0.0.0): Executed 56 of 56 SUCCESS (1.672 secs /
1.528 secs)
=============================== Coverage summary
===============================
Statements : 69.25% ( 903/1304 )
Branches : 40.43% ( 112/277 )
Functions : 48.89% ( 154/315 )
Lines : 67.72% ( 795/1174 )
================================================================================
=====
Done in 37.25s.
```

Now, let's run the Protractor end-to-end tests using the npm script. In order to run the `e2e` tests, we need to make sure that the server is running. If you have shut down the server which we started earlier, make sure to start it again by running `./gradlew` in a terminal. Now, open a new terminal and navigate to the application folder and execute the following command:

```
> yarn e2e
```

This will start protractor tests, which will open a new Chrome browser instance and execute the tests there. When finished, you should see something similar to the following in the console:

```
Started
..........
10 specs, 0 failures
Finished in 11.776 seconds

[00:02:57] I/launcher - 0 instance(s) of WebDriver still running
[00:02:57] I/launcher - chrome #01 passed
```

Summary

In this chapter, we saw how to create a monolithic web application using JHipster. We also walked through important aspects of the created source code and learned how to run the created application and the automated tests. We also browsed through the created modules and saw them in action. In the next chapter, we will see how we can utilize JHipster to model our business use case and generate entities for them. We will also learn about the **JHipster Domain Language (JDL)**.

4

Entity Modeling with JHipster Domain Language

In the previous chapter, we saw how we can use JHipster to generate a production-grade web application with a lot of awesome features, such as i18n, administration modules, account management, and so on. In this chapter, we will see how we can enrich that application with business entities and a model.

We will learn about the following in this chapter:

- **JHipster Domain Language (JDL)**
- JDL studio
- Entity and relationship modeling with JDL
- Entity generation

Introduction to JDL

JDL (http://www.jhipster.tech/jdl/) is used to create the domain model for a JHipster application. It provides a simple and user-friendly DSL to describe the entities and their relationships (for SQL databases only).

JDL is the recommended way to create entities for an application and can replace the entity generator provided by JHipster, which can be difficult to use when creating a lot of entities. The JDL is normally written in one or more files with a .jh extension.

Visit http://www.jhipster.tech/jdl/ for complete documentation on JDL.

If you prefer to work with UML and UML modeling tools, then check out JHipster-UML (`http://www.jhipster.tech/jhipster-uml/`), a tool that can create entities from popular UML tools.

DSL grammar for JDL

Now, let's see the JDL grammar. At the time of writing, JDL supports generating complete entity models with relationships and options such as DTO, service layer, and so on. The grammar can be broken down into the following:

- Entity declaration
- Relationship declaration
- Options declaration

In the following syntax, `[]` denotes optional and `*` denotes more than one can be specified.

Javadocs can be added to entity declarations and `/** */` Java comments can be added to fields and relationship declarations. JDL only comments can be added using `//` syntax.

It is also possible to define numerical constants in JDL, for example, `DEFAULT_MIN_LENGTH = 1`.

Entity modeling with JDL

The entity declaration is done using the following syntax:

```
entity <entity name> ([<table name>]) {
  <field name> <type> [<validation>*]
}
```

`<entity name>` is the name of the entity and will be used for class names and table names. Table names can be overridden using the optional `<table name>` parameter.

`<field name>` is the name of the fields (attributes) you want for the entity and `<type>` is the field type, as in String, Integer, and so on. Refer to `http://www.jhipster.tech/jdl/#available-types-and-constraints` for all supported field types. The ID field will be automatically created and hence need not be specified in JDL.

<validation> is optional and one or more <validation> for the fields can be specified depending on the validation supported by the field type. For validations such as max length and pattern, values can be specified in braces.

An example entity declaration would look like the following:

```
/**
 * This is customer entity javadoc comment
 * @author Foo
 */
entity Customer {
  /** Name field */
  name String required,
  age Integer,
  address String maxlength(100) pattern(/[a-Z0-9]+/)
}
```

Enumerations can also be declared using the following syntax:

```
enum <enum name> {
  <VALUE>*
}
```

Here is an example:

```
enum Language {
  ENGLISH, DUTCH, FRENCH
}
```

Relationship management

The relationship between entities can be declared using this syntax:

```
relationship <type> {
  <from entity>[{<relationship name>[(<display field>)] <validation>*}]
  to
  <to entity>[{<relationship name>[(<display field>)] <validation>*}]
}
```

The <type> is one from OneToMany, ManyToOne, OneToOne, or ManyToMany and as the name suggests, declares the relationship type between <from entity> and <to entity>.

<from entity> is the name of the owner entity of the relationship or the source. <to entity> is the destination of the relationship.

<relationship name> is optional and can be used to specify the field names to create for the relationship in the domain object. <display field> can be specified in braces to control the field of the entity to be shown in the drop-down menu on the generated web page, by default the ID field will be used. <validation> can be specified on the <from entity> or <to entity> and is optional. Currently, only required is supported.

OneToMany and ManyToMany relationships are always bidirectional in JHipster. In case of ManyToOne and OneToOne relationships, it is possible to create both bidirectional and unidirectional relationships. For unidirectional relationships, just skip the <relationship name> on the destination/to entity.

Multiple relationships of the same type can be declared within the same block, separated by a comma.

An example relationship declaration would look like the following:

```
entity Book
entity Author
entity Tag

relationship OneToMany {
  Author{book} to Book{writer(name) required},
  Book{tag} to Tag
}
```

The user is an existing entity in JHipster and it is possible to have certain relationships with the user. Many-to-many and one-to-one relations can be declared, but the other entity must be the source or owner. Many-to-one relations are also possible with a user entity.

DTO, service, and pagination options

JDL also allows us to declare entity related options easily. Options currently supported are:

- service: By default, JHipster generates REST Resource classes that call the entity repositories directly. This is the simplest option, but in real-world scenarios, we might need a service layer to handle business logic. This option lets us create a service layer with a simple Spring service bean class or with a traditional interface and implementation for the service bean. Possible values are serviceClass and serviceImpl. Choosing the latter will create an interface and implementation, which is preferred by some people.

- `dto`: By default, domain objects are directly used in the REST endpoints created, which may not be desirable in some situations and you might want to use an intermediatory **Data Transfer Object (DTO)** to have more control. JHipster lets us generate the DTO layer using Mapstruct (http://mapstruct.org/), an annotation preprocessor library that automatically generates the DTO classes. It is advisable to use a service layer when using DTO. A possible value is `mapstruct`. For more info visit: http://www.jhipster.tech/using-dtos/.

- `filter`: This option lets us enable JPA based filtering capabilities for the entity. This works only when a service layer is used. For more details, visit: http://www. jhipster.tech/entities-filtering/.

- `paginate`: This option lets us enable pagination for an entity. This enables pagination on the Resource layer and also implements a paging option on the client side. Possible values are pager, pagination, and infinite-scroll.

- `noFluentMethod`: This lets us disable Fluent API style setters for the generated entity domain objects.

- `skipClient/skipServer`: These options let us either skip the client-side code or server-side code during generation.

- `angularSuffix`: This option lets us specify a suffix for the folder and class names in the frontend code.

The general syntax for option declaration is <OPTION> <ENTITIES | * | all> [with <VALUE>] [except <ENTITIES>].

The following are some possible options and different syntax in which they can be declared:

```
entity A
entity B
...
entity Z

dto * with mapstruct
service A with serviceImpl
service B with serviceClass
paginate * with pagination except B, C
paginate B, C with infinite-scroll
filter A, B
```

JDL Studio

We will be using JDL Studio (`https://start.jhipster.tech/jdl-studio/`) to create our JDL file. It is an online web application built by the JHipster team for creating JDL files in a visual editor. The tool shows a visual representation of the created entity model and also lets you import/export JDL and capture image snapshots:

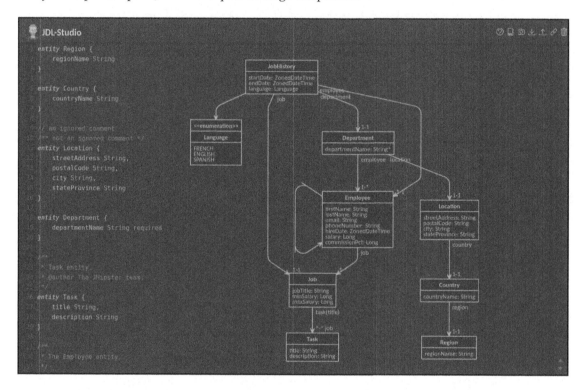

The tool also provides features such as syntax highlighting, auto-completion, error reporting, and Sublime Text-style keyboard shortcuts.

Navigate your favorite browser to `https://start.jhipster.tech/jdl-studio/` to open the application.

 Please note that by default this application stores the JDL in your browser's local storage. You can create an account with JHipster online if you want to save your JDL files to the cloud.

Use case entity model with explanation

Now, let's look at our use case and the entity model. Before that, clear the default JDL in the JDL Studio editor.

Entities

Let's start by defining our entities:

1. Copy the following snippet for `Product` and `ProductCategory` into the JDL Studio editor:

```
/** Product sold by the Online store */
entity Product {
    name String required
    description String
    price BigDecimal required min(0)
    size Size required
    image ImageBlob
}

enum Size {
    S, M, L, XL, XXL
}

entity ProductCategory {
    name String required
    description String
}
```

The `Product` entity is the core of the domain model; it holds product information such as `name`, `description`, `price`, `size`, and `image` which is a Blob. `name`, `price`, and `size` are required fields. `price` also has a min value validation. The `size` field is an enum with defined values.

The `ProductCategory` entity is used to group products together. It has `name` and `description` where `name` is a required field.

2. Add the following snippet for `Customer` into the JDL Studio editor:

```
entity Customer {
    firstName String required
    lastName String required
    gender Gender required
    email String required pattern(/^[^@\s]+@[^@\s]+\.[^@\s]+$/)
    phone String required
    addressLine1 String required
    addressLine2 String
    city String required
    country String required
}

enum Gender {
    MALE, FEMALE, OTHER
}
```

The `Customer` entity holds details of the customers using the online shopping portal. Most of the fields are marked as required, the `email` field has regex pattern validation. The `gender` field is an `enum`. This entity is related to the system user which we will see in detail soon.

3. Add the following snippet for `ProductOrder` and `OrderItem` into the JDL Studio editor:

```
entity ProductOrder {
    placedDate Instant required
    status OrderStatus required
    code String required
}

enum OrderStatus {
    COMPLETED, PENDING, CANCELLED
}

entity OrderItem {
    quantity Integer required min(0)
    totalPrice BigDecimal required min(0)
    status OrderItemStatus required
}

enum OrderItemStatus {
    AVAILABLE, OUT_OF_STOCK, BACK_ORDER
}
```

The `ProductOrder` and `OrderItem` entities are used to track product orders made by customers. `ProductOrder` holds the `placedDate` and `status`, and `code` of the order, which are all required fields, while `OrderItem` holds information about the `quantity`, `totalPrice`, and `status` of individual items. All fields are required and the `quantity` and `totalPrice` fields have min value validation. `OrderStatus` and `OrderItemStatus` are enum fields.

4. Add the following snippet for `Invoice` and `Shipment` into the JDL Studio editor:

```
entity Invoice {
    date Instant required
    details String
    status InvoiceStatus required
    paymentMethod PaymentMethod required
    paymentDate Instant required
    paymentAmount BigDecimal required
}

enum InvoiceStatus {
    PAID, ISSUED, CANCELLED
}

enum PaymentMethod {
    CREDIT_CARD, CASH_ON_DELIVERY, PAYPAL
}

entity Shipment {
    trackingCode String
    date Instant required
    details String
}
```

The `Invoice` and `Shipment` entities are used to track the invoice and shipping for the product orders, respectively. Most of the fields in `Invoice` are required and the `status` and `paymentMethod` fields are enums.

The enumerations are being used to contain the scope of certain fields, which gives more granular control over those fields.

Relationships

Now that we have defined our entities, let's add relationships between them:

1. Add the following snippet for relationships into the JDL Studio editor:

```
relationship OneToOne {
    Customer{user} to User
}
```

The first relationship declared is a unidirectional `OneToOne` between a `Customer` entity and the inbuilt `User` entity:

```
Customer (1) -----> (1) User
```

It means the `Customer` entity knows about the `User` and is the owner of the relationship but the `User` doesn't know about the `Customer` and hence we will not be able to obtain customers from a `User`. This lets us map customers to the `User` entity and use that for authorization purposes later ensuring one customer can be mapped only to one system user.

2. Add this snippet for relationships into the JDL Studio editor:

```
relationship ManyToOne {
    OrderItem{product} to Product
}
```

This one declares a unidirectional `ManyToOne` relationship from `OrderItem` to `Product`:

```
OrderItem (*) -----> (1) Product
```

It means the `OrderItem` knows their `Product` but `Product` does not know about `OrderItem`. This keeps the design clean as we don't want to know about orders from products for this use case. In the future, if we want to know the orders made for a product we could make this bi-directional.

3. Add the following snippet for relationship into the JDL Studio editor:

```
relationship OneToMany {
    Customer{order} to ProductOrder{customer},
    ProductOrder{orderItem} to OrderItem{order},
    ProductOrder{invoice} to Invoice{order},
    Invoice{shipment} to Shipment{invoice},
    ProductCategory{product} to Product{productCategory}
}
```

This declaration is interesting, as we have multiple `OneToMany` declarations:

```
Customer (1) <-----> (*) ProductOrder
ProductOrder (1) <-----> (*) OrderItem
ProductOrder (1) <-----> (*) Invoice
Invoice (1) <-----> (*) Shipment
ProductCategory (1) <-----> (*) Product
```

They are all bidirectional, meaning both the source entity and destination entity know about each other.

We declare that a `Customer` can have multiple ProductOrders, `ProductOrder` can have multiple OrderItems and Invoices, `Invoice` can have many `Shipment`, and `ProductCategory` can have many Products. From the destination entity, the source entities are mapped as `ManyToOne`.

Options for entities

Add the following snippet for options into the JDL Studio editor:

```
service * with serviceClass
paginate Product, Customer, ProductOrder, Invoice, Shipment, OrderItem with
pagination
```

In the options, we keep it simple and declare that we want a service class for all entities. We also enabled pagination for some of the entities that may get a lot of entries over time.

The diagram shows the complete model, with all the entities and their relationships as shown in JDL Studio:

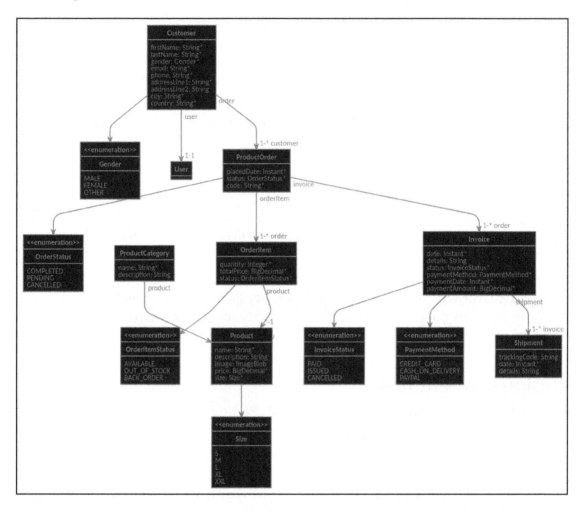

Now, let's download this JDL file to our file system:

1. Click on the download button in the upper-right-hand corner of the JDL Studio application.
2. Save the file with the name `online-store.jh` inside the `online-store` directory where we created our application in the previous chapter.

Entity generation with JHipster

Now, it's time to generate the domain model with our JDL. We will use the `import-jdl` command from JHipster for this.

Open your favorite Terminal application and navigate to the `online-store` folder where we created the application earlier. Then, execute the `import-jdl` command:

```
> cd online-store
> jhipster import-jdl online-store.jh
```

This will trigger the entity creation process and you will be asked to confirm the overwriting of existing files with changes. Take a look at the following screenshot:

```
Found the .jhipster/OrderItem.json configuration file, entity can be automatically generated!

The entity OrderItem is being updated.

Found the .jhipster/Invoice.json configuration file, entity can be automatically generated!

The entity Invoice is being updated.

Found the .jhipster/Shipment.json configuration file, entity can be automatically generated!

The entity Shipment is being updated.
    create src/main/resources/config/liquibase/changelog/20171128223527_added_entity_Product.xml
    create src/main/resources/config/liquibase/changelog/20171128223527_added_entity_constraints_Product.xml
    create src/main/java/com/mycompany/store/domain/Product.java
    create src/main/java/com/mycompany/store/repository/ProductRepository.java
    create src/main/java/com/mycompany/store/web/rest/ProductResource.java
    create src/main/java/com/mycompany/store/service/ProductService.java
    create src/test/java/com/mycompany/store/web/rest/ProductResourceIntTest.java
  conflict src/main/resources/config/liquibase/master.xml
? Overwrite src/main/resources/config/liquibase/master.xml? (ynaxdH)
```

Enter *a* to confirm the overwrite of all files with changes. Once the files are generated, JHipster will trigger a `yarn webpack:build` step to rebuild the client side code. Once done you will see a success message like the following:

```
Entity generation completed
Entity generation completed
Entity generation completed
Entity generation completed
Entity generation completed
Entity generation completed
Entity generation completed
Congratulations, JHipster execution is complete!
```

Running `git status` on the Terminal shows us that five files were modified and a lot of new files added. Let's commit the changes to Git. Execute the commands shown here:

```
> git add --all
> git commit -am "generated online store entity model"
```

Generated code walkthrough

Now let's take a look at what has been generated. Let's open the application code in our favorite IDE/editor. Let's take a look at what has been generated for the `Product` entity.

You might have noticed that there is a `.jhipster` folder at the root of the project and if you look into it you will see a bunch of JSON files. Let's look at `Product.json`. It holds metadata about the generated entity and is used by JHipster to regenerate and edit an entity when needed:

```json
{
    "fluentMethods": true,
    "relationships": [
        {
            "relationshipType": "many-to-one",
            "relationshipName": "productCategory",
            "otherEntityName": "productCategory",
            "otherEntityField": "id"
        }
    ],
    "fields": [
        {
            "fieldName": "name",
            "fieldType": "String",
            "fieldValidateRules": [
```

```
                "required"
            ]
        },
        {
            "fieldName": "description",
            "fieldType": "String"
        },
        {
            "fieldName": "price",
            "fieldType": "BigDecimal",
            "fieldValidateRules": [
                "required",
                "min"
            ],
            "fieldValidateRulesMin": 0
        },
        {
            "fieldName": "size",
            "fieldType": "Size",
            "fieldValues": "S,M,L,XL,XXL",
            "fieldValidateRules": [
                "required"
            ]
        },
        {
            "fieldName": "image",
            "fieldType": "byte[]",
            "fieldTypeBlobContent": "image"
        }
    ],
    "changelogDate": "20180114123458",
    "javadoc": "Product sold by the Online store",
    "entityTableName": "product",
    "dto": "no",
    "pagination": "pagination",
    "service": "serviceClass",
    "jpaMetamodelFiltering": false
}
```

Server-side source code

Now let's look at the server-side code generated.

Domain class for the entity

In the `src/main/java/com/mycompany/store/domain` folder, you will find the entity domain object. Open `Product.java`:

```java
@ApiModel(description = "Product sold by the Online store")
@Entity
@Table(name = "product")
@Cache(usage = CacheConcurrencyStrategy.NONSTRICT_READ_WRITE)
public class Product implements Serializable {

    private static final long serialVersionUID = 1L;

    @Id
    @GeneratedValue(strategy = GenerationType.IDENTITY)
    private Long id;

    @NotNull
    @Column(name = "name", nullable = false)
    private String name;

    @Column(name = "description")
    private String description;

    @Lob
    @Column(name = "image")
    private byte[] image;

    @Column(name = "image_content_type")
    private String imageContentType;

    @NotNull
    @DecimalMin(value = "0")
    @Column(name = "price", precision=10, scale=2, nullable = false)
    private BigDecimal price;

    @NotNull
    @Enumerated(EnumType.STRING)
    @Column(name = "jhi_size", nullable = false)
    private Size size;

    @ManyToOne
    private ProductCategory productCategory;
```

```
    // jhipster-needle-entity-add-field - JHipster will add fields
    here, do not remove

    ... // getters

    public Product name(String name) {
        this.name = name;
        return this;
    }

    ... // setters

    // jhipster-needle-entity-add-getters-setters - JHipster will add
getters and setters here, do not remove

    ... // equals, hashcode and toString methods
}
```

The entity class defines the fields and relationships.

```
@ApiModel(description = "Product sold by the Online store")
```

This annotation is used by Swagger to show useful documentation when the entity is used in an endpoint:

```
@Entity
@Table(name = "product")
```

These are JPA annotations declaring the POJO as an entity and mapping it to an SQL table:

```
@Cache(usage = CacheConcurrencyStrategy.NONSTRICT_READ_WRITE)
```

This is a Hibernate annotation, which lets us enable level 2 cache for this entity. In our case using Hazelcast:

```
@Id
@GeneratedValue(strategy = GenerationType.IDENTITY)
private Long id;
```

The id field is special and is mapped as a generated value field. Depending on the DB, this field will use a native generation technique or a sequence provided by Hibernate. Since we are using MySQL, it will use the native DB primary key generation technique:

```
@Column(name = "name", nullable = false)
```

This JPA annotation is used to map columns to fields and it can also be used to declare properties such as nullable, precision, scale, unique, and so on for the field:

```
@NotNull
@DecimalMin(value = "0")
```

These are Bean validation annotations enabling validation for the fields:

```
@Lob
@Column(name = "image")
private byte[] image;

@Column(name = "image_content_type")
private String imageContentType;
```

The image field is a Blob and it is marked by the Lob type since we are using MySQL. It also has an additional field to hold the content type information:

```
@Enumerated(EnumType.STRING)
```

The Enumerated annotation is used to map Enum fields. These are stored as simple varchar fields in the DB:

```
@ManyToOne
private ProductCategory productCategory;
```

The relationships are mapped using annotations such as `@ManyToOne`, `@OneToMany`, `@OneToOne`, and `@ManyToMany`.

Here, `ProductCategory` is mapped as `ManyToOne`; on the other side of the relationship Product is mapped as `OneToMany` as shown here:

```
@OneToMany(mappedBy = "productCategory")
@JsonIgnore
@Cache(usage = CacheConcurrencyStrategy.NONSTRICT_READ_WRITE)
private Set<Product> products = new HashSet<>();
```

As you can see, the relationship also specifies a cache for it. It tells Jackson to ignore the field while converting to JSON to avoid a circular reference since `ProductCategory` is already mapped in `Product` entity:

```
public Product name(String name) {
    this.name = name;
    return this;
}
```

This is a fluent setter generated by default along with the standard setter. This can be turned off by specifying the `noFluentMethod` for the entity in JDL. Fluent methods are handy as they let us chain setters as follows for more concise code:

```
new Product().name("myProduct").price(10);
```

The corresponding table definitions and constraints are created using Liquibase and can be found in `src/main/resources/config/liquibase/changelog` with the file names `<timestamp>_added_entity_Product` and `<timestamp>_added_entity_constraints_Product.xml`, which automatically get applied to the database when we reload or start the application again.

Repository interface for the entity

In the `src/main/java/com/mycompany/store/repository` folder, you will find the entity repository service. Open `ProductRepository.java`:

```
@Repository
public interface ProductRepository extends JpaRepository<Product, Long> {

}
```

The repository service is just an empty interface that extends the `JpaRepository` class. Since it is a Spring Data repository, the implementation is automatically created, allowing us to do all CRUD actions using this simple interface declaration. Additional repository methods can be added here easily. We will see about that in the next chapter.

Service class for the entity

Since we opted to generate service classes for our entities, let's look at one. In the `src/main/java/com/mycompany/store/service` folder, you will find the entity repository service. Open `ProductService.java`:

```
@Service
@Transactional
public class ProductService {

    private final Logger log =
LoggerFactory.getLogger(ProductService.class);

    private final ProductRepository productRepository;

    public ProductService(ProductRepository productRepository) {
        this.productRepository = productRepository;
```

```
        }

    . . .

  }
```

The service uses constructor injection to get its dependencies, which are automatically injected by Spring during bean instantiation. The service is also marked as `@Transactional` to enable transaction management for data access. The service defines CRUD action methods. For example, the `findAll` method calls the equivalent repository method while adding a read-only transaction rule to it. You can see that the method already supports pagination and returns the results as `Page`. The `Page` and `Pageable` objects are provided by Spring and let us easily control pagination:

```java
@Transactional(readOnly = true)
public Page<Product> findAll(Pageable pageable) {
    log.debug("Request to get all Products");
    return productRepository.findAll(pageable);
}
```

Resource class for the entity

In the `src/main/java/com/mycompany/store/web/rest` folder you will find the entity resource service. Open `ProductResource.java`:

```java
@RestController
@RequestMapping("/api")
public class ProductResource {
    . . .
}
```

The resource acts as the controller layer and in our case, it serves the REST endpoints to be used by our client-side code. The endpoint has a base mapping to `"/api"`:

```java
@GetMapping("/products")
@Timed
public ResponseEntity<List<Product>> getAllProducts(Pageable pageable) {
    log.debug("REST request to get a page of Products");
    Page<Product> page = productService.findAll(pageable);
    HttpHeaders headers =
    PaginationUtil.generatePaginationHttpHeaders(page,
    "/api/products");
    return new ResponseEntity<>(page.getContent(), headers,
    HttpStatus.OK);
}
```

All the CRUD actions have equivalent mapping methods here, for example, the `getAllProducts` maps to the `findAll` from our service. The resource also handles pagination by adding appropriate headers for pagination.

Client side

The client-side resources for the entity are created in the `src/main/webapp/app/entities` folder. Let's take a look at the code created for the `Product` entity in the `product` folder.

TypeScript model class for the entity

Let's look at the TypeScript model generated in `product.model.ts`. This maps directly to the domain object:

```
export class Product implements IProduct {
    constructor(
        public id?: number,
        public name?: string,
        public description?: string,
        public imageContentType?: string,
        public image?: any,
        public price?: number,
        public size?: Size,
        public productCategory?: IProductCategory
    ) {
    }
}
```

The fields are all optional making it possible to create an object instance without any values. You will also see that the enums are also generated alongside the model in the file.

Angular services for the entity

The `ProductService` is an Angular service that interacts with our REST endpoints and created in `product.service.ts`:

```
@Injectable()
export class ProductService {

    private resourceUrl = SERVER_API_URL + 'api/products';

    constructor(private http: HttpClient) { }
```

```
    ...

    query(req?: any): Observable<HttpResponse<Product[]>> {
        const options = createRequestOption(req);
        return this.http.get<Product[]>(
            this.resourceUrl,
            { params: options, observe: 'response' }
        )
        .map((res: HttpResponse<Product[]>) =>
this.convertArrayResponse(res));
    }


    ...
}
```

As you can see, the service has a constructor with dependencies injected following a similar pattern as our server-side code. There are methods mapping all the CRUD actions to the backend REST Resource. The HTTP calls make use of RxJS Observables to provide an asynchronous streaming API, which is much better than a Promise based API.

There is also `ProductPopupService` defined in `product-popup.service.ts`, a utility service to open popup dialogs for entity editing and deletion.

Angular components of the entity

For an entity, there are six component classes generated in four files and four HTML files that are used in the components.

`ProductComponent`, defined in `product.component.ts` handles the main listing screen. It uses `product.component.html`, as the template. The component manages the view and their actions. It also calls multiple services to fetch data and to do other actions such as alerts and event broadcasts:

```
@Component({
    selector: 'jhi-product',
    templateUrl: './product.component.html'
})
export class ProductComponent implements OnInit, OnDestroy {
    ...
}
```

`product-dialog.component.ts` defines `ProductDialogComponent` and `ProductPopupComponent`, which handle the create/edit dialog page using template `product-dialog.component.html`:

```
@Component({
    selector: 'jhi-product-dialog',
    templateUrl: './product-dialog.component.html'
})
export class ProductDialogComponent implements OnInit {
    ...
}

@Component({
    selector: 'jhi-product-popup',
    template: ''
})
export class ProductPopupComponent implements OnInit, OnDestroy {
    ...
}
```

`ProductDetailComponent` handles the detail view screen using `product-detail.component.html` as the template and is defined in `product-detail.component.ts`.

`ProductDeleteDialogComponent` and `ProductDeletePopupComponent` defined in `product-delete-dialog.component.ts` manages the delete popup dialog using `product-delete-dialog.component.html` as the template.

Angular route for the entity

We need a route declaration so that we can access the entity pages. This is declared in `product.route.ts`.

For example, this declares the detail view of the entity:

```
{
    path: 'product/:id',
    component: ProductDetailComponent,
    data: {
        authorities: ['ROLE_USER'],
        pageTitle: 'storeApp.product.home.title'
    },
    canActivate: [UserRouteAccessService]
}
```

The data attribute is used to pass metadata such as allowed roles and page titles to the component. The `UserRouteAccessService` defined in the `canActivate` attribute decides whether a user has the authorization to view the page and uses the authorities metadata and authentication details to verify. Routes having a popup, declares the `outlet: 'popup'` attribute.

Angular module for the entity

Finally, we have a module for the entity. Angular modules can be used to consolidate all components, directives, pipes, and services of an entity so that they can be imported into other modules easily. The `StoreProductModule` module is defined in `product.module.ts`:

```
@NgModule({
    imports: [
        StoreSharedModule,
        RouterModule.forChild(ENTITY_STATES)
    ],
    declarations: [
        ProductComponent,
        ProductDetailComponent,
        ProductDialogComponent,
        ProductDeleteDialogComponent,
        ProductPopupComponent,
        ProductDeletePopupComponent,
    ],
    entryComponents: [
        ProductComponent,
        ProductDialogComponent,
        ProductPopupComponent,
        ProductDeleteDialogComponent,
        ProductDeletePopupComponent,
    ],
    providers: [
        ProductService,
        ProductPopupService,
        ProductResolvePagingParams,
    ],
    schemas: [CUSTOM_ELEMENTS_SCHEMA]
})
export class StoreProductModule {}
```

The module declares the components and registers services provided by it. The module also imports shared modules so that it can access shared services and components. The module is imported by the `StoreEntityModule` defined in `entity.module.ts` under `src/main/webapp/app/entities`.

Generated pages

Let's start the application to view the generated pages. In the Terminal, execute the Gradle command the follows:

```
> ./gradlew
```

This will start the server in development mode locally. Since the `import-jdl` step already compiled the frontend code, we don't have to run `yarn start` just to see the new pages, but please note that for further development it is better to use `yarn start` along with the preceding command. If you had the server already running while generating the entities, then no need to run this command, instead just compile the source again using the `./gradlew compileJava` command. Using your IDE and Spring devtools will hot reload the application for you. If you had `yarn start` running then a hot reload will take place on the client side as well, otherwise, it will just refresh the page. We will see more about hot reloading in the next chapter.

Once you see the following message, the server is ready and we can navigate to the URL `http://localhost:8080` in our favorite browser:

```
-------------------------------------------------------------
        Application 'store' is running! Access URLs:
        Local: http://localhost:8080
        External: http://192.168.2.7:8080
        Profile(s): [swagger, dev]
-------------------------------------------------------------
```

If you are not already logged in, sign in using the default admin user with the password `admin` by clicking on the **Sign in** link on the home page. Once logged in, click on the **Entities** link in the menu and you will see all our entities listed there:

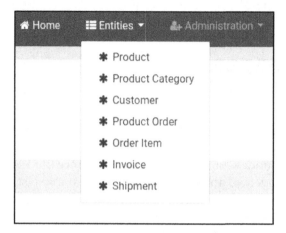

Click on the **Product** and you will see the **Products** listing screen. It doesn't have any items yet as we haven't created any:

Let's create an entity, click on the **Create a new Product** button on the screen and you will see the **Create or edit a Product** popup dialog:

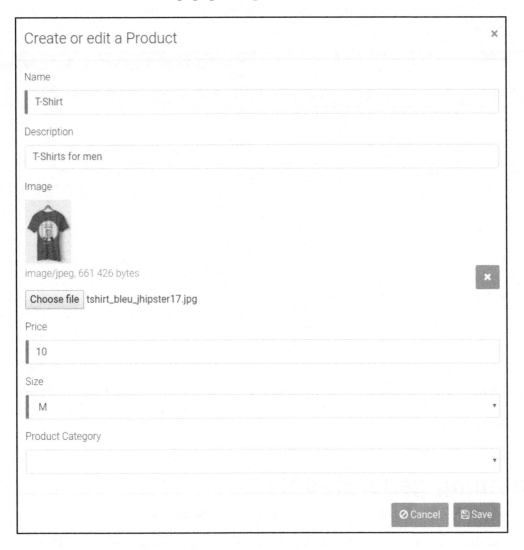

Create or edit a Product   ✕

Name

| T-Shirt

Description

| T-Shirts for men

Image

image/jpeg, 661 426 bytes   ✕

Choose file | tshirt_bleu_jhipster17.jpg

Price

| 10

Size

| M   ▾

Product Category

| ▾

⊘ Cancel   💾 Save

Enter `Name`, `Description`, `Price`, and `Size`. Choose an image by clicking on the **Choose file** button. Don't worry about **Product Category** as we haven't created any yet. Now click on **Save** and the popup will disappear and the listing screen will be refreshed with the success message:

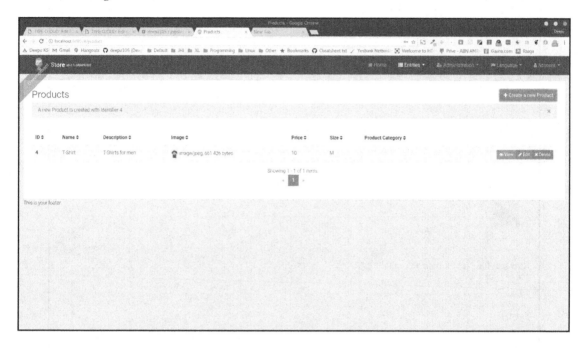

The **Products** screen now shows our new entity with buttons for **View**, **Edit**, and **Delete**. There are also pagination links on the bottom. Explore the **View**, **Edit**, and **Delete** buttons by clicking on each of them.

Running generated tests

Let's run all the tests to make sure the generated test code works fine.

Let's run the server-side unit/integration tests, client-side Karma unit tests, and Protractor e2e tests using the command-line. In a new Terminal, navigate to the application source folder and execute these commands. They should finish with a success message. Make sure you have the application running, as e2e tests will need it. If the application is not running first start it by running `./gradlew` in a Terminal:

```
> ./gradlew test && yarn test && yarn e2e
```

Summary

In this chapter, we saw how to model and create entities using JDL. We also walked through important aspects of the created source code. We also browsed through the created entity modules and saw them in action. In the next chapter, we will see how we can utilize JHipster to further develop the application and include specific business logic and tweaks. We will also learn about some of the technologies used in more depth.

5

Customization and Further Development

In the previous chapter, we saw how to use the JHipster Domain Language to model and generate our domain model. We also learned about entity relationships and the `import-jdl` sub-generator. In this chapter, we will see how we can further customize and add business logic to the generated application to suit our needs. We will learn about:

- Live reload with Spring DevTools and BrowserSync
- Customizing the angular frontend for an entity
- Editing an entity created using the JHipster entity generator
- Changing the look and feel of the application using a Bootstrap theme
- Adding a new i18n language using the JHipster language generator
- Customizing the generated REST API to add additional role-based authorization with Spring Security
- Creating new Spring Data JPA queries and methods

Live reload for development

When developing an application, one of the most annoying and time-consuming parts is recompiling the code and restarting the servers to see the code changes we have made. Traditionally, JavaScript code used to be easier, as it didn't need any compilation and you could just refresh the browser and see the changes. However, even though current MVVM stacks make the client side more important than before, they also introduce side effects, such as transpiling of client-side code, and more. So, if you are refactoring a field for an entity, you would traditionally need to do the following tasks to see the changes in your browser:

1. Compile the server-side Java code.
2. Apply the table changes to the database.
3. Recompile the client-side code.
4. Restart the application server.
5. Refresh the browser.

This takes a lot of time, is frustrating to do for every small change, and results in you making more changes before checking them, hence affecting productivity.

What if I told you that you don't have to do any of these, and all of this could happen automatically as you save your changes using your IDE? That would be awesome, wouldn't it?

With JHipster you get exactly that. JHipster uses Spring Boot DevTools, webpack dev server, and BrowserSync to enable a nice live reload feature for the end-to-end code.

Let's take a quick look at the technologies used.

Spring Boot DevTools

Spring Boot DevTools (`https://docs.spring.io/spring-boot/docs/current/reference/html/using-boot-devtools.html`) enables Spring Boot applications to reload the embedded server when there is a change in the classpath. It states the following—*The aim of this module is to try and improve the development-time experience when working on Spring Boot applications*, and it does exactly that. It uses a custom classloader to restart the application when a class is updated and recompiled, and since the server is hot reloaded it is much faster than a cold restart.

It isn't as cool as JRebel or similar technologies, which do instant reload, but it beats doing it manually and doesn't require any extra configuration to enable it.

JHipster DevTools is automatically enabled in the `dev` profile, using an IDE that can automatically recompile classes on saving. The DevTools will ensure the application is reloaded and up to date. Since Liquibase is used, any schema updates using proper changelogs will also get updated. Make sure not to change existing changelogs as it will cause a checksum error. Application reloads can also be triggered by simply using the commands `mvnw compile` or `gradlew compileJava` depending on the build tool used.

> If you choose a NoSQL DB, such as MongoDB, Cassandra, or Couchbase, JHipster provides database migration tools for those as well.

Webpack dev server and BrowserSync

Webpack dev server (`https://github.com/webpack/webpack-dev-server`) provides a simple Express server using webpack dev middleware, and supports live reloads when assets change. Webpack dev middleware supports features such as hot module replacement and in memory file access.

> In Webpack Version 4 and above a new alternative called **webpack-serve** (`https://github.com/webpack-contrib/webpack-serve`) is used instead of Webpack dev server. It uses native WebSocket support in newer browsers.

BrowserSync (`https://browsersync.io/`) is a Node.js tool that helps in browser testing by synchronizing file changes and interactions of the web page across multiple browsers and devices. It provides features such as auto-reload on file changes, synchronized UI interactions, scrolling, and so on. JHipster integrates BrowserSync with Webpack dev server to provide a productive development setup. It makes testing a web page on different browsers and devices super easy. Changes to CSS are loaded without a browser refresh.

To use live reload on the client side you need to run `yarn start`, which will start the development server and open up a browser pointing to `http://localhost:9000`. Notice the port `9000`. BrowserSync will be using this port, while the application backend will be served at `8080`, which all requests will be proxied through via webpack dev middleware.

Open another browser, for example, Firefox if BrowserSync has opened Chrome already or vice versa. Now place them side by side and play around with the application. You will see your actions are replicated, thanks to BrowserSync. Try changing some code and save the file to see live reload in action.

Setting up live reload for an application

Let's start the perfect development setup for the application we created. In a terminal, start the server in dev mode by running `./gradlew` and in another terminal, start the client side development server by running `yarn start`.

Now when you make any changes on the server side simply run `./gradlew compileJava` or if you are using an IDE click on the compile button.

With IntelliJ IDEA, files are automatically saved and so you can set up *Ctrl + S* to compile the classes giving you a nice workflow. In Eclipse, saving a class automatically compiles it.

When you make changes on the client side, simply save the file and webpack dev server and BrowserSync will do the rest.

Customizing the Angular frontend for an entity

Now that we have our entity domain model created and working, let's make it more usable. The Product listing screen has a table view generated by JHipster; it is sufficient for simple CRUD operations but isn't the best-suited user experience for end users who want to browse our product listing. Let's see how we can easily change to something more appealing. We will also add a nice client-side filter option to filter the listing. We will be using both Angular and Bootstrap features for this.

First, let's find the source code that we would need to edit. In your favorite editor/IDE navigate to `src/main/webapp/app/entities/product`:

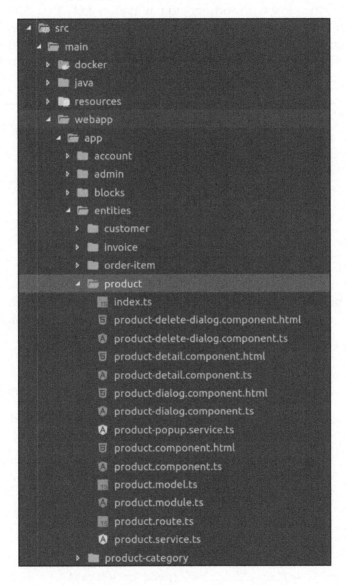

Let's start by customizing the `product.component.html` file to update the UI view of the product listing. The HTML code currently renders a table view and uses some Angular directives to enhance the view with sorting and pagination. Let's first change the view from a table into a list, but first open the development web server from BrowserSync, if it's not already open, by navigating to `http://localhost:9000`. Log in and navigate to **Entities** | **Product Category** and create a category, then navigate to **Entities** | **Product** and create few new products so that we have something to list:

We can use the Bootstrap List group (`https://getbootstrap.com/docs/4.0/components/list-group/`) component for this purpose. Let's use the following snippet and change the view. Replace the `div` with `class="table-responsive"` with the following code:

```
<div *ngIf="products">
    <div class="list-group">
        <a [routerLink]="['../product', product.id ]"
            class="list-group-item list-group-item-action flex-column
            align-items-start"
            *ngFor="let product of products; trackBy: trackId">
            <div class="d-flex w-100 justify-content-between">
                <h5 class="mb-1">{{product.name}}</h5>
                <small *ngIf="product.productCategory">
                    <a [routerLink]="['../product-category',
                    product.productCategory?.id ]" >
                        {{product.productCategory?.id}}
                    </a>
                </small>
            </div>
            <small class="mb-1">{{product.description}}</small>
            <p class="mb-1">Price: {{product.price}}</p>
            <small>
                Size:
                <span jhiTranslate="{{'storeApp.Size.' +
                product.size}}">
                    {{product.size}}
```

```
                </span>
            </small>
        </a>
    </div>
</div>
```

As you can see, we are iterating the products using the Angular directive `*ngFor="let product of products; trackBy: trackId"` on the anchor element so that the element is created for each product in the list. We wrap this in a `*ngIf="products"` directive so that the view is rendered only when the product's object is defined. The `[routerLink]="['../product', product.id ]"` directive will create a href for the anchor using the Angular router so that we can navigate to the particular product route. We then use properties from the product in template strings to be rendered using `{{product.name}}` syntax. As you save the code, you might notice that the view refreshes automatically, thanks to BrowserSync.

> The `trackBy` function used in `ngFor` lets Angular decide which items are added or removed from a collection. This improves rendering performance as Angular can now figure out which items need to be added or removed from DOM exactly, without having to recreate the entire collection. Here, we provide `trackId` as the function to uniquely identify an item in the collection.

This will produce the following:

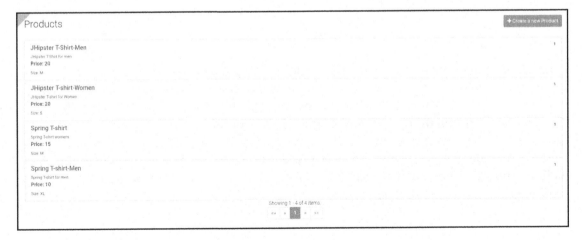

While it's a good start, it's not enough. So, let's go in and make it better. Let's add the image to the listing first. Modify the code to add Bootstrap rows and columns, as shown in the following code, the original code rendering the content is moved into the second column and remains unchanged:

```
<div *ngIf="products">
    <div class="list-group">
        <a [routerLink]="['../product', product.id ]" class="list-group-
item list-group-item-action flex-column align-items-start"
            *ngFor="let product of products; trackBy: trackId">
            <div class="row">
                <div class="col-2 col-xs-12 justify-content-center">
                    <img [src]="'data:' + product.imageContentType +
                    ';base64,' + product.image"
                        style="max-height:150px;" alt="product image"/>
                </div>
                <div class="col col-xs-12">
                    <div class="d-flex w-100 justify-content-between">
                        ...
                    </div>
                    <small class="mb-1">{{product.description}}</small>
                    <p class="mb-1">Price: {{product.price}}</p>
                    <small>
                        ...
                    </small>
                </div>
            </div>
        </a>
    </div>
</div>
```

Take a look at the code highlighted in bold. We added a Bootstrap row (https://getbootstrap.com/docs/4.0/layout/grid/) with two column divs, the first div takes up two columns in a 12 column grid specified by col-2, while we also say that when the display is **xs (extra small)** the div tag should take 12-columns using col-xs-12. The second div is kept responsive by specifying just col so it takes the remaining available columns after the first div, and when the display is extra small it takes up 12 columns as well. The image inside the first column div uses a data URL as src to render the image. Now we have an even better view:

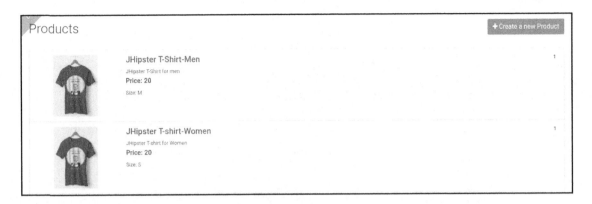

We can polish it further. We can use the Angular currency pipe (`https://angular.io/api/common/CurrencyPipe`) for the price and remove the redundant label for it by changing to `{{product.price | currency:'USD'}}`. We can add a label for the category shown on the right-hand side of the list as well.

Finally, we can add the **Edit** and **Delete** buttons back, but we need to show them only for users who have the role ADMIN so that normal users will only be able to view the product listing. We can copy the HTML code for `edit` and `delete` buttons from the original table. The final code will be as follows:

```
<div *ngIf="products">
    <div class="list-group">
        <a [routerLink]="['../product', product.id ]"
            class="list-group-item list-group-item-action flex-column
            align-items-start"
            *ngFor="let product of products; trackBy: trackId">
            <div class="row">
                <div class="col-2 col-xs-12 justify-content-center">
                    <img [src]="'data:' + product.imageContentType +
                    ';base64,' + product.image"
                        style="max-height:150px;" alt="product image"/>
                </div>
                <div class="col col-xs-12">
                    <div class="d-flex w-100 justify-content-between">
                        <h5 class="mb-1">{{product.name}}</h5>
                        <small *ngIf="product.productCategory">
                            <a [routerLink]="['../product-category',
                                product.productCategory?.id ]" >
                                Category: {{product.productCategory?.id}}
                            </a>
                        </small>
                    </div>
```

```
            <small class="mb-1">{{product.description}}</small>
      <p class="mb-1">{{product.price | currency:'USD'}}</p>
          <small>
              Size:
              <span jhiTranslate="{{'storeApp.Size.' +
              product.size}}">
                  {{product.size}}
              </span>
          </small>
          <div *jhiHasAnyAuthority="'ROLE_ADMIN'">
              <button type="submit"
                      [routerLink]="['/',
                          { outlets: { popup: 'product/'+
                          product.id + '/edit'} }]"
                      replaceUrl="true"
                      queryParamsHandling="merge"
                      class="btn btn-primary btn-sm">
                  <span class="fa fa-pencil"></span>
                  <span class="d-none d-md-inline"
jhiTranslate="entity.action.edit">Edit</span>
              </button>
              <button type="submit"
                      [routerLink]="['/',
                          { outlets: { popup: 'product/'+
                          product.id + '/delete'} }]"
                      replaceUrl="true"
                      queryParamsHandling="merge"
                      class="btn btn-danger btn-sm">
                  <span class="fa fa-remove"></span>
                  <span class="d-none d-md-inline"
jhiTranslate="entity.action.delete">Delete</span>
              </button>
          </div>
      </div>
   </div>
 </a>
 </div>
</div>
```

The *jhiHasAnyAuthority="'ROLE_ADMIN'" directive is provided by JHipster and can be used to control presentation based on user roles. By default, JHipster provides ROLE_ADMIN and ROLE_USER, but controlling this only on the client side is not secure as it can be easily bypassed, so we should secure this on the server side as well. We will look at this later in the chapter. Log out and log in again using the user account to see the directive in action:

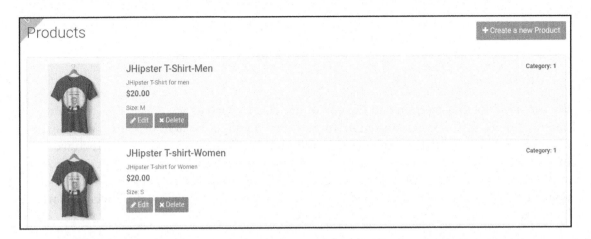

Now, let's also add the `*jhiHasAnyAuthority="'ROLE_ADMIN'"` directive to the create button element.

Now that our view is much better, let's bring back the sorting functionality we originally had. Since we do not have table headers anymore we can use some buttons to sort based on certain fields that are important.

Let's use Bootstrap button group (`https://getbootstrap.com/docs/4.0/components/button-group/`) for this. Place the following snippet above the `<div class="list-group">` element we created earlier:

```
<div class="mb-2 d-flex justify-content-end align-items-center">
    <span class="mx-2 col-1">Sort by</span>
    <div class="btn-group" role="group"
        jhiSort [(predicate)]="predicate" [(ascending)]="reverse"
            [callback]="transition.bind(this)">
        <button type="button" class="btn btn-light" jhiSortBy="name">
            <span jhiTranslate="storeApp.product.name">Name</span>
            <span class="fa fa-sort"></span>
        </button>
        <button type="button" class="btn btn-light" jhiSortBy="price">
            <span jhiTranslate="storeApp.product.price">Price</span>
            <span class="fa fa-sort"></span>
        </button>
        <button type="button" class="btn btn-light" jhiSortBy="size">
            <span jhiTranslate="storeApp.product.size">Size</span>
            <span class="fa fa-sort"></span>
        </button>
        <button type="button" class="btn btn-light"
          jhiSortBy="productCategory.id">
            <span
```

```
jhiTranslate="storeApp.product.productCategory">Product Category</span>
            <span class="fa fa-sort"></span>
        </button>
    </div>
</div>
```

We can use Bootstrap margin and flexbox utility classes such as `mb-2 d-flex justify-content-end align-items-center` to position and align the item properly. We use the `btn-group` class on a div element to group our button elements together on which we have placed the `jhiSort` directive and its bound properties such as `predicate`, `ascending`, and `callback`. On the buttons themselves, we use the `jhiSortBy` directive to specify which field it would use to sort. Now our page looks as follows, where products are sorted by price:

Finally, let's add some good old client-side filtering for the page.

 JHipster provides an option to enable server-side filtering using JPA metamodel. Another option is to enable Elasticsearch, for which JHipster will automatically create full-text search fields for every entity. So for any serious filtering requirements, you should use these.

First, let's add a new instance variable called `filter` of type string to the `ProductComponent` class in the `product.component.ts` file:

```
export class ProductComponent implements OnInit, OnDestroy {

    ...
    filter: string;

    constructor(
        ...
    ) {
    ...
    }
    ...
}
```

Now, let's use this variable in the `product.component.html` file. Add the highlighted snippet from the following code to the `div` we created for the sort-by buttons:

```
<div class="mb-2 d-flex justify-content-end align-items-center">
    <span class="mr-2 col-2">Filter by name</span>
    <input type="search" class="form-control" [(ngModel)]="filter">
    <span class="mx-2 col-1">Sort by</span>
    <div class="btn-group" role="group"
        ...
    </div>
</div>
```

We bound the filter variable to an input element using the `ngModel` directive, and using `[()]` ensures two-way binding on the variable.

 `[(ngModel)]="filter"` creates a two-way binding, `[ngModel]="filter"` creates a one-way binding from model to view, and `(ngModel)="filter"` creates a one-way binding from view to model.

Finally, update the `ngFor` directive on our list-group-item element as follows. We use a pipe provided by JHipster to filter the list using the name field of the product:

```
*ngFor="let product of (products | pureFilter:filter:'name'); trackBy:
trackId"
```

That's it, and we get a shiny filter option on our screen:

The UX is much better than before but for a real-world use case you could build a much better UI for the client-facing website, with features to add items to a cart, pay for items online, and so on, and leave this part for the back office use. Let's commit this to `git`: this is very important for managing changes to the project later. Run the following commands:

```
> git add --all
> git commit -am "update product listing page UI"
```

Editing an entity using the JHipster entity sub-generator

While looking through the generated entity screens, we might realize that there are some minor issues that affect the user experience. For example, on the product screens we have a relationship to a product category but when choosing the product category from the drop-down menu during creation, or when showing the category in the list, we show the category by its ID, which is not user-friendly. It would be nice if we could show the product category name instead. This is the default JHipster behavior but it can be customized while defining the relationships. Let's see how we can make our generated screens more user-friendly by editing the JDL model. This will overwrite existing files, but since we are using `git` we can easily cherry-pick the changes we made, we will see how this is done in a moment.

In our JDL, we defined relationships between entities using the following code:

```
relationship OneToOne {
    Customer{user} to User
}

relationship ManyToOne {
  OrderItem{product} to Product
}

relationship OneToMany {
    Customer{order} to ProductOrder{customer},
    ProductOrder{orderItem} to OrderItem{order},
    ProductOrder{invoice} to Invoice{order},
    Invoice{shipment} to Shipment{invoice},
    ProductCategory{product} to Product{productCategory}
}
```

By specifying the field to use for displaying the relationship in JDL using the (<field name>) syntax as follows, we can change how the client-side code displays relationships:

```
relationship OneToOne {
    Customer{user(login)} to User
}

relationship ManyToOne {
  OrderItem{product(name)} to Product
}

relationship OneToMany {
    Customer{order} to ProductOrder{customer(email)},
    ProductOrder{orderItem} to OrderItem{order(code)},
    ProductOrder{invoice} to Invoice{order(code)},
    Invoice{shipment} to Shipment{invoice(code)},
    ProductCategory{product} to Product{productCategory(name)}
}
```

Let's run this using the import-jdl command. The command only generates entities that underwent changes from the last run. But before we run let's also switch to a new branch, because it's a good practice to do major changes on a separate branch and merge them back so you have more control:

```
> git checkout -b entity-update-display-name
> jhipster import-jdl online-store.jh
```

Read more about Git flow here: `https://guides.github.com/introduction/flow/`.

Accept the changes to the files and wait for the build to finish. Now, let's look at the entity pages to verify that the display names are used properly and create some entities to try it out. Now we realize that the `Invoice` entity has empty drop-down menus, and that is because the `Invoice` entity does not have a field called **code**. Since we use `{{invoice.order?.code}}` in the template the symbol `?` makes Angular skip undefined values preventing errors in rendering.

This is easy to fix. Sometimes we might want to make a small change to an entity after we have created it using JDL and the `import-jdl` command. The best way would be to make the change in JDL and regenerate it using the import JDL command as we saw in the previous code. Now there is also another option, the entity sub generator, which can yield the same result. For the sake of familiarizing yourself with this option, let's use that to add the field to our `Invoice` entity:

1. Run the following command:

   ```
   > jhipster entity Invoice
   ```

2. From the options select **Yes, add more fields and relationships**:

   ```
   Using JHipster version installed globally
   Executing jhipster:entity Invoice
   Options:

   Found the .jhipster/Invoice.json configuration file, entity can be
   automatically generated!

   The entity Invoice is being updated.

   ? Do you want to update the entity? This will replace the existing
   files for this entity, all your custom code will be overwritten
     Yes, re generate the entity
   ❯ Yes, add more fields and relationships
     Yes, remove fields and relationships
     No, exit
   ```

3. Select **Yes** for the next question and provide the field name, type, and validation in the questions that follow:

```
Generating field #7

? Do you want to add a field to your entity? Yes
? What is the name of your field? code
? What is the type of your field? String
? Do you want to add validation rules to your field? Yes
? Which validation rules do you want to add? Required


================== Invoice ==================
Fields
date (Instant) required
details (String)
status (InvoiceStatus) required
paymentMethod (PaymentMethod) required
paymentDate (Instant) required
paymentAmount (BigDecimal) required
code (String) required

Relationships
shipment (Shipment) one-to-many
order (ProductOrder) many-to-one


Generating field #8

? Do you want to add a field to your entity? (Y/n)
```

4. Select **n** for the prompts that follow to add more fields and relationships. Accept the proposed file changes and that's it, we are done.
5. Now just make sure to update the JDL so that the entity `Invoice` has `code String required` as a field.

> You could also run `jhipster export-jdl online-store.jh` to export the current model back to the JDL.

Now that we have displayed entity relationships properly, we also need to make sure certain entities have relationship values mandatory. For example, for customers it should be mandatory to have a user, `ProductOrder` should have a customer, order item should have an order, Invoice should have an order, and finally, the shipment should have an invoice. Since JHipster supports making relationships required, we can make these changes using JDL. Update the relationships to the following snippet in `online-store.jh`:

```
relationship OneToOne {
    Customer{user(login) required} to User
}

relationship ManyToOne {
    OrderItem{product(name) required} to Product
}

relationship OneToMany {
    Customer{order} to ProductOrder{customer(email) required},
    ProductOrder{orderItem} to OrderItem{order(code) required},
    ProductOrder{invoice} to Invoice{order(code) required},
    Invoice{shipment} to Shipment{invoice(code) required},
    ProductCategory{product} to Product{productCategory(name)}
}
```

Now, run `jhipster import-jdl online-store.jh` and accept the proposed updates. Make sure to check what has changed using the `git diff` command or your Git UI tool.

Let's commit this step so that it can be rolled back if required:

```
> git add --all
> git commit -am "entity relationships display names and required update"
```

Now we have a problem, regenerating the entities overwrote all the files and that means we lost all the changes we made for the product listing page, but since we use `git` it's easy to get it back. So far, our project has only a few commits, so it will be easy to cherry-pick the commit we made for the product listing UI change and apply it back on top of the current codebase. However, in real-world scenarios, there could be a lot of changes before you can regenerate the JDL, and so it will require some effort to verify and merge the required changes back. Always rely on pull requests so that you can see what has changed and others can review and find any issues.

Let's cherry-pick the changes that we need.

Refer to the documentation for cherry-picking advanced options at: `https://git-scm.com/docs/git-cherry-pick`.

Since the commit we need is the last one on the master we can simply use `git cherry-pick master`. We could also switch to the master and use the `git log` command to list the commits, then copy the commit hash of the required commit and use that with `git cherry-pick <commit-sha>`.

Now, this results in merge conflicts, as the `product.component.html` file was updated in the commit we picked on our current branch tip. We need the incoming change from the commit but also need to update the product category display name from ID to code, so let's accept the incoming change and make a manual update from `{{product.productCategory?.id}}` to `{{product.productCategory?.name}}`.

Resolve the conflict by staging the file and commit. Now we can merge the branch into the master:

```
> git add src/main/webapp/app/entities/product/product.component.html
> git commit -am "cherrypick: update product listing page UI"
> git checkout master
> git merge --no-ff entity-update-display-name
```

If you are new to Git, it is advisable to use a UI tool such as SourceTree or GitKraken to cherry-pick and resolve merge conflicts. IDEs such as IntelliJ and editors such as VSCode, also provide good options for these.

Now our page view should be good:

Of course, we could also make it more user-friendly by making the product listing our home page. But for now, let's skip that.

Since we were working on the client-side code we didn't pay attention to the server-side code that was changed during this. We need to compile the Java code to reload our server. Let's run `./gradlew compileJava`.

Unfortunately, we receive an error during the reload regarding a failure to update the database changelogs by Liquibase due to a checksum error:

```
liquibase.AsyncSpringLiquibase : Liquibase could not start correctly, your
database is NOT ready: Validation Failed:
     5 change sets check sum
config/liquibase/changelog/20180114123500_added_entity_Customer.xml::201801
14123500-1::jhipster was: 7:3e0637bae010a31ecb3416d07e41b621 but is now:
7:01f8e1965f0f48d255f613e7fb977628
config/liquibase/changelog/20180114123501_added_entity_ProductOrder.xml::20
180114123501-1::jhipster was: 7:0ff4ce77d65d6ab36f27b229b28e0cda but is
now: 7:e5093e300c347aacf09284b817dc31f1
config/liquibase/changelog/20180114123502_added_entity_OrderItem.xml::20180
114123502-1::jhipster was: 7:2b3d9492d127add80003e2f7723903bf but is now:
7:4beb407d4411d250da2cc2f1d84dc025
config/liquibase/changelog/20180114123503_added_entity_Invoice.xml::2018011
4123503-1::jhipster was: 7:5afaca031815e037cad23f0a0f5515d6 but is now:
7:fadec7bfabcd82dfc1ed22c0ba6c6406
config/liquibase/changelog/20180114123504_added_entity_Shipment.xml::201801
14123504-1::jhipster was: 7:74d9167f5da06d3dc072954b1487e11d but is now:
7:0b1b20dd4e3a38f7410b6b3c81e224fd
```

This is due to the changes made to the original changelog by JHipster. In an ideal world, new schema changes should be done in new changelogs so that Liquibase can apply them, but JHipster doesn't generate this by default yet. For local development using an H2 DB we can run `./gradlew clean` to clear the DB and start the application again, but in real use cases you might be using an actual DB, and you would want to retain the data, so we would have to handle this manually here using the diff features provided by Liquibase.

JHipster provides an integration for Liquibase in both Gradle and Maven builds. You can make use of it to create new changelogs and to create diff changelogs. In cases like these, when we would like to resolve conflicts while retaining data, the Liquibase diff feature is our friend. With Gradle, you could run the `./gradlew liquibaseDiffChangeLog` command to create a diff changelog of your changesets and the database. You can add this changeset to the `src/main/resources/config/liquibase/master.xml` file and it will get applied the next time you restart your server. By default, the command is configured to run against your development database, if you would like to do this against your production database just update the liquibaseCommand command definition in the `gradle/liquibase.gradle` file with the details of the production DB. Refer to `http:/ /www.jhipster.tech/development/#using-a-database` for more.

If you want to clear checksums in your DB, use the `./gradlew liquibaseClearChecksums` task.

Changing the look and feel of the application

The good thing about using Bootstrap is that it lets us easily change the look and feel of the application using any available Bootstrap themes. Let's see how we can install a cool theme for our application, then we will also fine tune the styles to fit our needs using Sass variables provided by Bootstrap.

There are hundreds of Bootstrap themes out there. Since we are using Bootstrap 4 it is important to pick a theme that is made for Bootstrap 4.

Bootswatch is a nice collection of themes for Bootstrap; check it out to see all the available themes at: `https://bootswatch.com/`.

Let's use a Bootswatch theme called **materia**.

In your terminal, run `yarn add bootswatch` to install all the themes. Don't worry; we will only import the theme that we want to use so you do not have to worry about installing all themes.

Now let's import this using Sass. Open `src/main/webapp/content/scss/vendor.scss` and find the line `@import 'node_modules/bootstrap/scss/bootstrap';` and add the following code highlighted in bold:

```scss
// Override Boostrap variables
@import "bootstrap-variables";
@import 'node_modules/bootswatch/dist/materia/variables';
// Import Bootstrap source files from node_modules
@import 'node_modules/bootstrap/scss/bootstrap';
@import "node_modules/bootswatch/dist/materia/bootswatch";
```

The name of the theme here is materia, you can use any theme available in Bootswatch here. Make sure that name is in all lowercase. Also, notice the order of imports. It is important that we import the theme variables after importing Bootstrap variables and themes after importing the Bootstrap theme so that SASS variables and styles are overridden properly.

We can customize the theme further by overriding Bootstrap variables defined in `src/main/webapp/content/scss/_bootstrap-variables.scss`.

You can override any variable supported by Bootstrap. The full list of supported variables can be found in `node_modules/bootstrap/scss/_variables.scss`.

For example, let's change some colors as follows, in `_bootstrap-variables.scss`:

```scss
$primary: #032b4e;
$success: #1df54f;
$info: #17a2b8;
$warning: #ffc107;
$danger: #fa1a30;
```

There might be some UI glitches when you apply a new theme, you could solve them by updating the generated SASS files.

For example, add the following CSS to `src/main/webapp/content/scss/global.scss` to fix the glitch in checkboxes that we got after the theme change:

```scss
.form-check-input {
    height: 18px;
    width: 18px;
}
```

We now have a cool new theme:

Further reference can be found at: `https://getbootstrap.com/docs/4.0/getting-started/theming/`.

Let's commit this:

```
> git add --all
> git commit -am "update bootstrap theme using bootswatch"
```

Adding a new i18n language

Since we enabled i18n support for our application we can add new i18n languages easily, at any time, using the JHipster language generator. Let's add a new language to our application.

In the terminal, switch to a new branch and run the following command:

```
> git checkout -b add-french-language
> jhipster languages
```

You will now see a prompt like this, where you can choose any available language listed:

```
Using JHipster version installed locally in current project's node_modules
Executing jhipster:languages
Options:
```

```
Languages configuration is starting
? Please choose additional languages to install (Press <space> to select,
<a> to toggle all, <i> to inverse selection)
>O  Arabic (Libya)
 O  Armenian
 O  Catalan
 O  Chinese (Simplified)
 O  Chinese (Traditional)
 O  Czech
 O  Danish
(Move up and down to reveal more choices)
```

Let's select French here for now. Accept the file changes proposed and we are good to go. Once the application automatically refreshes you can see the new language in the language drop-down menu in the application menu. Now, wasn't that easy!

Now there is a problem, since we have some entities and we added a new language. We will need to get i18n French files for entities as well. We can do this easily by running the `jhipster --with-entities` command, which will regenerate the application along with entities. Now make sure to carefully stage only changes that you need (i18n related JSON files) from the diff and discard the remaining changes. The following are the files and folders that need to be staged:

`.yo-rc.json`

`src/main/resources/i18n/messages_fr.properties`

`src/main/webapp/app/shared/language/find-language-from-key.pipe.ts`

`src/main/webapp/app/shared/language/language.constants.ts`

`webpack/webpack.common.js`

`src/main/webapp/i18n/fr`

Now, let's commit this and merge it back to the master. If we have picked only i18n related changes we shouldn't have any merge conflicts:

```
> git add --all
> git commit -am "add French as additional language"
> git merge --no-ff add-french-language
```

Authorization with Spring Security

As you may have noticed, when it comes to generated code, JHipster doesn't provide much in terms of role-based security, authorization management, and so on. This is intentional, as these heavily depend on the use case and most often associated with the business logic of the application. So, it would be better if this was hand-coded by the developers as part of the business code.

Normal users have ROLE_USER and admin users have ROLE_ADMIN assigned in user management. For our use case there are few security holes that we need to take care of:

- Normal users should only have access to view the product listing, product order, order item, invoice, and shipment
- Normal users should not have access to create/edit/delete entities via the CRUD API
- Normal users should not be able to access the product order, order item, invoice, and shipment of other users

We could overcome these issues using features provided by Spring Security.

Limiting access to entities

First, let's limit the access for normal users. This can be done easily at the API level using Spring Security. Add the following snippet to the configure method of src/main/java/com/mycompany/store/config/SecurityConfiguration.java.

Add it right before the line .antMatchers("/api/**").authenticated(). The position is very important:

```
.antMatchers("/api/customers").hasAuthority(AuthoritiesConstants.ADMIN)
.antMatchers("/api/product-
categories").hasAuthority(AuthoritiesConstants.ADMIN)
```

We specify that when the request path matches api/customers or api/product-categories the user should have ROLE_ADMIN to access them. Now sign out and log in as user and try to access the customer entity page. Look at the console in your browser's development tools and you should see a 403 Forbidden error for calls made to GET http://localhost:9000/api/customers.

Now that our backend handles this properly let's hide these entries in the menu for normal users. Let's add a `*jhiHasAnyAuthority="'ROLE_ADMIN'"` directive to the elements for customer and product category in `src/main/webapp/app/layouts/navbar/navbar.component.html`.

Now only admin users will see these items on the menu.

Limiting access to create/edit/delete entities

Now we need to ensure that only admin users can edit entities, normal users should only be able to view entities authorized to them. For this, it would be better to handle it at the API level using the Spring Security `PreAuthorize` annotation. Let's start with the order item. Go to `src/main/java/com/mycompany/store/web/rest/OrderItemResource.java` and add `@PreAuthorize("hasAuthority('ROLE_ADMIN')")` to methods `createOrderItem`, `updateOrderItem`, and `deleteOrderItem`:

```
@DeleteMapping("/order-items/{id}")
@Timed
@PreAuthorize("hasAuthority('ROLE_ADMIN')")
public ResponseEntity<Void> deleteOrderItem(@PathVariable Long id) {
    ...
}
```

We are asking Spring Security interceptors to provide access to these methods only when the user has `ROLE_ADMIN`. The `PreAuthorize` annotation stops access before executing the method. Spring Security also provides `PostAuthorize` and more general `Secured` annotations. More about these can be found in the Spring Security documentation at: `https://projects.spring.io/spring-security/`.

Compile the backend using `./gradlew compileJava` or using the IDE. Now go to the order items page and try to create an order item. You will get an `POST http://localhost:9000/api/order-items 403 (Forbidden)` error from the API call on the web console. Now let's add the annotation to all the entity Resource class create, update, and delete methods. You could skip customer and product category entities as they are entirely forbidden to the `ROLE_USER` already.

Let's also hide the create, edit, and delete buttons from the Angular views using the `*jhiHasAnyAuthority="'ROLE_ADMIN'"` directive.

Limiting access to data of other users

Now, this is a little more tricky, as this requires us to change code at the service layer on the backend, but it is not hard. Let's get right to it.

Let's start with the product order entity. Let's modify the `findAll` method in `src/main/java/com/mycompany/store/service/ProductOrderService.java` as follows:

```
@Transactional(readOnly = true)
public Page<ProductOrder> findAll(Pageable pageable) {
    log.debug("Request to get all ProductOrders");
    if (SecurityUtils.isCurrentUserInRole(AuthoritiesConstants.ADMIN))
{
        return productOrderRepository.findAll(pageable);
    } else
        return productOrderRepository.findAllByCustomerUserLogin(
            SecurityUtils.getCurrentUserLogin().get(),
            pageable
        );
}
```

As you can see, we modified the original call to `productOrderRepository.findAll(pageable)` so that we call it only when the current user has the `Admin` role, else we call `findAllByCustomerUserLogin`, but our generated `ProductOrderRepository` interface does not have this method yet so let's add that. In `src/main/java/com/mycompany/store/repository/ProductOrderRepository.jav a` let's add a new method as follows. Currently, the interface doesn't have any methods and only uses methods inherited from `JpaRepository`:

```
Page<ProductOrder> findAllByCustomerUserLogin(String login, Pageable pageable);
```

There is a lot of magic going on here. This is a Spring Data interface and hence, we can simply write a new method and expect Spring Data to create an implementation for this automatically; we just need to follow the naming conventions. In our use case, we need to find all product orders where the user relationship for the customer has the same login as our current logged in user. In SQL, this would be as follows:

```
select * from product_order po cross join customer c cross join jhi_user u
where po.customer_id=c.id and c.user_id=u.id and u.login=:login
```

In simple terms, we could say *find all product orders where* `customer.user.login` *equals* `login` and that is exactly what we have written as the `findAllByCustomerUserLogin` method. The entity under operation is implicit, hence the product order is omitted. By providing the Pageable parameter we tell Spring Data to provide us a page from the paginated list of entities. You can refer to the Spring Data docs (`https://docs.spring.io/spring-data/jpa/docs/current/reference/html/`) for more information.

While calling the `productOrderRepository.findAllByCustomerUserLogin` method we can pass the current user login using the `SecurityUtils.getCurrentUserLogin()` method. The SecurityUtils class is generated by JHipster as well, as it has useful methods such as `getCurrentUserLogin`, `getCurrentUserJWT`, `isAuthenticated`, and `isCurrentUserInRole`.

That is it. Now log in as admin and create two new users, create two customers, and create product orders for each of them. Then log out and log in again as the default user and see if you can see the product order for the newly created user.

Now let's make similar updates for other services. The repository methods for those would be as follows:
For `src/main/java/com/mycompany/store/repository/InvoiceRepository`:

```
Page<Invoice> findAllByOrderCustomerUserLogin(String login, Pageable
pageable);
```

For `src/main/java/com/mycompany/store/repository/OrderItemRepository`:

```
Page<OrderItem> findAllByOrderCustomerUserLogin(String login, Pageable
pageable);
```

For `src/main/java/com/mycompany/store/repository/ShipmentRepository`:

```
Page<Shipment> findAllByInvoiceOrderCustomerUserLogin(String login,
Pageable pageable);
```

Now we need to make similar changes for `findOne` methods on the services.

For the `ProductOrderService` it would be as follows:

```
@Transactional(readOnly = true)
public ProductOrder findOne(Long id) {
    log.debug("Request to get ProductOrder : {}", id);
    if (SecurityUtils.isCurrentUserInRole(AuthoritiesConstants.ADMIN))
{
        return productOrderRepository.findOne(id);
```

```
    } else
        return productOrderRepository.findOneByIdAndCustomerUserLogin(
            id,
            SecurityUtils.getCurrentUserLogin().get()
        );
}
```

As you can see, we changed the methods to find one by ID and customer user login. The repository method for the same would be as follows:

```
ProductOrder findOneByIdAndCustomerUserLogin(Long id, String login);
```

For src/main/java/com/mycompany/store/repository/InvoiceRepository:

```
Invoice findOneByIdAndOrderCustomerUserLogin(Long id, String login);
```

For src/main/java/com/mycompany/store/repository/OrderItemRepository:

```
OrderItem findOneByIdAndOrderCustomerUserLogin(Long id, String login);
```

For src/main/java/com/mycompany/store/repository/ShipmentRepository:

```
Shipment findOneByIdAndInvoiceOrderCustomerUserLogin(Long id, String login);
```

The same queries can be written using the @Query annotation provided by Spring Data as well.

That's it. We have implemented a good role-based authorization logic for the application.

Let's commit this checkpoint:

```
> git add --all
> git commit -am "update role based authorization logic"
```

In a real-world scenario, the changes we have made so far are not enough for an e-commerce website. But since our aim is to learn JHipster and its supported tools rather than to create a feature perfect application, consider this a minimum viable product. To make this e-commerce application usable, we would need to build more features, such as a shopping cart, invoice generation, customer registration, and so on. Why don't you take it up as an assignment and see if you can build more features for this application? This would be part of the next steps to take once you finish the book. The use case and instructions will be detailed in Chapter 14, *Best Practices with JHipster*.

Summary

In this chapter, we saw how we can easily customize a web application created using JHipster. We also learned about Angular and Bootstrap when we customized our Product listing page. In addition to this, we saw how to secure our application with role-based authorization using Spring Security. We also learned about Spring Data and used Git to manage our source code properly. We saw our application evolving with business logic and becoming more user-friendly. In the next chapter, we will see how we can integrate continuous integration with our application using Jenkins.

6
Testing and Continuous Integration

Now that we have scaffolded and developed our e-commerce application, it's time to make it ready for deployment to our production environment. Before that, there are two important aspects of engineering that we need to look at, *quality* and *stability*. In this chapter, we will see how this can be achieved using modern DevOps practices, such as continuous integration and automated testing.

We will also see the following:

- Fixing and running tests
- **CI/CD (continuous integration/continuous deployment)** tools
- Setting up CI with Jenkins using the JHipster CI-CD sub-generator

 DevOps is a software engineering practice that unifies software development (Dev) and software operation (Ops). The main focus of DevOps is automation and monitoring at all stages of software engineering, such as development, integration, testing, deployment, and infrastructure management. DevOps is one of the most trending engineering practices of this decade, and continuous integration and continuous deployment are two of its core aspects.

Fixing and running tests

Before we dive into continuous integration tools, let's first make sure that our tests are working and still pass after the changes we made in the previous chapter. In an ideal world, where software development is done using practices such as **TDD (Test-driven development)**, writing and fixing tests is done along with the development of the code, and specs are written before you develop the actual code. You should try to follow this practice so that you write failing tests first for an expected result, and then develop code that will make the tests pass. Since our tests were autogenerated by JHipster we can at least make sure that they are working when we make changes to the generated code.

> JHipster can also generate performance tests using Gatling for the entities. It is very useful, and a must if you are developing a high-availability and high-volume website. This can be enabled when creating the application. See http://www.jhipster.tech/running-tests/ for more details.

Let's run our unit and integration tests to see if any of them fail:

1. Head over to your terminal and navigate to the online-store folder first.
2. Let's first run the server-side tests using Gradle:

   ```
   > ./gradlew test
   ```

   Note that JHipster generates both unit tests and integration tests for the server side. The unit tests, files named *UnitTest.java, are simple JUnit tests intended for unit testing functions. The integration tests, files named *IntTest.java, are intended for testing a Spring component using the entire Spring environment. They are run with the SpringRunner class and normally start up the Spring environment, configure all the required beans, and run the test.

Some of our tests failed with the following error trace:

```
com.mycompany.store.web.rest.ProductOrderResourceIntTest > getProductOrder
FAILED
    java.lang.AssertionError at ProductOrderResourceIntTest.java:229

com.mycompany.store.web.rest.ProductOrderResourceIntTest >
getAllProductOrders FAILED
    java.lang.AssertionError at ProductOrderResourceIntTest.java:213

com.mycompany.store.web.rest.ProductOrderResourceIntTest >
getNonExistingProductOrder FAILED
    java.lang.AssertionError at ProductOrderResourceIntTest.java:242
```

```
com.mycompany.store.web.rest.ShipmentResourceIntTest > getAllShipments
FAILED
    java.lang.AssertionError at ShipmentResourceIntTest.java:176

com.mycompany.store.web.rest.ShipmentResourceIntTest > getShipment FAILED
    java.lang.AssertionError at ShipmentResourceIntTest.java:192

com.mycompany.store.web.rest.ShipmentResourceIntTest >
getNonExistingShipment FAILED
    java.lang.AssertionError at ShipmentResourceIntTest.java:205

com.mycompany.store.web.rest.InvoiceResourceIntTest > getInvoice FAILED
    java.lang.AssertionError at InvoiceResourceIntTest.java:309

com.mycompany.store.web.rest.InvoiceResourceIntTest > getNonExistingInvoice
FAILED
    java.lang.AssertionError at InvoiceResourceIntTest.java:326

com.mycompany.store.web.rest.InvoiceResourceIntTest > getAllInvoices FAILED
    java.lang.AssertionError at InvoiceResourceIntTest.java:289

com.mycompany.store.web.rest.OrderItemResourceIntTest >
getNonExistingOrderItem FAILED
    java.lang.AssertionError at OrderItemResourceIntTest.java:247

com.mycompany.store.web.rest.OrderItemResourceIntTest > getAllOrderItems
FAILED
    java.lang.AssertionError at OrderItemResourceIntTest.java:218

com.mycompany.store.web.rest.OrderItemResourceIntTest > getOrderItem FAILED
    java.lang.AssertionError at OrderItemResourceIntTest.java:234
2018-02-11 13:55:55.693 INFO 27458 --- [ Thread-10]
c.m.store.config.CacheConfiguration : Closing Cache Manager

217 tests completed, 12 failed
```

You could also run the tests from your IDE so that you have a better error message and failure report. Select the entire src/test folder, right-click, and select **Run all tests**.

3. These are expected to fail as we changed the `Resource` classes for these entities in the previous chapter to handle authorizations, and the failure means that it's working perfectly. Fortunately, it's not difficult to fix the tests using Spring. We can use the `@WithMockUser` annotation provided by the Spring test context to provide a mock user for our tests. Add the annotation with user details as highlighted in the following code to all the failing test classes:

```
@RunWith(SpringRunner.class)
@SpringBootTest(classes = StoreApp.class)
@WithMockUser(username="admin", authorities={"ROLE_ADMIN"},
password = "admin")
public class InvoiceResourceIntTest {
...
}
```

4. We are providing a mock user with the `ADMIN` role here. Add the same to `OrderItemResourceIntTest`, `ProductOrderResourceIntTest`, and `ShipmentResourceIntTest`. Run the tests again and they should pass.

5. Commit the changes made by running `git commit -am "fix server side tests with mockUser"`.

6. Now let's make sure our client-side Karma unit tests are working. Since we didn't make any logic changes on the client-side there shouldn't be any failures. Run the following command:

```
> yarn test
```

7. All tests should pass. Let's head over to `src/test/javascript/spec/app/entities/product/product.component.spec.ts`. We use the Jasmine Framework for our tests. The existing test has the following structure. The `beforeEach` block sets up the Angular `TestBed`:

```
...

describe('Component Tests', () => {
    describe('Product Management Component', () => {
        ...
        beforeEach(() => {
            TestBed.configureTestingModule({
                ...
            })
            .overrideTemplate(ProductComponent, '')
            .compileComponents();
            ...
        });
```

```
        it('Should call load all on init', () => {
            . . .
        });
        . . .
    });

});
```

8. Now let's make sure our protractor e2e tests are working. Run the following commands in two separate terminals. Start the server first. Let's clear the database as well by a running clean task so that tests run on a fresh setup. Since we are running a clean task we also need to run the webpackBuildDev task to rebuild the client side:

    > **./gradlew clean webpackBuildDev bootRun**

9. Now run the e2e tests:

    > **yarn e2e**

    If you prefer not to run scripts via Yarn or NPM, you could also run them via Gradle using the node integration provided by JHipster. For example, instead of yarn e2e, you could run ./gradlew yarn_e2e, and instead of yarn test you could run ./gradlew yarn_test. This is useful if you do not want to install NodeJS and Yarn and want everything to be managed for you by Gradle. If you choose Maven instead of Gradle the same feature is available for that as well.

10. All tests should pass here as well. But if you look at the generated e2e tests, for example, look at src/test/javascript/e2e/entities/customer.spec.ts, you will see that a test is commented out. Some tests are commented out during generation if an entity has a required relationship field, as we would have to create a relationship first and set its value for the test to work. Let's focus on only the Customer page test. Uncomment the test named **should create and save Customers** and change the describe function to fdescribe on the test file, so that only this test file is executed:

    ```
    fdescribe('Customer e2e test', () => {
        . . .
    });
    ```

11. Now execute `yarn e2e` and we should see one failing test. First, let's fix the email field by providing a valid email format:

```
it('should create and save Customers', () => {
    ...
    customerDialogPage.setEmailInput('email@email.com');
    expect(customerDialogPage.getEmailInput()).toMatch('email@email.com
');
    ...
});
```

12. Run `yarn e2e` again and this time it should pass. But since we have a one-to-one relationship between user and customer the test will fail if we run it again, hence we need to delete the row created after it. Let's add a test case for a delete action. In the `CustomerComponentsPage` class defined in the file (if you are using JHipster 5, this class will be available under `src/test/javascript/e2e/page-objects/customer-page-object.ts`), add a new property and methods as follows:

```
table = element.all(by.css('.table-responsive tbody tr'));
getTable() {
    return this.table;
}

deleteFirstItem() {
    this.table.first().element(by.css('button.btn-
    danger')).click();
}
```

13. Now
add `expect(customerComponentsPage.getTable().isPresent()).toBeT ruthy();` as the last line in our previous test to confirm if the row was created. Then add the following test to delete the row:

```
it('should create and save Customers', () => {
    ...
    expect(customerComponentsPage.getTable().isPresent()).toBeTruthy();
});

    it('should delete Customers', () => {
        customerComponentsPage.deleteFirstItem();
        const deleteBtn = element.all(by.css('.modal-footer
        .btn.btn-danger'));
        deleteBtn.click();
    expect(customerComponentsPage.getTable().isPresent()).toBeFalsy();
```

```
    });
```

14. Run `yarn e2e` again to verify. Do not forget to remove the `fdescribe` from the file so that all tests get executed. Congratulations! You added you first protractor e2e tests.
15. Similarly, fix the commented out e2e tests in other files under `src/test/javascript/e2e/entities` as well. This is part of the *next steps* assignment.

Continuous integration

Having automated testing ensures that we are creating bug-free code, and also ensures that there are no regressions introduced from new code. JHipster helps to an extent, by creating unit and integration tests for the generated code, but in real use cases, it won't be sufficient. We would have to add server-side unit tests for the business logic that we introduce and integration tests for new APIs we add. You will also have to add more unit tests for business logic handled on the client side and e2e tests, as JHipster only generates a few sample tests for you and doesn't know anything about your business logic.

The more tests you have, more confident you will be changing code, with fewer chances of regression.

Testing and continuous integration is an integral part of full-stack development and is an important aspect of DevOps. Testing should be considered as important as developing features to build a quality product. Continuous integration is nothing more than continuously merging and testing your new code changes in an isolated environment against your master/main/stable codebase to identify potential bugs and regression. It is achieved by running automated unit, integration, end-to-end, and other test suites against the code. For example, if you are working with Git, these are typically run for every commit you make to your master branch and/or for every pull request, you create.

Once we have automated tests, we can make use of continuous integration practices to make sure that any new code we introduce doesn't cause any regression in our stable code base. This will give us the confidence to merge new code and deploy that to production.

Modern DevOps teams often go a step further and do continuous delivery (continuous integration + continuous deployment). They often define CI/CD pipelines, which continuously integrate, test, and deploy code to production in a fully automated way.

 Teams with a good continuous integration and continuous deployment setup can deliver more features more frequently with fewer bugs.

Have I stressed the importance of continuous integration enough?

CI/CD tools

JHipster provides excellent support for the well-known CI/CD tools. Let's take a look at the options available first.

Jenkins

Jenkins (`https://jenkins.io/`) is one of the leading CI/CD tools out there. It is free and open source. It is an automation server written in Java and supports integration with various version control tools, such as Git, CVS, SVN, and so on. Jenkins has a huge plugin ecosystem and this makes it one of the most flexible platforms. Jenkins can be used for building projects, running automated tests, automating deployment, and so on. It is available as an executable binary for various platforms and as Docker images. Blue Ocean is the latest UI interface for Jenkins giving it a much-needed breath of fresh air. Jenkins has the concept of a pipeline, achieved by using multiple plugins and a Groovy DSL to define the CI/CD pipeline. Jenkins pipeline plugins provide a comprehensive DSL-based configuration that can be defined in a file called a `Jenkinsfile`.

Travis CI

Travis CI (`https://travis-ci.org/`) is an open source hosted **PaaS (Platform as a Service)** solution for CI/CD. It is free for public/OSS projects and needs a subscription for use by private/enterprise projects. It supports applications written in a variety of languages and platforms, and is heavily used by open source projects, including JHipster, for their continuous integration needs. It has excellent integration with version control tools and offers an enterprise version as well. It is very easy to set up and use, and has a simple YAML-based configuration. Advanced setups are typically done using shell scripts that can be triggered by the YAML configuration using hooks.

GitLab CI

GitLab CI (`https://about.gitlab.com/features/gitlab-ci-cd/`) is a CI/CD solution available as part of GitLab, a web UI on top of Git. It is well integrated into the platform and is an excellent choice when using GitLab. It is free and open source for use by public projects and has an enterprise version as well. It has both a hosted solution and binaries to be used on-premises.

CircleCI

CircleCI (`https://circleci.com/`) is another open source CI/CD solution that offers both a hosted PaaS and on-premises option. It has free options for small teams and subscription plans for bigger teams and enterprises. The configuration is simple and YAML-based, similar to Travis CI. It provides options to choose different OS environments for the builds and is very easy to set up.

Setting up Jenkins

Let's use Jenkins as the CI tool for our application. We first need to set up a local Jenkins instance:

If you are already familiar with Docker, you can use the official Docker image provided by Jenkins and can skip the following steps. The Docker image will be automatically generated by JHipster when creating the CD/CI pipeline in the following section. Visit `http://www.jhipster.tech/setting-up-ci-jenkins2/` for more details.

1. Let's download the latest binary from `http://mirrors.jenkins.io/war-stable/latest/jenkins.war`.
2. Now open a terminal and navigate to the folder where the file was downloaded.
3. Execute `java -jar jenkins.war --httpPort=8989` from the terminal to start a Jenkins server. The port should not conflict with our application port. The default password will be printed on the console. Make a copy of it.
4. Navigate to `https://localhost:8989` and paste the password copied before.
5. Click on the **Install suggested plugins** button on the next page and wait for the plugin installation to complete.
6. Create an admin user on the next page and complete.

Now that our Jenkins server is ready, let's go ahead and create a Jenkins pipeline for our project.

Creating a Jenkins pipeline using JHipster

We can create the `Jenkinsfile` for our project using the `ci-cd sub-generator` from JHipster:

1. In a terminal, navigate to the online-store folder first. Now run the following command:

   ```
   > jhipster ci-cd
   ```

2. You will be asked to select from a list of options as follows:

   ```
   Welcome to the JHipster CI/CD Sub-Generator
   ? What CI/CD pipeline do you want to generate? (Press <space> to
   select, <a> to toggle all, <i> to inverse selection)
   ```

```
>O  Jenkins pipeline
 O  Travis CI
 O  GitLab CI
 O  CircleCI
```

3. Let's select **Jenkins pipeline** from it. Next, we will have an option to choose additional stages:

```
? What CI/CD pipeline do you want to generate? Jenkins pipeline
? Jenkins pipeline: what tasks/integrations do you want to include?
>O Perform the build in a Docker container
 O Analyze code with Sonar
 O Send build status to GitLab
 O Build and publish a Docker image
```

4. Let's skip this, as we won't be needing these for now, and proceed. Next, we will be asked if we need to automatically deploy to Heroku from our CI/CD pipeline:

```
? What CI/CD pipeline do you want to generate? Jenkins pipeline
? Jenkins pipeline: what tasks/integrations do you want to include?
? Deploy to heroku?
>O In Jenkins pipeline
```

5. Let's choose this option as we will need it later. Once the option is selected JHipster will generate the files and log the following output on the console.

```
      create Jenkinsfile
      create src/main/docker/jenkins.yml
      create src/main/resources/idea.gdsl
Congratulations, JHipster execution is complete!
```

If you want to use Travis instead of Jenkins you can do so by choosing the **Travis** option and then publishing the repository to GitHub as a public repository. Once published go to `https://github.com/<username>/<repoName>/settings/installations` and add Travis CI as a service and follow the instructions. You can now see automated builds when you make commits. Refer to `https://docs.travis-ci.com/user/getting-started/` for details.

As you can see, we got a `Jenkinsfile` generated at the root and Docker image for Jenkins created in the `src/main/docker` directory. We also got an `idea.gdsl` file, which is used by IntelliJ Idea for autocompletion.

The Jenkinsfile and its stages

Let's take a look at the generated `Jenkinsfile`, which has our pipeline definitions using the Groovy DSL:

```groovy
#!/usr/bin/env groovy

node {
    stage('checkout') {
        checkout scm
    }

    stage('check java') {
        sh "java -version"
    }

    stage('clean') {
        sh "chmod +x gradlew"
        sh "./gradlew clean --no-daemon"
    }

    stage('install tools') {
        sh "./gradlew yarn_install -PnodeInstall --no-daemon"
    }

    stage('backend tests') {
        try {
            sh "./gradlew test -PnodeInstall --no-daemon"
        } catch(err) {
            throw err
        } finally {
            junit '**/build/**/TEST-*.xml'
        }
    }

    stage('frontend tests') {
        try {
            sh "./gradlew yarn_test -PnodeInstall --no-daemon"
        } catch(err) {
            throw err
        } finally {
            junit '**/build/test-results/karma/TESTS-*.xml'
        }
    }

    stage('packaging') {
        sh "./gradlew bootRepackage -x test -Pprod -PnodeInstall --
```

```
        no-daemon"
        archiveArtifacts artifacts: '**/build/libs/*.war',
        fingerprint: true
    }

    stage('deployment') {
        sh "./gradlew deployHeroku --no-daemon"
    }
}
```

We have multiple stages defined running in a sequence, highlighted in bold; there are eight to be exact. It starts with a checkout of the branch from version control ending with deployment to Heroku (we will see more about this in the following chapter).

The steps are quite straightforward as most of it is just triggering a Gradle task. Let's look at each of them:

```
stage('checkout') {
    checkout scm
}
```

The checkout stage does a local checkout of the source code revision that triggered the build:

```
stage('check java') {
    sh "java -version"
}
```

This check java stage just prints the Java version installed on the Jenkins environment:

```
stage('clean') {
    sh "chmod +x gradlew"
    sh "./gradlew clean --no-daemon"
}
```

The clean stage first grants execution permission for the Gradle wrapper on a Unix-like OS and then executes the Gradle clean task. The --no-daemon flag disables the Gradle daemon feature, which is not required in a CI environment:

```
stage('install tools') {
    sh "./gradlew yarn_install -PnodeInstall --no-daemon"
}
```

The install tools stage makes sure that NodeJS and all the NPM modules are installed by running yarn install via Gradle.

The `-PnodeInstall` flag ensures that NodeJS is installed first if not done already:

```
stage('backend tests') {
    try {
        sh "./gradlew test -PnodeInstall --no-daemon"
    } catch(err) {
        throw err
    } finally {
        junit '**/build/**/TEST-*.xml'
    }
}
```

The **backend tests** stage runs all the server-side integration and unit tests by triggering the Gradle test task. It will fail the Jenkins pipeline when there is an error and register the test reports on the Jenkins web UI using the JUnit plugin after the test run is complete:

```
stage('frontend tests') {
    try {
        sh "./gradlew yarn_test -PnodeInstall --no-daemon"
    } catch(err) {
        throw err
    } finally {
        junit '**/build/test-results/karma/TESTS-*.xml'
    }
}
```

Similar to previously, the frontend tests stage runs the client-side unit tests by triggering the yarn test command via a `Gradle` task. It will also fail the pipeline on an error and register the test reports on the Jenkins web UI:

```
stage('packaging') {
    sh "./gradlew bootRepackage -x test -Pprod -PnodeInstall --no-daemon"
    archiveArtifacts artifacts: '**/build/libs/*.war', fingerprint: true
}
```

The `packaging` stage triggers the Gradle `bootRepackage` task with the `prod` profile and archives the created WAR files with a unique fingerprint:

```
stage('deployment') {
    sh "./gradlew deployHeroku --no-daemon"
}
```

The final stage is for `deployment` and it also uses a Gradle task for this. We will see this in detail in the following chapter. For now, let's comment out this stage. We will re-enable it later.

Now let's commit everything to `git` by running these commands. Make sure you are on the master branch, else `commit` and merge the branch with the master:

```
> git add --all
> git commit -am "add Jenkins pipeline for ci/cd"
```

Setting up the Jenkinsfile in a Jenkins server

Now that our `Jenkinsfile` is ready, let's set up CI/CD for our application. First, we need to upload our application to a GIT server, such as GitHub, GitLab, or BitBucket. Let's use GitHub (`https://github.com/`) for this. Make sure you have an account created in GitHub first:

1. In GitHub, create a new repository (`https://github.com/new`); let's call it online-store. *Do not* check the **Initialize this repository with a README** option. Once created, you will see instructions to add code. Let's go with the option of **push an existing repository from the command line** by running the following commands inside our online-store application folder. Do not forget to replace `<username>` with your actual GitHub username:

   ```
   > cd online-store
   > git remote add origin
   https://github.com/<username>/online-store.git
   > git push -u origin master
   ```

2. Now go to the Jenkins server web UI by visiting `http://localhost:8989/` and create a new job using the **create new jobs** link.

3. Enter a name, select **Pipeline** from the list, and click **OK**:

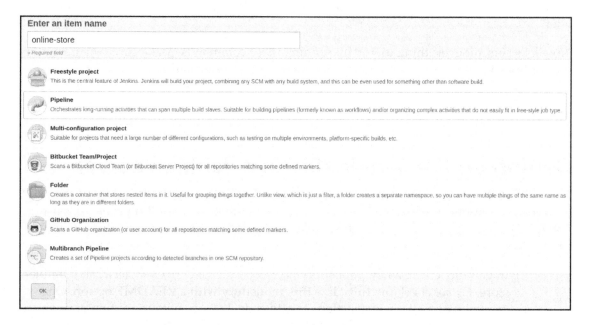

4. Then, on the next page, do the following:
    1. Scroll down or click on the **Build Triggers** section.
    2. Select the **Poll SCM** checkbox.
    3. Enter **H/01 * * * *** as the cron schedule value so that Jenkins polls our repository every minute and builds if there are new commits:

5. Next, on the same page:
   1. Scroll down or click on the **Pipeline** section.
   2. Select **Pipeline script from SCM** for the **Definition** field from the drop-down menu.
   3. Select **Git** for the **SCM** field from the drop-down menu.
   4. Add the **Repository URL** for the application.
   5. Finally, click **Save**:

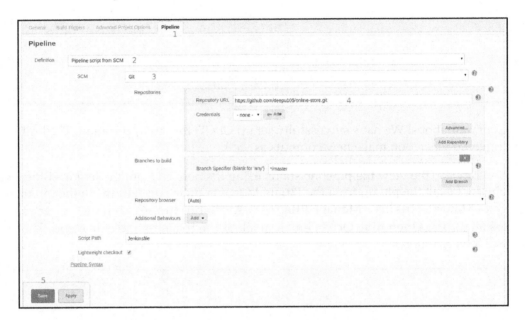

6. Click on **Build Now** to trigger a new build to test our pipeline:

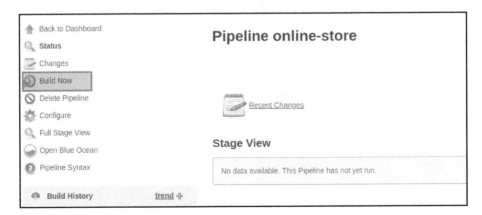

We should now see a build has started and its progress on the web UI as in the following screenshot:

Congratulations! We have successfully set up CI/CD for our application. The builds will get triggered when you make new commits as well.

You can also the view the pipeline status using the new UI from the Jenkins Blue Ocean plugin. Install the plugin from the Plugin Manager (Click on **Jenkins** in the top menu and go to **Manage Jenkins | Manage Plugins | Available** and search for `Blue Ocean` and install it). The **Open Blue Ocean** link is available on the left-hand side menu. The builds will look as follows:

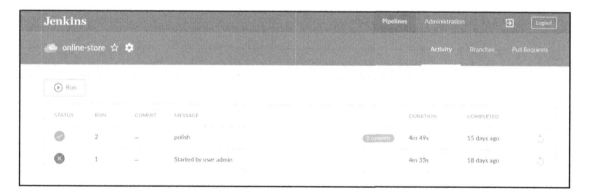

Click on a build to view the pipeline. You can click on each stage on the progress indicator to list the steps from that stage, and then expand the list items to view the logs from that step:

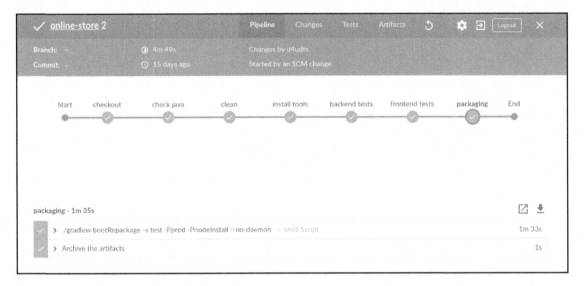

Summary

In this chapter, we looked at what CI/CD is, and the tools supported by JHipster. We also learned how to set up Jenkins and created our CI/CD pipeline using JHipster and Jenkins. We also fixed our automated tests and made them run on the CI server.

In the next chapter, we will see how to deploy our application to *production* using a cloud-hosting provider such as Heroku.

7
Going into Production

Our application is almost ready and it's time to go into production. Since this is the age of cloud computing, we will be deploying our application to a cloud provider—Heroku, to be specific. Before we go on and deploy intended for Linux, but it is possible to use it with Mac and Windows using tools such as our application into production, we need to make sure our application is production ready in our local environment. It would also be beneficial to make ourselves familiar with technologies and tools that will be useful at this stage.

In this chapter, we will learn about the following:

- An introduction to Docker
- Starting the production database with Docker
- An introduction to Spring profiles
- Packaging the application for local deployment
- Upgrading to the newest version of JHipster
- An introduction to the deployment options supported by JHipster
- Production deployment to Heroku cloud

An Introduction to Docker

Docker is one of the most disruptive technologies to have taken center stage in the world of DevOps in recent times. Docker is a technology that enables operating-system-level virtualization or containerization, and is also open source and free to use. Docker is intended for Linux, but it is possible to use it with Mac and Windows using tools such as Docker for Mac and Docker for Windows.

Docker containers

When we talk about containers in the Docker world, we are technically talking about Linux containers. As stated by Red Hat on their website (`https://www.redhat.com/en/topics/containers/whats-a-linux-container`):

> *A Linux container is a set of processes that are isolated from the rest of the system, running from a distinct image that provides all files necessary to support the processes. By providing an image that contains all of an application's dependencies, it is portable and consistent as it moves from development to testing, and finally to production.*

Though the concept is not new, Docker makes it possible to create containers that are easy to build, deploy, version, and share. A Docker container only contains dependencies that are required for the application to run on the host OS; it shares the OS and other dependencies for the host system hardware. This makes a Docker container lighter than a **virtual machine** (**VM**) in terms of size and resource usage as it doesn't have to ship an entire OS and emulate virtual hardware. Hence, Docker made virtual machines obsolete in many of the traditional use cases that were handled using VM technologies. This also means that, with Docker, we will be able to run more applications on the same hardware compared to running with VMs. Docker containers are instances of a docker image, which is a set of layers which describes the application that is being containerized. They contain the code, runtime, libraries, environment variables, and configuration files needed to run the application.

The Dockerfile

A Dockerfile is a set of instructions that tells Docker how to build a Docker image. By running the `docker build` command on a specific Dockerfile, we will produce a docker image that can be used to create Docker containers. Existing docker images can be used as a base for new Dockerfiles, hence letting you reuse and extend existing images.

The following code is from the Dockerfile of our application:

```
FROM openjdk:8-jre-alpine

ENV SPRING_OUTPUT_ANSI_ENABLED=ALWAYS \
    JHIPSTER_SLEEP=0 \
    JAVA_OPTS=""

CMD echo "The application will start in ${JHIPSTER_SLEEP}s..." && \
    sleep ${JHIPSTER_SLEEP} && \
    java ${JAVA_OPTS} -Djava.security.egd=file:/dev/./urandom -jar /app.war

EXPOSE 8080 5701/udp

ADD *.war /app.war
```

The `FROM` instruction specifies the base image to use while initializing the build. Here, we specify open JDK 8 as our Java runtime.

The `ENV` instruction is used to set environment variables, and the `CMD` instruction is used to specify commands to be executed.

The `EXPOSE` instruction is used to specify the port that the container listens to during runtime.

Visit `https://docs.docker.com/engine/reference/builder/` for a complete reference.

The Docker Hub

Docker Hub (`https://hub.docker.com/`) is the online registry provided by Docker. It can be used to publish public and private docker images. This makes sharing and reusing docker images extremely easy.

To get a docker image from the registry, we just need to run `docker pull <image-name>`.

This makes it easy to use third-party tools without having to install them locally by just pulling and running the container from the registry.

Docker compose

Docker compose is a tool in the Docker platform that is used to define and run multi-container applications. It lets us define how a container will behave when it is run in production, and also lets us define other services that it depends on and how services work with each other. Each application is a service as it defines the behavior of the container, for example, what port it runs on, what environment variables it uses, and so on. A YAML file is used for this. A single `docker.compose.yml` file can define all the services that are required for a multi-container application and can then be started with a single command. We will see more about Docker and docker -compose in `Chapter 11`, *Deploying with Docker Compose*.

 Visit `https://docs.docker.com/get-started/` to learn more about Docker.

The following table is a list of useful commands for Docker and Docker compose:

`docker build -t myapp:1.0.`	**Build an image from the Dockerfile in the current directory and tag the image**
`docker images`	List all images that are locally stored with the Docker engine
`docker pull alpine:3.4`	Pull an image from a registry
`docker push myrepo/myalpine:3.4`	Push an image to a registry
`docker login`	Log in to a registry (the Docker Hub, by default)

`docker run --rm -it -p 5000:80 -v /dev/code alpine:3.4 /bin/sh`	Run a docker container **--rm**: Remove container automatically after it exits **-it**: Connect the container to the Terminal **-p**: Expose port 5000 externally and map to port 80 **-v**: Create a host mapped volume inside the container **alpine:3.4**: The image from which the container is instantiated **/bin/sh**: The command to run inside the container
`docker stop myApp`	Stop a running container
`docker ps`	List the running containers
`docker rm -f $(docker ps -aq)`	Delete all running and stopped containers
`docker exec -it web bash`	Create a new bash process inside the container and connect it to the Terminal
`docker logs --tail 100 web`	Print the last 100 lines of a container's logs
`docker-compose up`	Start the services defined in the `docker-compose.yml` file in the current folder
`docker-compose down`	Stop the services defined in the `docker-compose.yml` file in the current folder

Starting the production database with Docker

JHipster creates a Dockerfile for the application and provides `docker-compose` files for all the technologies we choose, such as the database, search engine, Jenkins, and so on, under `src/main/docker`:

```
├── app.yml - Main compose file for the application
├── Dockerfile - The Dockerfile for the application
├── hazelcast-management-center.yml - Compose file hazelcast management
center
├── jenkins.yml - Compose file for Jenkins
├── mysql.yml - Compose file for the database that we choose.
```

└──── **sonar.yml** - COmpose file for SonarQube.

Let's see how we can start our production database using Docker from the compose file provided under `src/main/docker/mysql.yml`. You will need to use a Terminal for the following instructions:

1. Run `docker --version` and `docker-compose --version` to ensure these are installed.
2. Run `docker ps` to list the running containers. If you are not already running any containers, you should see an empty list.
3. Let's start the DB by running `docker-compose -f src/main/docker/mysql.yml up`.

You will see the following console output:

```
$ docker-compose -f src/main/docker/mysql.yml up
Recreating docker_store-mysql_1 ...
Recreating docker_store-mysql_1 ... done
Attaching to docker_store-mysql_1
store-mysql_1  | 2018-03-03T14:10:42.518245Z 0 [Note] mysqld (mysqld 5.7.20) starting as process 1 ...
store-mysql_1  | 2018-03-03T14:10:42.521178Z 0 [Note] InnoDB: PUNCH HOLE support available
store-mysql_1  | 2018-03-03T14:10:42.521196Z 0 [Note] InnoDB: Mutexes and rw_locks use GCC atomic builtins
store-mysql_1  | 2018-03-03T14:10:42.521206Z 0 [Note] InnoDB: Uses event mutexes
store-mysql_1  | 2018-03-03T14:10:42.521204Z 0 [Note] InnoDB: GCC builtin __atomic_thread_fence() is used for memory barrier
store-mysql_1  | 2018-03-03T14:10:42.521209Z 0 [Note] InnoDB: Compressed tables use zlib 1.2.3
store-mysql_1  | 2018-03-03T14:10:42.521213Z 0 [Note] InnoDB: Using Linux native AIO
store-mysql_1  | 2018-03-03T14:10:42.521832Z 0 [Note] InnoDB: Number of pools: 1
store-mysql_1  | 2018-03-03T14:10:42.527272Z 0 [Note] InnoDB: Using CPU crc32 instructions
store-mysql_1  | 2018-03-03T14:10:42.524890Z 0 [Note] InnoDB: Initializing buffer pool, total size = 128M, instances = 1, chunk size = 128M
store-mysql_1  | 2018-03-03T14:10:42.531726Z 0 [Note] InnoDB: Completed initialization of buffer pool
store-mysql_1  | 2018-03-03T14:10:42.533641Z 0 [Note] InnoDB: If the mysqld execution user is authorized, page cleaner thread priority can be changed.
store-mysql_1  | 2018-03-03T14:10:42.548765Z 0 [Note] InnoDB: Highest supported file format is Barracuda.
store-mysql_1  | 2018-03-03T14:10:42.550433Z 0 [Note] InnoDB: Log scan progressed past the checkpoint lsn 12213183
store-mysql_1  | 2018-03-03T14:10:42.550454Z 0 [Note] InnoDB: Doing recovery: scanned up to log sequence number 12213192
store-mysql_1  | 2018-03-03T14:10:42.550458Z 0 [Note] InnoDB: Database was not shutdown normally!
store-mysql_1  | 2018-03-03T14:10:42.550461Z 0 [Note] InnoDB: Starting crash recovery.
```

> If you want to run the service in the background, pass the -d flag to the command. `docker-compose -f src/main/docker/mysql.yml up -d` will let you continue to use the same Terminal without having to switch to another.

Now if you run `docker ps` again, it should list the database service that we started:

```
$ docker ps
CONTAINER ID    IMAGE          COMMAND                 CREATED        STATUS          PORTS                     NAMES
f16976e9f661    mysql:5.7.20   "docker-entrypoint..."  6 minutes ago  Up 4 seconds    0.0.0.0:3306->3306/tcp    docker_store-mysql_1
```

An introduction to Spring profiles

Before we prepare our application for production, let's talk a little bit about Spring profiles.

Spring profiles (`https://docs.spring.io/spring/docs/current/spring-framework-reference/core.html#beans-definition-profiles-java`) let you change the way your application behaves based on environments. This is achieved using the `@Profile` annotations and profile-specific configuration files, which can be activated by specifying the `spring.profiles.active` property. Based on the profile that we set here, Spring will choose the appropriate `application.properties/application.yml` files and will include/exclude components that are included/excluded for the specific profile using the `@Profile` annotation in the Java source code. For example, if we set `spring.profiles.active=prod`, all the Spring components that have `@Profile("prod")` will be instantiated and any component that has `@Profile("!prod")` will be excluded. Similarly, Spring will load and use the `application-prod.yml` or `application-prod.properties` file if it is available on the classpath.

JHipster configures a `dev` and `prod` profile by default and includes an `application-dev.yml` and `application-prod.yml` in the `src/main/resources/config` folder, along with the base `application.yml` file. JHipster goes a step further and provides a `dev` and `prod` profile for the Gradle build as well (Available for Maven as well) so that we can build/run the application for a particular profile, which is very handy. Here are the profile and database configurations defined in the `application-dev.yml` file:

```
...

spring:
    profiles:
        active: dev
        include: swagger
    ...
    datasource:
        type: com.zaxxer.hikari.HikariDataSource
        url: jdbc:h2:file:./build/h2db/db/store;DB_CLOSE_DELAY=-1
        username: store
        password:
    ...
```

The following profiles are available in a JHipster application:

dev	Tuned for development and productivity, it enables Spring dev tools, in-memory databases, and so on
prod	Tuned for production, it focuses on performance and stability
swagger	Enables Swagger documentation for the API
no-liquibase	Disables Liquibase, and is useful in production environments where you don't want Liquibase to run

Packaging the application for local deployment

Now let's build our application and deploy it locally. This can be done in two ways, either using Docker or by building and executing a WAR file.

Building and deploying using Docker

Let's use a Gradle task to build our docker image.

Use the `./gradlew tasks` command to list all available tasks.

1. In your Terminal, go to the project root folder and execute; `./gradlew bootRepackage -Pprod buildDocker`:
   - **bootRepackage**: Builds an executable archive (WAR) file for the application
   - **-Pprod**: Specifies the profile to use
   - **buildDocker**: Builds a docker image based on the Dockerfile present in the `src/main/docker` folder

If you are using JHipster Version 5 or above, use `bootWar` instead of the `bootRepackage` command in Gradle.

2. Once the task is completed successfully, we can deploy our app by running:

```
> docker-compose -f src/main/docker/app.yml up
```

This will also start the MySQL DB if you haven't started it already. If you already have it running from the previous step, then `docker-compose` will just skip it.

Our application will be ready once we see the following output in the console. As you can see, it's running with the `prod` and `swagger` profiles:

```
store-app_1    | ----------------------------------------------------------
store-app_1    |     Application 'store' is running! Access URLs:
store-app_1    |     Local:          http://localhost:8080
store-app_1    |     External:       http://172.18.0.2:8080
store-app_1    |     Profile(s):     [prod, swagger]
store-app_1    | ----------------------------------------------------------
store-app_1    |
```

Visit `http://localhost:8080` in your favorite browser to see the application in action.

Building and deploying an executable archive

If you prefer not to use Docker, then we could deploy the app with a production profile locally by completing the following steps:

1. First, make sure that MySQL DB is running from the previous step; otherwise, start it using `docker-compose -f src/main/docker/mysql.yml up -d`.
2. Now let's create an executable archive for the prod profile by running `./gradlew bootRepackage -Pprod`.
3. Once the build is successful, there will be two archives (WAR) created under `build/libs`. The `store-0.0.1-SNAPSHOT.war` file is an executable archive which can be run directly on a JVM, and the `store-0.0.1-SNAPSHOT.war.original` is a normal WAR file that can be deployed to a server such as JBoss or Tomcat.
4. Let's use the executable archive. Just run `./build/libs/store-0.0.1-SNAPSHOT.war` to start the application. If you are on Windows, run `java -jar build/libs/store-0.0.1-SNAPSHOT.war`.

Once the application starts up, you will see the URL printed on the console.
Visit `http://localhost:8080` in your favorite browser to see the application in action.

Upgrading to the newest version of JHipster

JHipster provides an upgrade sub-generator (`http://www.jhipster.tech/upgrading-an-application/`) to help you upgrade an application with a new JHipster version of it. It is quite useful as it automates a lot of manual steps for you, and the only thing you need to do is resolve merge conflicts if there are any after the upgrade is complete. Let's upgrade our application, shall we?

1. In your Terminal, execute the `jhipster upgrade` command. The upgrade process will start if there is a new version of JHipster available; otherwise the process will exit.

Once the process starts, you will see a detailed console log of what is going on. As you can see, this sub-generator uses the global JHipster version instead of the local one, unlike other sub-generators:

```
Using JHipster version installed globally
Executing jhipster:upgrade
Options:
Welcome to the JHipster Upgrade Sub-Generator
This will upgrade your current application codebase to the latest JHipster
version
Looking for latest generator-jhipster version...
yarn info v1.5.1
4.14.1
Done in 0.16s.
 New generator-jhipster version found: 4.14.1
     info git rev-parse -q --is-inside-work-tree
 Git repository detected
     info git status --porcelain
     info git rev-parse -q --abbrev-ref HEAD
     info git rev-parse -q --verify jhipster_upgrade
     info git checkout --orphan jhipster_upgrade
 Created branch jhipster_upgrade
     info Removing .angular-cli.json
     ...
 Cleaned up project directory
Installing JHipster 4.13.3 locally
     info yarn add generator-jhipster@4.13.3 --dev --no-lockfile --ignore-
scripts
```

```
yarn add v1.5.1
...
Done in 6.16s.
 Installed generator-jhipster@4.13.3
Regenerating application with JHipster 4.13.3...
warning package.json: No license field
/home/deepu/Documents/jhipster-book/online-store/node_modules/.bin
     info "/home/deepu/Documents/jhipster-book/online-
store/node_modules/.bin/jhipster" --with-entities --force --skip-install
Using JHipster version installed globally
Running default command
Executing jhipster:app
Options: withEntities: true, force: true, skipInstall: true, with-entities:
true, skip-install: true
...
Server application generated successfully.
...
Client application generated successfully.
...
Entity generation completed
...
Congratulations, JHipster execution is complete!
 Successfully regenerated application with JHipster 4.13.3
     info Removing src/main/resources/keystore.jks
     info git add -A
     info git commit -q -m "Generated with JHipster 4.13.3" -a --allow-
empty
 Committed with message "Generated with JHipster 4.13.3"
     info git checkout -q master
 Checked out branch "master"
     info git --version
     info git merge --strategy=ours -q --no-edit --allow-unrelated-
histories jhipster_upgrade
 Current code has been generated with version 4.13.3
     info git checkout -q jhipster_upgrade
 Checked out branch "jhipster_upgrade"
Updating generator-jhipster to 4.14.1 . This might take some time...
     info yarn add generator-jhipster@4.14.1 --dev --no-lockfile --ignore-
scripts
...
Done in 30.40s.
 Updated generator-jhipster to version 4.14.1
     info Removing .angular-cli.json
     ...
 Cleaned up project directory
Regenerating application with JHipster 4.14.1...
/home/deepu/Documents/jhipster-book/online-store/node_modules/.bin
     info "/home/deepu/Documents/jhipster-book/online-
```

```
store/node_modules/.bin/jhipster" --with-entities --force --skip-install
Using JHipster version installed globally
Running default command
Executing jhipster:app
Options: withEntities: true, force: true, skipInstall: true, with-entities:
true, skip-install: true
...
Entity generation completed
Congratulations, JHipster execution is complete!
```
 Successfully regenerated application with JHipster 4.14.1
```
      info Removing src/main/resources/keystore.jks
      info git add -A
      info git commit -q -m "Generated with JHipster 4.14.1" -a --allow-
empty
```
 Committed with message "Generated with JHipster 4.14.1"
```
      info git checkout -q master
  Checked out branch "master"
```
Merging changes back to master...
```
      info git merge -q jhipster_upgrade
  Merge done!
      info git diff --name-only --diff-filter=U package.json
```
WARNING! There are conflicts in package.json, please fix them and then run yarn
```
  Start your Webpack development server with:
yarn start


      info git diff --name-only --diff-filter=U
  Upgraded successfully.
```
WARNING! Please fix conflicts listed below and commit!
gradle/wrapper/gradle-wrapper.properties
package.json
src/test/java/com/mycompany/store/web/rest/CustomerResourceIntTest.java
```

Congratulations, JHipster execution is complete!
```

The sub-generator does the following in order:

1. Checks whether there is a new version of JHipster available (not applicable if you are using `--force`).
2. Checks whether the application is already initialized as a GIT repository; otherwise, JHipster will initialize one for you and commit the current codebase to the master branch.
3. Checks to ensure that there are no uncommitted local changes in the repository. The process will exit if it finds any uncommitted changes.
4. Checks whether a `jhipster_upgrade` branch exists. If not, a branch is created.

5. Checks out the `jhipster_upgrade` branch.

6. Upgrades JHipster to the latest available version globally.

7. Cleans the current project directory.

8. Regenerates the application using the `jhipster --force --with-entities` command.

9. Commits the generated code to the `jhipster_upgrade` branch.

10. Merges the `jhipster_upgrade` branch back to the original branch from where the `jhipster upgrade` command was launched.

Let's see what has changed after the upgrade before we resolve the merge conflicts. See the changes staged. Carefully check the changes to make sure everything is in order, especially in the files where we made customizations earlier. My changelog looks like this; note that I truncated the bottom as there were 147 updated files:

Thankfully, we have only three conflicts and hence they should be easy to resolve. The conflict in `package.json` arises from the change we made to integrate Bootswatch. Carefully resolve the conflict stage in the file and move on to next file.

Once all the conflicts are resolved, stage the files and commit them:

```
> git add --all
> git commit -am "update to latest JHipster version"
```

Ensure that everything works. Run the server-side and client-side tests using `./gradlew test && yarn && yarn test`, and start the application to verify this by running the `./gradlew clean webpackBuildDev bootRun` command.

An introduction to deployment options supported by JHipster

Now that we have verified our production builds by deploying it locally, let's see how we can take it to actual production by using a cloud service. JHipster supports most of the cloud platforms out of the box, and provides special sub-generator commands for the popular ones such as Heroku, Cloudfoundry, and AWS.

JHipster also supports platforms such as Openshift, Google Cloud (using Kubernetes), and Rancher, but let's see them in upcoming chapters as they are more geared towards microservices. In theory, though, you could use them for Monolith deployments as well.

Heroku

Heroku (`https://www.heroku.com/`) is the cloud platform from Salesforce. It lets you deploy, manage, and monitor your applications on the cloud. Heroku has a focus on Applications rather than on containers and supports languages ranging from NodeJS to Java to Go. JHipster provides the Heroku sub-generator, which was built and is maintained by Heroku, making it easy to deploy JHipster apps to Heroku cloud. It makes use of the Heroku CLI, and you need a Heroku account to use it. The sub-generator can be used to deploy and update your application to Heroku.

Visit `http://www.jhipster.tech/heroku/` for more info.

Cloud Foundry

Cloud Foundry is a multi-cloud computing platform governed by Cloud Foundry Foundation. It was originally created by VMWare, and is now under Pivotal, the company behind Spring Framework. It offers a multi-cloud solution which is currently supported by **Pivotal Cloud Foundry (PCF)**, **Pivotal Web Services (PWS)**, Atos Canary, SAP cloud platform, and IBM Bluemix among others. The platform is open source and hence can be used to set up your own private instance. JHipster provides a sub-generator to deploy JHipster applications to any Cloud Foundry provider easily. It makes use of the Cloud Foundry command line tool.

Visit `http://www.jhipster.tech/cloudfoundry/` for more info.

Amazon Web Services

Amazon Web Services (AWS) is the leading cloud computing platform that offers platform, software, and infrastructure as a service. AWS offers Elastic Beanstalk as a simple platform to deploy and manage your applications on the cloud. JHipster provides a sub-generator to deploy JHipster applications to AWS or Boxfuse (`http://www.jhipster.tech/boxfuse/`), an alternative service.

Visit `http://www.jhipster.tech/aws/` for more info.

Production deployment to Heroku cloud

We need to choose a cloud provider. For this demo, let's choose Heroku.

 Though the Heroku account is free and you get free credits, you will have to provide your credit card information to use MySQL and other add-ons. You will only be charged if you exceed the free quota.

Let's deploy our application to Heroku by completing the following steps:

1. First, you need to create an account in Heroku (`https://signup.heroku.com/`). It is free and you get free credits as well.
2. Install the Heroku CLI tool by following `https://devcenter.heroku.com/articles/heroku-cli`.
3. Verify that the Heroku CLI is installed fine by running `heroku --version`.

4. Login to Heroku by running `heroku login`. When prompted, enter your Heroku email and password.

5. Now run the `jhipster heroku` command. You will start seeing questions.

6. Choose a name you like when asked **Name to deploy as: (store)**. By, default it will use the application name. Try to choose a unique name since the Heroku namespace is shared.

7. Next, you will be asked to choose a region—**On which region do you want to deploy?** Choose between US and EU, and proceed.

8. The generator will create the required files and accept changes suggested by the Gradle build files.

The console output will look like this:

```
$ jhipster heroku
Using JHipster version installed locally in current project's node_modules
Executing jhipster:heroku
Options:
Heroku configuration is starting
? Name to deploy as: jhbook-online-store
? On which region do you want to deploy ? eu

Using existing Git repository

Heroku CLI deployment plugin already installed

Creating Heroku application and setting up node environment
heroku create jhbook-online-store --region eu
https://jhbook-online-store.herokuapp.com/ | https://git.heroku.com/jhbook-online-store.git

Provisioning addons
Created jawsdb:kitefin --as DATABASE

Creating Heroku deployment files
   create src/main/resources/config/bootstrap-heroku.yml
   create src/main/resources/config/application-heroku.yml
   create Procfile
   create gradle/heroku.gradle
 conflict build.gradle
? Overwrite build.gradle? overwrite
   force build.gradle

Building application
Parallel execution is an incubating feature.
```

The generated `.yml` files add Heroku-specific configurations for the application. The `Procfile` contains the specific command that will be executed on Heroku for the application. The Gradle build is also modified to include dependencies required by Heroku.

After generating the files, it will build the application and will start uploading artifacts. This may take several minutes based on your network latency. Once this has been successfully completed, you should see the following screen:

```
Deploying application

Uploading your application code.
This may take several minutes depending on your connection speed...
Uploading store-0.0.1-SNAPSHOT.war
-----> Packaging application...

       - app: jhbook-online-store
       - including: build/libs/store-0.0.1-SNAPSHOT.war
-----> Creating build...
       - file: slug.tgz
       - size: 49MB
-----> Uploading build...
       - success
-----> Deploying...
remote:
remote: -----> heroku-deploy app detected
remote: -----> Installing JDK 1.8... done
remote: -----> Discovering process types
remote:        Procfile declares types -> web
remote:
remote: -----> Compressing...
remote:        Done: 100.1M
remote: -----> Launching...
remote:        Released v4
remote:        https://jhbook-online-store.herokuapp.com/ deployed to Heroku
remote:
-----> Done

Your app should now be live. To view it run
       heroku open
And you can view the logs with this command
       heroku logs --tail
After application modification, redeploy it with
       jhipster heroku
Congratulations, JHipster execution is complete!
```

Now run the `heroku open` command to open the deployed application in a browser. That's it, you have successfully deployed your application to Heroku with a few commands.

When you update the application further, you can rebuild the package using `./gradlew -Pprod bootRepackage` and then redeploy it using the `heroku deploy:jar --jar build/libs/*war` command.

Don't forget to commit the changes made to `git` by executing the following command:

```
> git add --all
> git commit -am "add heroku configuration"
```

Summary

Deployment to production is one of the most important phases of application development, and is the most crucial one as well. With the help of JHipster, we deployed our application to a cloud provider with ease. We also learned about Docker and the various other deployment options available. We also made use of the upgrade sub-generator to keep our application up-to-date with JHipster.

So far, we've seen how we can develop and deploy a monolithic e-commerce application using JHipster. We started with a monolith and, in the upcoming chapters, we will see how we can scale our application into a microservice architecture with the help of JHipster. In the next chapter, we will learn about different microservice technologies and tools. So, stay tuned!

8
Introduction to Microservice Server-Side Technologies

Wasn't it easy to develop a production-ready monolithic application with JHipster? So far, we have created an application from scratch, added a few entities with JDL Studio, and then deployed it to the production environment along with tests. We have also added a continuous integration and continuous delivery pipeline. Wasn't the experience faster, easier, and better than coding everything from scratch?

So what's next? Yes, you guessed it right—**microservices**!

Microservices is the buzzword everywhere these days. Many companies out there are trying to solve their problems with microservices. We already saw an overview of the benefits of microservices in `Chapter 1`, *Introduction to Modern Web Application Development*.

In this chapter, we will look at the following:

- Benefits of microservices over monoliths
- Components that we need for building a complete microservices architecture

In this chapter, we will see how the monolithic application we created earlier can be converted into a microservice application.

After that, we will see how easy it is to create a microservice architecture using the options JHipster provides.

Microservice applications versus monoliths

The benefits of microservice architectures can be better understood by comparing them with monolithic architectures.

 The benefits of microservices over monoliths are phenomenal when they are designed and deployed correctly.

It is not as simple as splitting a monolithic application based on structure, component, or functionality and then deploying them as individual services. This will not work out. Converting a monolithic application or even a monolithic design into microservices needs a clear vision of the product. It includes knowledge of what part of the project will change and what part will be consistent. We must have low-level details, such as which entities we should group together and those that can be separated.

This clearly illustrates the need for an ever-evolving model. It is much easier to split the technologies used in the application, but not the interdependent models or the business logic of the application. So it is essential to place the project's primary focus on core domain and its logic.

Microservices should be independent. They will fail when a component is tightly coupled with another. The trickiest part is identifying and segregating the components.

When we have done that, it offers the following benefits over monolithic applications.

The monolithic code is a single unit. Thus, all parts of the application share the same memory. For a bigger system, we need to have a bigger infrastructure. When the application grows, we need to scale the infrastructure as needed. The scaling of an already bigger infrastructure is always a difficult and costlier task for operations.

Even though they have all the necessary code to handle anything in the product at a single place (no need to worry about latency or availability), it is difficult to handle the resources that it consumes to run and it is definitely not scalable. If any one part of the application fails, then the whole product will be impacted. When any one thread or query of the product clings on to the memory, then the impact will be seen by millions of our customers.

Microservices, on the other hand, require less memory to run since we are splitting the application into smaller components, which in turn reduces the infrastructure's cost. For example, it is cheaper to run 10 2GB instances (costs ~$170 per month on AWS) than running a single 16 GB instance (costs ~$570 per month on AWS). Each component runs in its own environment, which makes microservices much more developer-friendly and cloud-native. Similarly, microservices also increase the throughput across services. A memory intensive operation on one service will not affect any other service.

Monolithic architecture, over a period of time, will remove the agility of a team, which will delay the application rollout. This means people will tend to invest more time to find a workaround to fix a problem when a new feature is added, or something in the existing feature breaks. The monolithic architecture will bring a greater amount of inefficiency that in turn increases the technical debt.

Microservices, on the other hand, reduce the technical debt in terms of architecture since everything is reduced to individual components. Teams tend to be more agile and they will find handling changes easier.

The less code there is, the fewer bugs there are, meaning less pain and a shorter time to fix.

Monolithic applications are more time consuming to work with. Imagine there is a big monolithic application and you have to reverse an *if condition* in your service layer. After changing the code, it has to be built, which usually takes a few minutes, and then you must test the entire application, which will reduce the team's performance.

You can reboot or reload an application in seconds for a microservice architecture. When you have to reverse an *if condition*, you need not wait for minutes to build and deploy the application to test, you can do it in seconds. This will decrease the time it takes to do mundane tasks.

Faster iterations/releases and decreased downtime are the key things to increase user engagement and user retention, which in turn results in better revenue.

A human mind (unless you are superhuman) can handle only a limited amount of information. So cognitively, microservices help people to reduce the clutter and focus on the functionality. This enables better productivity and faster rollouts.

Embracing microservices will:

- Maximize productivity
- Improve agility
- Improve customer experience
- Speed up development/unit testing (if designed properly)
- Improve revenue

Building blocks of a microservice architecture

Running a microservice architecture requires a lot of components/features and involves a lot of advanced concepts. For the sake of understanding these concepts, imagine we have a microservice-based application for our e-commerce shopping website. This includes the following services:

- Pricing services: Responsible for giving us the price of the product based on demand
- Demand services: Responsible for calculating the demand for the product based on the sales and stocks left
- Inventory services: Responsible for tracking the quantity left in the inventory
- Many other services

Some of the concepts we will see in this section are:

- Service registry
- Service discovery
- Health check
- Dynamic routing and resiliency
- Security (authentication and authorization)
- Fault tolerance and failover

Service registry

Microservices are independent, but many use cases will need them to be interdependent. This means for some services to work properly they need data from another service, which in turn may or may not depend on other services or sources.

For example, our pricing service will directly depend on the demand service, which in turn depends on the inventory service. But these three services are completely independent, that is they can be deployed on any host, port, or location and scaled at will.

If the pricing service wants to communicate with the demand service, it has to know the exact location to which it can send requests to get the required information. Similarly, the demand service should know about the inventory service's details in order to communicate.

So we need a service registry that registers all other services and their locations. All services should register themselves to this registry service when the service is started and deregister itself when the service goes down.

 The service registry should act as a database of services, recording all the available instances and their details.

Service discovery

The service registry has details of the services available. But in order to find out where the required service is and which services to connect, we need to have service discovery.

When the pricing service wants to communicate with the demand service, it needs to know the network location of the demand service. In the case of traditional architecture, this is a fixed physical address but in the microservices world, this is a dynamic address that is assigned and updated dynamically.

The pricing service (client) will have to locate the demand service in the service registry and determine the location and then load balance the request o the available demand service. The demand service, in turn, will respond to the request of the requested client (pricing service).

Service discovery is used to discover the exact service to which the client should connect to, in order to get the necessary details.

Service discovery helps the API gateway to discover the right endpoint for a request.

They will also have a load balancer, which regulates the traffic and ensures the high availability of the services.

Based on the location where load balancing happens, the service discovery is classified into:

- **Client-side discovery pattern**

  The load balancing will happen on the client service side. The client service will determine where to send the request and the logic of load balancing will be in the client service. For example, Netflix Eureka (`https://github.com/Netflix/eureka`) is a service registry. It provides endpoints to register and discover the services.

  When the pricing service wants to invoke the demand service, it will connect to the service registry and then find the available services. Then, based on the load balancing logic configured, the pricing service (client) will determine which demand service to request.

  The services will then do an intelligent and application-specific load balancing. On the downside, this adds an extra layer of load balancing in every service, which is an overhead:

- **Server-side discovery pattern**

  The pricing service will request the load balancer to connect to the demand service. Then, the load balancer will connect to the service registry to determine the available instance, and then route the request based on the load balancing configured.

  For example, in Kubernetes, each pod will have its own server or proxy. All the requests are sent through this proxy (which has a dedicated IP and port associated with it).

  The load balancing logic is moved away from the service and isolated into a separate service. On the downside, it requires yet another highly available service to handle the requests.

Health check

In the microservices world, instances can start, change, update, and stop at random. They can also scale up and down based on their traffic and other settings. This requires a health check service that will constantly monitor the availability of the services.

Services can send their status periodically to this health check service, and this keeps a track of the health of the services. When a service goes down, the health check service will stop getting the heartbeat from the service. Then, the health check service will mark the service down and cascade the information to the service registry. Similarly, when the service resumes, the heartbeat is sent to the health check service. Upon receiving a few positive heartbeats, the service is marked UP and then the information is sent to the service registry.

The health check service can check for health in two ways:

- **Push configuration**: All the services will send their heartbeat periodically to the health check service
- **Pull configuration**: A single health check service instance will query for the availability of the systems periodically

This also requires a **high availability system**. All the services should connect to this service to share their heartbeat and this has to connect to the service registry to tell them whether a service is available or not.

Dynamic routing and resiliency

The health check services will track the health of available services and send details to the service registry about the health of services.

Based on this, services should intelligently route requests to healthy instances and shut down the traffic to unhealthy instances.

Since the services dynamically change their location (address /port), every time a client wants to connect to the service, it should first check for the availability of the services from the service registry. Every connection to the client will also need to have a timeout added to it, beyond which the request has to be served or it has to be retried (configured) to another instance. This way we can minimize the *cascading failure*.

Security

When a client invokes the available service, we need to validate the request. In order to prevent unwanted requests from piling up, we should have an additional layer of **security**. The requests from the client should be authenticated and authorized to call the other service, to prevent unauthorized calls to the service. The service should, in turn, decrypt the request, understand whether it is valid or invalid, and do the rest.

In order to provide secure microservices, it should have the following characteristics:

- Confidentiality: Allow only the authorized clients to access and consume the information.
- Integrity: Can guarantee the integrity of the information that it receives from the client and ensure that it is not modified by a third-party (for example, when a gateway and a service is talking to each other, no party can tamper with or alter the messages that are sent between them. This a classic man-in-the-middle attack).
- Availability: A secure API service should be highly available.
- Reliability: Should handle the requests and process them reliably.

 For more information on MITM, or man-in-the-middle attacks check, the following link: `https://www.owasp.org/index.php/Man-in-the-middle_attack`.

Fault tolerance and failover

In a microservice architecture, there might be many reasons for a fault. It is important to handle faults or failovers gracefully, as follows:

- When the request takes a long time to complete, have a predetermined timeout instead of waiting for the service to respond.
- When the request fails, identify the server, notify the service registry, and stop connecting to the server. This way, we can prevent other requests from going to that server.
- Shut down the service when it is not responding and start a new service to make sure services are working as expected.

This can be achieved using the following:

- **Fault tolerance** libraries, which prevent cascading failures by isolating the remote instance and services that are not responding or taking a longer time than in the SLA to respond. This prevents other services from calling the failed or unhealthy instances.
- **Distributed tracing system** libraries help to trace the timing and latency of the service or system, and highlight any discrepancies with the agreed SLA. They also help you to understand where the performance bottleneck is so that you can act on this.

JHipster provides options to fulfill many of the preceding concepts. The most important of them are as follows:

- JHipster Registry
- HashiCorp Consul
- JHipster Gateway
- JHipster console
- Prometheus
- JHipster UAA server

JHipster Registry

JHipster provides JHipster Registry (`http://www.jhipster.tech/jhipster-registry/`) as the default **service registry**. The JHipster Registry is a runtime application that all microservice applications register with and get their configuration from. It also provides additional features such as monitoring and health check dashboards.

JHipster Registry is made up of the following:

- Netflix Eureka server
- Spring cloud config server

Netflix Eureka server

Eureka (`https://github.com/Netflix/eureka`) consists of the following:

- The Eureka server

Eureka is a REST-based service. It is used for locating services for load balancing and failover middle tiers.

Eureka servers help to load balance among the instances. They are more useful in a cloud-based environment where the availability is intermittent. On the other hand, traditional load balancers help in load balancing the traffic between known and fixed instances.

- The Eureka client

Eureka provides a Eureka client, which makes the interaction between servers seamless. It is a Java-based client.

Eureka acts as a **middle tier** *load balancer* that helps to load balance the host of a middle-tier services. They provide a simple round robin-based load balancing by default. The load balancing algorithm can be customized as needed with a wrapper.

They cannot provide sticky sessions. They also fit perfectly for client-based load balancing scenarios (as seen earlier).

Eureka has no restriction on the communication technology. We can use anything, such as Thrift, HTTP, or any RPC mechanisms, for communication.

Imagine our application is in different AWS Availability Zones. We register a Eureka cluster in each of the zones that holds information about available services in that region only and start the Eureka server in each zone to handle zone failures.

All the services will register themselves to the Eureka server and send their heartbeats. When the client no longer sends a heartbeat, the service is taken out of the registry itself and the information is passed across the Eureka nodes in the cluster. Then, any client from any zone will look up the registry information to locate it and then make any remote calls. Also, we need to ensure that Eureka clusters between regions do not communicate with each other.

Eureka prefers availability over consistency. That is when the services are connected to the Eureka server and it shares the complete configuration between the services. This enables services to run even when the Eureka server goes down. In production, we have to run Eureka in a high availability cluster for better consistency.

Eureka also has the ability to add or remove the servers on the fly. This makes it the right choice for service registry and service discovery.

Spring cloud config server

In a microservice architecture, the services are dynamic in nature. They will go down and come up based on traffic or any other configuration. Due to this dynamic nature, there should be a separate, *highly available* server that holds the essential configuration details that all the servers need to know.

For example, our pricing service will need to know where the registry service is and how it has to communicate to the registry service. The registry service, on the other hand, should be highly available. If for any reason the server has to go down, we will spin up a new server. The pricing service needs to communicate with the config service in order to find out about the registry service. On the other hand, when the registry service is changed, it has to communicate the changes to the config server, which will then cascade the information to all the necessary services.

Spring cloud config server (`https://github.com/spring-cloud/spring-cloud-config`) provides server and client-side support for external configuration.

With the cloud config server, we have a central place to manage all our external properties across all environments. The concept is similar to Spring-based environment property source abstractions on both client and server. They fit for any application running in any language.

They are also helpful for carrying the configuration data between various (development/test/production) environments and help to migrate much easier.

Spring config server has a HTTP, resource-based API for external configuration. They will encrypt and decrypt property values. They bind to the config server and initialize a Spring environment with remote property sources. The configuration can be stored in a Git repository or in a file system.

HashiCorp Consul

Consul (`https://www.consul.io/`) is primarily a service discovery client from Hashicorp. It focuses on consistency. Consul is completely written in Go.

This means it will have a lower memory footprint. Added to that, we can also use Consul with services written in any programming language.

The main advantages of using Consul are as follows:

- It has a lower memory footprint
- It can be used with services that are written in any programming language
- It focuses on consistency rather than availability

Consul also provides service discovery, failure detection, multi-data center configuration, and storage.

 This is an alternative option to JHipster Registry. There is an option to choose between JHipster Registry and Consul during application creation.

Eureka (JHipster Registry) requires each application to use its APIs for registering and discovering themselves. It focuses on availability over consistency. It supports only applications or services written in Spring Boot.

On the other hand, Consul runs as an agent in the services, and checks the health information and a few other extra operations listed previously.

Service discovery

Consul can provide a service and other clients can use Consul to discover the providers of a given service. Using either DNS or HTTP, applications can easily find the services that they depend on.

Health discovery

Consul clients can provide any number of health checks, either associated with a given service or with the local node. This information can be used by a health check service to monitor services' health, and it is in turn used to discover the service components and route traffic away from unhealthy hosts and towards the healthy hosts.

K/V store

Consul has an easy-to-use HTTP API that makes it simple for applications to use Consul's key/value store for dynamically configuring services, electing the leader when the current leader goes down, and segregating containers based on features.

Multiple data centers

Consul supports multiple data centers out of the box. This means you do not have to worry about building additional layers of abstraction to grow to multiple regions.

Consul should be a distributed and highly available service. Every node that provides services to Consul runs a consul agent, which is mainly responsible for health checking. These agents will then talk with one or more Consul servers, which collect and add this information. These servers will also elect a leader among themselves.

Thus, Consul serves as a service registry, service discovery, health check, and K/V store.

JHipster Gateway

In a microservice architecture, we need an entry point to access all the running services. So we need a service that acts as a gateway. This will proxy or route clients' requests to the respective services. In JHipster, we provide JHipster Gateway for that.

JHipster Gateway is a microservice application that can be generated. It integrates Netflix Zuul and Hystrix in order to provide routing, filtering, security, circuit breaking, and so on.

Netflix Zuul

In a microservice architecture, Zuul is a front door for all the requests (gatekeeper). It acts as an edge service application. Zuul is built to enable *dynamic routing, monitoring, resiliency, and security* among the services. It also has the ability to dynamically route requests as needed.

Trivia: In *Ghostbusters*, Zuul is the gatekeeper.

Zuul works based on different types of filter that enable us to quickly and nimbly apply functionality to our edge service.

These filters help us to perform the following functions:

- Authentication and security: To identify each resource's authentication requirements and to reject requests that do not satisfy the requirements
- Insights and monitoring: To track data and statistics at the edge and to give an insight into the production application
- Dynamic routing: To dynamically route requests to different backend clusters as needed based on health and other factors
- Multi-regional resiliency (AWS): To route requests across AWS regions in order to diversify our Elastic Load Balancer usage and move our edge closer to our members

For even more information on Zuul, please check `https://github.com/Netflix/zuul/wiki`.

Hystrix

Hystrix (`https://github.com/Netflix/Hystrix`) is a latency and fault tolerance library designed to isolate points of access to remote systems, services, and third-party libraries, stop cascading failures; and enable resilience in complex distributed systems where failure is inevitable.

Hystrix is designed to do the following:

- Stop failure cascades in a complex distributed system
- Protect the system from the failures of dependencies over the network
- Control the latency of the system
- Recover rapidly and fail faster to prevent cascading
- Fall back and gracefully degrade when possible
- Enable near-real-time monitoring, alerting, and operational control

Applications in complex distributed architectures have a lot of dependencies, each of which will inevitably fail at some point. If the host application is not isolated from these external failures, it risks being taken down with them.

JHipster Console

The JHipster Console (`https://github.com/jhipster/jhipster-console`) is a monitoring solution for microservices built using the ELK stack. It comes bundled with preset dashboards and configuration. It is provided as a runtime component in the form of a Docker image.

 The ELK Stack is made up of Elasticsearch, Logstash, and Kibana.

Logstash can be used to normalize the data (usually from logs) and then Elasticsearch is used to process the same data faster. Finally, Kibana is used to visualize the data.

Elasticsearch

Elasticsearch is a widely used search engine in data analytics. It helps you to extract data really fast from data haystacks. It also helps to provide real-time analytics and data extraction. It is highly scalable, available, and multi-tenanted.

It also provides full text-based searches saved as a document. These documents, in turn, will be updated and modified based on any changes to the data. This, in turn, will provide a faster search and analyze the data.

Logstash

Logstash (`https://www.elastic.co/products/logstash`) will take the logs, process them, and convert them into output. They can read any type of logs, such as system logs, error logs, and app logs. They are the **heavy working** component of this stack, which helps to store, query, and analyze the logs.

They act as a pipeline for event processing and are capable of processing huge amounts of data with the filters and, along with Elasticsearch, deliver results really fast. JHipster makes sure that the logs are in the correct format so that they can be grouped and visualized in the correct way.

Kibana

Kibana (`https://www.elastic.co/products/kibana`) forms the frontend of the ELK stack. It is used for data visualization. It is merely a log data dashboard. It is helpful in visualizing the trends and patterns in data that are otherwise tedious to read and interpret. It also provides an option to share/save, which makes visualization of the data more useful.

Zipkin

Zipkin (`https://zipkin.io/`) is a distributed tracing system. Microservice architecture always has latency problems, and a system is needed to troubleshoot the latency problem. Zipkin helps to solve the problem by collecting timing data. Zipkin also helps to search the data.

All registered services will report timing data to Zipkin. Zipkin creates a dependency diagram based on the received traced requests for each of the applications or services. Then, it can be used to analyze, spot an application that takes a long time to resolve, and fix it as needed.

When a request is made, the trace instrumentation will record tags, add the trace headers to the request, and finally record the timestamp. Then, the request is sent to the original destination and the response is sent back to the trace instrumentation, which then records the duration and shares the result with the Zipkin collector, which is responsible for storing the information.

By default, JHipster will generate the application with Zipkin disabled, but this can be enabled in the application-`<env>.yml` file.

Prometheus

In a microservice architecture, we need to monitor our services continuously and any issues should cause alerts immediately. We need a separate service that will continuously monitor and alert us whenever something weird happens.

Prometheus consists of the following:

- Prometheus server, which is responsible for scraping and storing the time series data
- Libraries to instrument the application code
- A push gateway for supporting short-lived jobs

- An exporter to Grafana to visualize data
- An alert manager
- Other support tools

 Prometheus is an alternative to JHipster console. It provides monitoring and alerting support. This requires running a Prometheus server separately for more information. To get started with Prometheus, visit `https://prometheus.io/`.

It provides multi-dimensional data models, which are time series and are identified by metric name and key-value pair. It has a flexible dynamic query language. It supports pulling time series out of the box and pushing time series via an intermediary gateway. It has multiple modes of graphing and dashboard support.

It is helpful in finding out problems when there is an outage. Since it is autonomous and does not depend on any remote services, the data is sufficient for finding where the infrastructure is broken.

It is helpful in recording the time series data and monitoring either via machine or highly dynamic Service Oriented Architecture.

Some things to consider when choosing Prometheus over JHipster Console are as follows:

- Prometheus is very good at exploiting the metrics of your application and will not monitor logs or traces. JHipster console, on the other hand, uses the ELK stack and monitors the logs, traces, and metrics of your application.
- Prometheus can be used to query a huge amount of time series data. ELK on JHipster console is much more versatile in terms of tracking and searching the metrics and logs.
- JHipster console uses Kibana to visualize the data while Prometheus uses Grafana (`https://grafana.com/`) to visualize the metrics.

JHipster UAA server

JHipster user accounting and authorizing (UAA) services are merely an OAuth2 server that can be used for *centralized identity management*. In order to access the protected resource and also to avoid unwanted access to the APIs, there has to be an authorization server that authorizes the request and provides access to the resource.

OAuth2 is an authorization framework that provides access to the request based on tokens. Clients request access to a service; if the user is authorized, the application receives an authorization grant. After receiving the grant, the client requests a token from the authorization server. Once the token is received, the client will then request the resource server gets the necessary information.

JHipster supports both standard LDAP protocols and is invoked via JSON APIs.

JHipster UAA is a user accounting and authorizing service for securing JHipster microservices using the OAuth2 authorization protocol.

JHipster UAA is a JHipster generated application consisting of user and role management. It also has a full-fledged OAuth2 authorization server. This is flexible and completely customizable.

Security is essential in a microservice architecture. The following are the basic requirements for securing microservices.

They should be authenticated in one place. Users should experience the entire experience as a single unit. Once the end user logs in to the application, they should be able to access whatever they have access to. They should hold session-related information throughout the time they are logged in to the system.

The security service should be stateless. Irrespective of the service, the security service should be capable of providing authentication for requests.

They also need to have the ability to provide authentication to machines and users. They should be able to distinguish them and trace them. Their function should be authorizing the incoming request rather than identifying the end user.

Since the underlying services are scalable, security services should also have the ability to scale up and down based on requirements.

They should, of course, be safe from attacks. Any known vulnerability should be fixed and updated as and when required.

The previous requirements were satisfied by using the OAuth2 protocol.

JHipster UAA is a centralized server that helps to authenticate and authorize users. They also have session-related information and the role-based access control with the help of a user and role management that is available inside the system.

The OAuth2 protocol, in general, provides the token for authenticating based on the details provided, which makes them stateless and able to authenticate a request from any source.

Summary

So far, we have seen the benefits of a microservice architecture over monolithic applications, and the components that we need to run a microservice application such as JHipster Registry, Consul, Zuul, Zipkin, the ELK stack, Hystrix, Prometheus, and the JHipster UAA server. In our next chapter, we will see how to build microservices using JHipster. We will also learn how we can choose the previous components and how easy it is to set them up with JHipster.

9

Building Microservices with JHipster

Now, it's time to build a full-fledged microservices stack. So far, we have generated, developed, and deployed a monolithic application using JHipster, and in the previous chapter, we saw the benefits offered by a microservice stack. In this chapter, we will look at how to build microservices with JHipster.

We will start by converting our monolithic store application into a microservice gateway application. Next, we will add a new functionality to our e-commerce shop as a separate microservice application. We will then see how these applications communicate with each other and work as a single application for our end users.

In this chapter, we will:

- Generate a Gateway application:
  - Run through the generated code
  - See a brief introduction to JWT
- Generate a microservice application:
  - Invoice service
  - Notification service

Application architecture

We built an online e-commerce shop using JHipster in `Chapter 3`, *Building Monolithic Web Applications* with JHipster. It was built as a monolith since the scope was small and it was an easier choice to start with. Let's say that our e-commerce store has grown tremendously in terms of users and scope, resulting in a more demanding situation. The team is finding it difficult to roll out features faster with the monolithic architecture, and would like to have more control over individual parts of the application.

One of the solutions to this problem would be to adopt a microservice architecture. The application was created using JHipster; the option to move to microservices is much easier to accomplish. JHipster follows the **proxy microservice pattern** in which there is an aggregator/proxy in front of the services, which acts as the gateway for the end users. In much simpler terms, JHipster creates a gateway (which handles all the user requests) and the individual services that talk via the gateway to the users.

This said, we need to have a gateway service, along with one or a few microservice applications that can run alone.

Our customers are facing some issues regarding invoicing, since it is taking longer for the system to respond. Customers are also complaining that they are not receiving notifications so they can track their orders. To solve this, we will remove the invoice service from our monolithic application and make it a separate service, and then create a separate **Notification Service** that will take care of the notifications. For the former, we will stick with the same SQL database. For the latter, we will use the NoSQL database.

Let's have a look at the application architecture that we are going to generate:

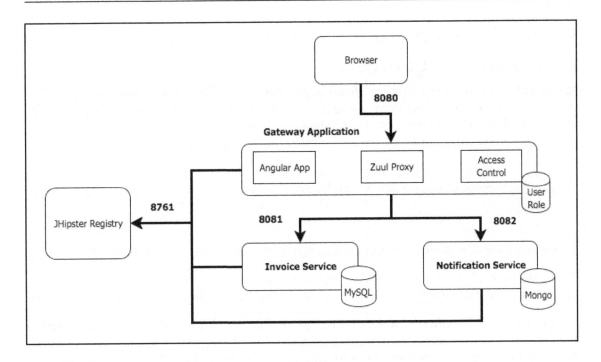

Gateway application generation

We will start by converting the monolithic application that we have generated into a microservice gateway application.

Even though microservices are made up of different services inside, for end users it should be a single, unified product. There are a lot of services that are designed to work in a lot of different ways, but there should be a single entry point for users. Thus, we need a gateway application, since they form the frontend of your application.

Segregate the internal contracts and services from external users. We may have application-level internal services that we shouldn't expose to external users, so these can be masked away. This also adds another level of security to the application.

Easier to mock services for testing help validate the services independently in integration testing.

Converting a monolithic application to a microservice gateway

We already have our monolithic application generated, as well as our entities. As a part of monolithic application generation, we have already selected some options via JHipster CLI. We will stick to the same options (the database, authentication type, package name, i18n, and so on) when we generate the microservice gateway application.

 Note: We will see how the customizations that we applied in the monolithic app can be applied to the gateway later.

It's coding time now, so let's start building a gateway application using JHipster CLI.

The first step here is to convert the monolithic app into a microservice gateway application with almost the same configuration that we used when we created a monolithic application.

Let's move to the Terminal (Command Prompt, if you are using Windows) now, and start by navigating to the folder where we created the monolithic application. Once you're in the folder, create a new Git branch so that we can do a clean merge back to master once we are done:

```
> cd e-commerce-app/online-store
> git checkout -b gateway-conversion
```

Now, open the `.yo-rc.json` file in your favorite text editor or IDE and change the following value:

```
"searchEngine": false,                    19   "searchEngine": false,
"messageBroker": false,                   20   "messageBroker": false,
"serviceDiscoveryType": false,            21 + "serviceDiscoveryType": "eureka",
"buildTool": "gradle",                    22   "buildTool": "gradle",
"enableSocialSignIn": false,              23   "enableSocialSignIn": false,
"enableSwaggerCodegen": false,            24   "enableSwaggerCodegen": false,
"jwtSecretKey": "6e7e481b0f8c547a543060764db3834caa87199a",  25  "jwtSecretKey": "6e7e481b0f8c547a543060764db3834caa87199a",
"clientFramework": "angularX",            26   "clientFramework": "angularX",
"useSass": true,                          27   "useSass": true,
"clientPackageManager": "yarn",           28   "clientPackageManager": "yarn",
"applicationType": "monolith",            29 + "applicationType": "gateway",
"testFrameworks": [                       30   "testFrameworks": [
  "protractor"                            31     "protractor"
```

In order to make the monolith into a microservice gateway application, we can just change the preceding values in the `.yo-rc.json` file. We have added the service discovery type to Eureka since for monolithic applications, it is not mandatory to have service discovery.

Also, obviously, the next change is to change the application type from monolith to gateway.

Application generation

Now, let's run the `jhipster` command to generate the application:

```
Installing languages: en
conflict package.json
? Overwrite package.json? (ynaxdH)
  y) overwrite
  n) do not overwrite
  a) overwrite this and all others
  x) abort
  d) show the differences between the old and the new
  h) Help, list all options
Answer:
```

JHipster then asks whether you want to overwrite the conflicting files or use your existing ones, as well as a few other options. Users can use any one of the desired options.

Right now, we will choose option a. It will overwrite all of the other files, including the highlighted file.

> This prompt is extremely useful if you have a lot of custom code written on your application. You can choose the appropriate option to get the desired result.

```
Server application generated successfully.

Run your Spring Boot application:
  ./gradlew

Client application generated successfully.

Start your Webpack development server with:
  yarn start

Congratulations, JHipster execution is complete!
Application successfully committed to Git.
```

This will overwrite all the customizations we did in our monolithic application. We can easily bring them back into this branch by cherry picking the required changes from our master branch using GIT. You can follow a similar approach to the one we saw in Chapter 5, *Customization and Further Development*, for that. Once all changes are applied, we can merge this branch back into the master. You will have to do the same for entity files as well in Chapter 10, *Working with Microservices*.

Generating a new Gateway

If you do not want to convert the existing monolith and want to start fresh, then follow these steps.

In the Terminal, navigate to the e-commerce-app folder and create a new folder called app-gateway, change the directory to app-gateway, and run the jhipster command.

So, obviously, the first question is, **Which *type* of application would we like to create?** We will select the **Microservice gateway** (third option) and then click *Enter*:

```
? Which *type* of application would you like to create?
  Monolithic application (recommended for simple projects)
  Microservice application
> Microservice gateway
  JHipster UAA server (for microservice OAuth2 authentication)
```

Then, we will enter the base name of our application. We will use the name store:

```
? Which *type* of application would you like to create? Microservice gateway
? What is the base name of your application? (jhipster) store
```

Since we are working with microservices, there is a high risk of having port conflicts. In order to avoid them, JHipster will ask you to select a port for each microservice application (both gateway and application). By default, we will have 8080 as the port, but we can change the port as necessary. For now, we will use the default port since the gateway will run on 8080, similar to what our monolithic application had:

```
? Which *type* of application would you like to create? Microservice gateway
? What is the base name of your application? store
? As you are running in a microservice architecture, on which port would like your server to run? It should be unique to avoid port conflicts. (8080)
```

Then, we enter the package name for our application. We will use the default name that is available, which is `com.mycompany.store`:

```
? Which *type* of application would you like to create? Microservice gateway
? What is the base name of your application? store
? As you are running in a microservice architecture, on which port would like your server to run? It should be unique to avoid port conflicts. 8080
? What is your default Java package name? (com.mycompany.store) com.mycompany.store
```

For the next question, JHipster will ask you to configure the registry service. We will select the necessary registry service to configure, monitor, and scale our microservices and gateway application. We can either choose to use the JHipster registry or Consul. This is also optional; we don't need to choose any registry service here. We can then select **No service discovery**.

When you select **No service discovery**, the microservice URLs are hardcoded in the property files.

```
? Which *type* of application would you like to create? Microservice gateway
? What is the base name of your application? store
? As you are running in a microservice architecture, on which port would like your server to run? It should be unique to avoid port conflicts. 8080
? What is your default Java package name? com.mycompany.store
? Which service discovery server do you want to use? (Use arrow keys)
> JHipster Registry (uses Eureka, provides Spring Cloud Config support and monitoring dashboards)
  Consul
  No service discovery
```

For the next question, JHipster will ask you to select the authentication type. JHipster provides three options for the authentication type, which are JWT, OAuth2, and UAA server-based. JWT is stateless, while the UAA runs on a different server (and application altogether). OAuth2, on the other hand, will provide authorization tokens, while the authorization is done on the third-party system.

JHipster does provide an option to create a UAA server application.

We will look at JWT in more detail shortly. For now, we will select **JWT authentication**.

```
? Which *type* of application would you like to create? Microservice gateway
? What is the base name of your application? store
? As you are running in a microservice architecture, on which port would like your server to run? It should be unique to avoid port conflicts. 8080
? What is your default Java package name? com.mycompany.store
? Which service discovery server do you want to use? JHipster Registry (uses Eureka, provides Spring Cloud Config support and monitoring dashboards)
? Which *type* of authentication would you like to use? (Use arrow keys)
> JWT authentication (stateless, with a token)
  OAuth 2.0 / OIDC Authentication (stateful, works with Keycloak and Okta)
  Authentication with JHipster UAA server (the server must be generated separately)
```

We will select the database type next. We have an option to select either SQL and NoSQL. In terms of NoSQL, we can choose MongoDB or Cassandra. We will select the **SQL** database:

```
? Which *type* of application would you like to create? Microservice gateway
? What is the base name of your application? store
? As you are running in a microservice architecture, on which port would like your server to run? It should be unique to avoid port conflicts. 8080
? What is your default Java package name? com.mycompany.store
? Which service discovery server do you want to use? JHipster Registry (uses Eureka, provides Spring Cloud Config support and monitoring dashboards)
? Which *type* of authentication would you like to use? JWT authentication (stateless, with a token)
? Which *type* of database would you like to use? (Use arrow keys)
> SQL (H2, MySQL, MariaDB, PostgreSQL, Oracle, MSSQL)
  MongoDB
  Cassandra
  [BETA] Couchbase
```

Then, we will select the database that we will be using for production and development. JHipster provides an option to use a different database for your production and development environment. This really helps to kick-start application development faster and easier.

We will select a **MySQL** database for production:

```
? Which *type* of application would you like to create? Microservice gateway
? What is the base name of your application? store
? As you are running in a microservice architecture, on which port would like your server to run? It should be unique to avoid port conflicts. 8080
? What is your default Java package name? com.mycompany.store
? Which service discovery server do you want to use? JHipster Registry (uses Eureka, provides Spring Cloud Config support and monitoring dashboards)
? Which *type* of authentication would you like to use? JWT authentication (stateless, with a token)
? Which *type* of database would you like to use? SQL (H2, MySQL, MariaDB, PostgreSQL, Oracle, MSSQL)
? Which *production* database would you like to use? (Use arrow keys)
> MySQL
  MariaDB
  PostgreSQL
  Oracle (Please follow our documentation to use the Oracle proprietary driver)
  Microsoft SQL Server
```

Then, we will select **H2 with disk-based persistence** for development:

```
? Which *type* of application would you like to create? Microservice gateway
? What is the base name of your application? store
? As you are running in a microservice architecture, on which port would like your server to run? It should be unique to avoid port conflicts. 8080
? What is your default Java package name? com.mycompany.store
? Which service discovery server do you want to use? JHipster Registry (uses Eureka, provides Spring Cloud Config support and monitoring dashboards)
? Which *type* of authentication would you like to use? JWT authentication (stateless, with a token)
? Which *type* of database would you like to use? SQL (H2, MySQL, MariaDB, PostgreSQL, Oracle, MSSQL)
? Which *production* database would you like to use? MySQL
? Which *development* database would you like to use? (Use arrow keys)
> H2 with disk-based persistence
  H2 with in-memory persistence
  MySQL
```

Following the databases, we will select **yes** for the second level hibernate cache:

```
? Which *type* of application would you like to create? Microservice gateway
? What is the base name of your application? store
? As you are running in a microservice architecture, on which port would like your server to run? It should be unique to avoid port conflicts. 8080
? What is your default Java package name? com.mycompany.store
? Which service discovery server do you want to use? JHipster Registry (uses Eureka, provides Spring Cloud Config support and monitoring dashboards)
? Which *type* of authentication would you like to use? JWT authentication (stateless, with a token)
? Which *type* of database would you like to use? SQL (H2, MySQL, MariaDB, PostgreSQL, Oracle, MSSQL)
? Which *production* database would you like to use? MySQL
? Which *development* database would you like to use? H2 with disk-based persistence
? Do you want to use Hibernate 2nd level cache? (Y/n) y
```

Then, we will select **Gradle for building the backend**. We have an option to select **Gradle** for the backend development:

```
? Which *type* of application would you like to create? Microservice gateway
? What is the base name of your application? store
? As you are running in a microservice architecture, on which port would like your server to run? It should be unique to avoid port conflicts. 8080
? What is your default Java package name? com.mycompany.store
? Which service discovery server do you want to use? JHipster Registry (uses Eureka, provides Spring Cloud Config support and monitoring dashboards)
? Which *type* of authentication would you like to use? JWT authentication (stateless, with a token)
? Which *type* of database would you like to use? SQL (H2, MySQL, MariaDB, PostgreSQL, Oracle, MSSQL)
? Which *production* database would you like to use? MySQL
? Which *development* database would you like to use? H2 with disk-based persistence
? Do you want to use Hibernate 2nd level cache? Yes
? Would you like to use Maven or Gradle for building the backend?
  Maven
> Gradle
```

Then, we can select any other additional technologies that we need to use. JHipster provides an option to select Elasticsearch, using Hazelcast for clustered applications, WebSockets, and Swagger Codegen for API-based development and Kafka-based asynchronous messaging. We will select WebSockets here, similar to what we used in our monolithic store:

```
? Which *type* of application would you like to create? Microservice gateway
? What is the base name of your application? store
? As you are running in a microservice architecture, on which port would like your server to run? It should be unique to avoid port conflicts. 8080
? What is your default Java package name? com.mycompany.store
? Which service discovery server do you want to use? JHipster Registry (uses Eureka, provides Spring Cloud Config support and monitoring dashboards)
? Which *type* of authentication would you like to use? JWT authentication (stateless, with a token)
? Which *type* of database would you like to use? SQL (H2, MySQL, MariaDB, PostgreSQL, Oracle, MSSQL)
? Which *production* database would you like to use? MySQL
? Which *development* database would you like to use? H2 with disk-based persistence
? Do you want to use Hibernate 2nd level cache? Yes
? Would you like to use Maven or Gradle for building the backend? Gradle
? Which other technologies would you like to use?
  o Search engine using Elasticsearch
>o WebSockets using Spring Websocket
  o API first development using swagger-codegen
  o Asynchronous messages using Apache Kafka
```

Since our gateway application needs a user interface, for the next question we can choose the framework that we need to use for the client. We will select `Angular 5` for this:

```
? Which *type* of application would you like to create? Microservice gateway
? What is the base name of your application? store
? As you are running in a microservice architecture, on which port would like your server to run? It should be unique to avoid port conflicts. 8080
? What is your default Java package name? com.mycompany.store
? Which service discovery server do you want to use? JHipster Registry (uses Eureka, provides Spring Cloud Config support and monitoring dashboards)
? Which *type* of authentication would you like to use? JWT authentication (stateless, with a token)
? Which *type* of database would you like to use? SQL (H2, MySQL, MariaDB, PostgreSQL, Oracle, MSSQL)
? Which *production* database would you like to use? MySQL
? Which *development* database would you like to use? H2 with disk-based persistence
? Do you want to use Hibernate 2nd level cache? Yes
? Would you like to use Maven or Gradle for building the backend? Gradle
? Which other technologies would you like to use? WebSockets using Spring Websocket
? Which *Framework* would you like to use for the client? (Use arrow keys)
> Angular 5
  [BETA] React
```

Then, we will select whether we need to use a SASS-based preprocessor for the CSS. We will use SASS here, so we will select **y**:

```
? Which *type* of application would you like to create? Microservice gateway
? What is the base name of your application? store
? As you are running in a microservice architecture, on which port would like your server to run? It should be unique to avoid port conflicts. 8080
? What is your default Java package name? com.mycompany.store
? Which service discovery server do you want to use? JHipster Registry (uses Eureka, provides Spring Cloud Config support and monitoring dashboards)
? Which *type* of authentication would you like to use? JWT authentication (stateless, with a token)
? Which *type* of database would you like to use? SQL (H2, MySQL, MariaDB, PostgreSQL, Oracle, MSSQL)
? Which *production* database would you like to use? MySQL
? Which *development* database would you like to use? H2 with disk-based persistence
? Do you want to use Hibernate 2nd level cache? Yes
? Would you like to use Maven or Gradle for building the backend? Gradle
? Which other technologies would you like to use? WebSockets using Spring Websocket
? Which *Framework* would you like to use for the client? Angular 5
? Would you like to enable *SASS* support using the LibSass stylesheet preprocessor? (y/N) y
```

Then, we will select whether we need to enable internationalization support. We will select **yes** for this:

```
? Which *type* of application would you like to create? Microservice gateway
? What is the base name of your application? store
? As you are running in a microservice architecture, on which port would like your server to run? It should be unique to avoid port conflicts. 8080
? What is your default Java package name? com.mycompany.store
? Which service discovery server do you want to use? JHipster Registry (uses Eureka, provides Spring Cloud Config support and monitoring dashboards)
? Which *type* of authentication would you like to use? JWT authentication (stateless, with a token)
? Which *type* of database would you like to use? SQL (H2, MySQL, MariaDB, PostgreSQL, Oracle, MSSQL)
? Which *production* database would you like to use? MySQL
? Which *development* database would you like to use? H2 with disk-based persistence
? Do you want to use Hibernate 2nd level cache? Yes
? Would you like to use Maven or Gradle for building the backend? Gradle
? Which other technologies would you like to use? WebSockets using Spring Websocket
? Which *Framework* would you like to use for the client? Angular 5
? Would you like to enable *SASS* support using the LibSass stylesheet preprocessor? Yes
? Would you like to enable internationalization support? (Y/n) y
```

Then, we will choose **English** as our native language:

```
? Which *type* of application would you like to create? Microservice gateway
? What is the base name of your application? store
? As you are running in a microservice architecture, on which port would like your server to run? It should be unique to avoid port conflicts. 8080
? What is your default Java package name? com.mycompany.store
? Which service discovery server do you want to use? JHipster Registry (uses Eureka, provides Spring Cloud Config support and monitoring dashboards)
? Which *type* of authentication would you like to use? JWT authentication (stateless, with a token)
? Which *type* of database would you like to use? SQL (H2, MySQL, MariaDB, PostgreSQL, Oracle, MSSQL)
? Which *production* database would you like to use? MySQL
? Which *development* database would you like to use? H2 with disk-based persistence
? Do you want to use Hibernate 2nd level cache? Yes
? Would you like to use Maven or Gradle for building the backend? Gradle
? Which other technologies would you like to use? WebSockets using Spring Websocket
? Which *Framework* would you like to use for the client? Angular 5
? Would you like to enable *SASS* support using the LibSass stylesheet preprocessor? Yes
? Would you like to enable internationalization support? Yes
? Please choose the native language of the application (Use arrow keys)
> English
  Estonian
  Farsi
  French
  Galician
  German
  Greek
(Move up and down to reveal more choices)
```

Then, choose any other additional languages:

```
? Which *type* of application would you like to create? Microservice gateway
? What is the base name of your application? store
? As you are running in a microservice architecture, on which port would like your server to run? It should be unique to avoid port conflicts. 8080
? What is your default Java package name? com.mycompany.store
? Which service discovery server do you want to use? JHipster Registry (uses Eureka, provides Spring Cloud Config support and monitoring dashboards)
? Which *type* of authentication would you like to use? JWT authentication (stateless, with a token)
? Which *type* of database would you like to use? SQL (H2, MySQL, MariaDB, PostgreSQL, Oracle, MSSQL)
? Which *production* database would you like to use? MySQL
? Which *development* database would you like to use? H2 with disk-based persistence
? Do you want to use Hibernate 2nd level cache? Yes
? Would you like to use Maven or Gradle for building the backend? Gradle
? Which other technologies would you like to use? WebSockets using Spring Websocket
? Which *Framework* would you like to use for the client? Angular 5
? Would you like to enable *SASS* support using the LibSass stylesheet preprocessor? Yes
? Would you like to enable internationalization support? Yes
? Please choose the native language of the application English
? Please choose additional languages to install
  o Armenian
  o Catalan
  o Chinese (Simplified)
 >o Chinese (Traditional)
  o Czech
  o Danish
  o Dutch
(Move up and down to reveal more choices)
```

Then, select any other testing frameworks, such as Gatling, Cucumber, and/or Protractor, since this is required. We will select **Protractor** as the testing tool:

```
? Which *type* of application would you like to create? Microservice gateway
? What is the base name of your application? store
? As you are running in a microservice architecture, on which port would like your server to run? It should be unique to avoid port conflicts. 8080
? What is your default Java package name? com.mycompany.store
? Which service discovery server do you want to use? JHipster Registry (uses Eureka, provides Spring Cloud Config support and monitoring dashboards)
? Which *type* of authentication would you like to use? JWT authentication (stateless, with a token)
? Which *type* of database would you like to use? SQL (H2, MySQL, MariaDB, PostgreSQL, Oracle, MSSQL)
? Which *production* database would you like to use? MySQL
? Which *development* database would you like to use? H2 with disk-based persistence
? Do you want to use Hibernate 2nd level cache? Yes
? Would you like to use Maven or Gradle for building the backend? Gradle
? Which other technologies would you like to use? WebSockets using Spring Websocket
? Which *Framework* would you like to use for the client? Angular 5
? Would you like to enable *SASS* support using the LibSass stylesheet preprocessor? Yes
? Would you like to enable internationalization support? Yes
? Please choose the native language of the application English
? Please choose additional languages to install Chinese (Traditional)
? Besides JUnit and Karma, which testing frameworks would you like to use?
  o Gatling
  o Cucumber
 >o Protractor
```

Finally, JHipster asks us to install any other generators from the marketplace; we will select no here:

```
? Which *type* of application would you like to create? Microservice gateway
? What is the base name of your application? store
? As you are running in a microservice architecture, on which port would like your server to run? It should be unique to avoid port conflicts. 8080
? What is your default Java package name? com.mycompany.store
? Which service discovery server do you want to use? JHipster Registry (uses Eureka, provides Spring Cloud Config support and monitoring dashboards)
? Which *type* of authentication would you like to use? JWT authentication (stateless, with a token)
? Which *type* of database would you like to use? SQL (H2, MySQL, MariaDB, PostgreSQL, Oracle, MSSQL)
? Which *production* database would you like to use? MySQL
? Which *development* database would you like to use? H2 with disk-based persistence
? Do you want to use Hibernate 2nd level cache? Yes
? Would you like to use Maven or Gradle for building the backend? Gradle
? Which other technologies would you like to use? WebSockets using Spring Websocket
? Which *Framework* would you like to use for the client? Angular 5
? Would you like to enable *SASS* support using the LibSass stylesheet preprocessor? Yes
? Would you like to enable internationalization support? Yes
? Please choose the native language of the application English
? Please choose additional languages to install Chinese (Traditional)
? Besides JUnit and Karma, which testing frameworks would you like to use? Protractor
? Would you like to install other generators from the JHipster Marketplace? (y/N)
```

This will create all the necessary files and install the frontend dependencies using Yarn:

```
Server application generated successfully.

Run your Spring Boot application:
 ./gradlew

Client application generated successfully.

Start your Webpack development server with:
 yarn start

Congratulations, JHipster execution is complete!
Application successfully committed to Git.
```

Now, our gateway application is generated. JHipster will automatically commit the generated files to Git; if you wish to do this step yourself, you can do so by passing the `skip-git` flag during execution, for example, `jhipster --skip-git`, and executing the steps manually as follows:

```
> git init
> git add --all
> git commit -am "converted into gateway application"
```

Gateway configuration

The gateway application is generated in a similar fashion to the monolithic application, except for configurations related to Zuul proxy, Eureka Client, and Hystrix:

```
@ComponentScan
@EnableAutoConfiguration(exclude = {MetricFilterAutoConfiguration.class,
MetricRepositoryAutoConfiguration.class,
MetricsDropwizardAutoConfiguration.class})
@EnableConfigurationProperties({LiquibaseProperties.class,
ApplicationProperties.class})
@EnableDiscoveryClient
@EnableZuulProxy
public class GatewayApp {
...
}
```

We have selected the JHipster registry for our registry service. This will be a standalone registry server which other microservice applications and gateways will register itself:

- `@EnableDiscoveryClient` is added to Spring Boot's main class, which will enable the Netflix Discovery Client. The microservice applications and gateways need to register themselves to the registry service. It uses Spring Cloud's discovery client abstraction to interrogate its own host and port, and then adds them to the registry server.
- Zuul, on the other hand, is the gatekeeper. This helps route the authorized requests to the respective endpoints, limits the requests per route, and relays the necessary tokens to the microservice application.
- `@EnableZuulProxy` helps the microservice gateway application route the requests to the applicable microservice application based on the configurations provided in the `application.yml`:

```
zuul: # those values must be configured depending on the
application specific needs
    host:
        max-total-connections: 1000
        max-per-route-connections: 100
    semaphore:
        max-semaphores: 500
```

In the gateway app, we have specified the aforementioned settings for Zuul configuration. The maximum number of total connections that a proxy can hold open is kept at 1000. The maximum number of route connections that a proxy can hold open is kept at 100. Semaphore is kept to a maximum of 500. (Semaphore is like a counter that is used for synchronization between threads and processes.)

Access to the backend microservice endpoint is controlled by `AccessControlFilter`, which will check whether the request is authorized, and is allowed to request the endpoint:

```
public class AccessControlFilter extends ZuulFilter {
    ...
    public boolean shouldFilter() {
        ...
        return !isAuthorizedRequests(serviceUrl, serviceName,
        requestUri);
    }
    ...
}
```

Zuul, as a gatekeeper, also acts as a rate limiter. A rate-limiting filter is added to the generated application, which limits the number of HTTP calls that are made per client. This is enabled conditionally with:

```
@ConditionalOnProperty("jhipster.gateway.rate-limiting.enabled")
public static class RateLimitingConfiguration {
...
}
```

`SwaggerBasePathRewritingFilter` is also used, which will help to rewrite the microservice Swagger URL base path:

```
@Component
public class SwaggerBasePathRewritingFilter extends SendResponseFilter {
    @Override
    public Object run() {
        RequestContext ctx = RequestContext.getCurrentContext();
        if(!context.getResponseGzipped()) {
            context.getResponse().setCharacterEncoding("UTF-8");
        }
        // rewrite the base path and send down the response
    }
...
```

A `TokenRelayFilter` is added to remove the authorization from Zuul's ignore list. This will help to propagate the generated authorization token:

```
@Component
public class TokenRelayFilter extends ZuulFilter {
    @Override
    public Object run() {
        RequestContext ctx = RequestContext.getCurrentContext();
        Set<String> headers = (Set<String>) ctx.get("ignoredHeaders");
        // JWT tokens should be relayed to the resource servers
        headers.remove("authorization");
        return null;
    }
...
```

Each application should have a Eureka client that helps load balance the requests among the services, as well as sending health information to the Eureka Server or registries. The Eureka client is configured in `application-dev.yml` as follows:

```
eureka:
    client:
        enabled: true
        healthcheck:
            enabled: true
        fetch-registry: true
        register-with-eureka: true
        instance-info-replication-interval-seconds: 10
        registry-fetch-interval-seconds: 10
    instance:
        appname: gateway
        instanceId: gateway:${spring.application.instance-
id:${random.value}}
        lease-renewal-interval-in-seconds: 5
        lease-expiration-duration-in-seconds: 10
        status-page-url-path: ${management.context-path}/info
        health-check-url-path: ${management.context-path}/health
        metadata-map:
            zone: primary # This is needed for the load balancer
            profile: ${spring.profiles.active}
            version: ${info.project.version}
```

We have chosen to enable health checks and have the interval to register and replicate be within 10 seconds, as well as instances where we define the lease renewal interval and expiration duration.

We will configure timeout in Hystrix, beyond which the server is considered to be closed:

```
hystrix:
    command:
        default:
            execution:
                isolation:
                    thread:
                        timeoutInMilliseconds: 10000
```

If the server does not respond within 10 seconds, then the server is considered dead and is registered in the registry service. This makes sure no subsequent requests are sent to that server until the server is made active.

JWT authentication

We need to transfer information between microserves securely. The requests must be verified and signed digitally, where the applications verify the authenticity of the requests and respond to them.

We need to have a compact way to handle this information in the REST or HTTP world, since the information is required to be sent with each request. JWT is here to help. JWT is basically JSON web tokens in an open web standard that helps to securely transfer information between parties (applications). JWT will be signed using a secret, based on the HMAC algorithm, or with a public/private key. They are compact and self-contained.

 For advanced uses, we need to add Bouncy Castle (`librarieshttps://en.wikipedia.org/wiki/Bouncy_Castle_(cryptography)`).

Compact: They are small and can be sent to each request.

Self-contained: The payload contains all the necessary details about the user, which prevents us from querying the database for user authentication.

JWT consists of the header, payload, and signature. They are base64 encoded strings, separated by . (a period):

```
eyJhbGciOiJIUzI1NiIsInR5cCI6IkpXVCJ9.eyJzdWIiOiIxMjM0NTY3ODkwIiwibmFtZSI6Il
NlbmRpcCBLdW1hciBOIiwiYWRtaW4iOnRydWV9.ILwKeJ128TwDZmLGAeeY7qiROxA3kXiXOG4M
xTQVk_I

#Algorithm for JWT generation
HMACSHA256(
  base64UrlEncode(header) + "." +
  base64UrlEncode(payload),
)
```

How JWT works

When a user logs in to the system, a token is generated based on the payload (that is, the user information and secret key). The generated token is stored locally. For all future requests, this token is added to the request and the application will validate the token before responding to the request:

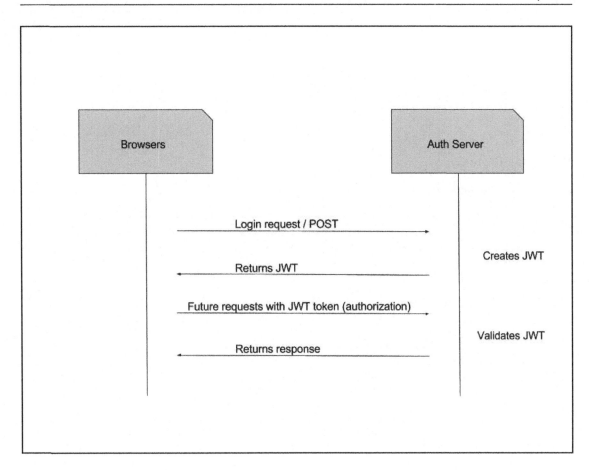

The token will be in this format:

```
Authorization: Bearer <token>
```

In JHipster, we use **JJWT (Java-based JSON Web Tokens)** from Okta. This is a simplified builder pattern-based library used to generate and sign the token as a producer, and parse and validate the token as a consumer.

Creating the token:

```
public class TokenProvider {
    ...
    public String createToken(Authentication authentication, Boolean
rememberMe) {
        ...
```

```
            return Jwts.builder()
                .setSubject(authentication.getName())
                .claim(AUTHORITIES_KEY, authorities)
                .signWith(SignatureAlgorithm.HS512, secretKey)
                .setExpiration(validity)
                .compact();
        }
    }
```

Validating the token:

```
    public boolean validateToken(String authToken) {
        try {
            Jwts.parser().setSigningKey(secretKey).parseClaimsJws(authToken);
            return true;
        } catch (SignatureException e) {
            log.info("Invalid JWT signature.");
            log.trace("Invalid JWT signature trace: {}", e);
        } catch (MalformedJwtException e) {
            log.info("Invalid JWT token.");
            log.trace("Invalid JWT token trace: {}", e);
        } catch (ExpiredJwtException e) {
            log.info("Expired JWT token.");
            log.trace("Expired JWT token trace: {}", e);
        } catch (UnsupportedJwtException e) {
            log.info("Unsupported JWT token.");
            log.trace("Unsupported JWT token trace: {}", e);
        } catch (IllegalArgumentException e) {
            log.info("JWT token compact of handler are invalid.");
            log.trace("JWT token compact of handler are invalid trace: {}", e);
        }
        return false;
    }
```

So far, we have created a gateway application, which will serve as a single point of entry for our application and services. Now, we will generate a microservice application using JHipster.

Microservice applications are *the* services. We will construct two sample services in this book and discuss the features that JHipster offers, one with the SQL database (MySQL) and the other with the NoSQL database (MongoDB). These services are individual and loosely coupled.

With JHipster, you can build microservice applications serving as REST endpoints.

Microservice application - Invoice Service with MySQL database

We can take the invoice service from our monolithic application, separate it, and make them separate microservice applications. Let's name it `Invoice Service`. This service is responsible for creating and tracking invoices.

Application generation

First, let's see how we can generate a microservices application. In the `e-commerce-app` folder, create a new folder where you will keep the microservices application. Let's name the folder `invoice`. Go into the directory and start creating the application by typing `jhipster`.

The first question we are asked is to select the type of application we would like to create. We have to choose **Microservice application** and then click *Enter*:

```
? Which *type* of application would you like to create?
  Monolithic application (recommended for simple projects)
> Microservice application
  Microservice gateway
  JHipster UAA server (for microservice OAuth2 authentication)
```

Then, you need to give a base name to your application. We will go with the default application name, `invoice` (by default, JHipster selects a folder name the same as the application name):

```
? Which *type* of application would you like to create? Microservice application
? What is the base name of your application? (jhipster) invoice
```

Then, we will select the default port in which the application has to run. By default, JHipster prompts `8081` as the default port for microservices, since we use `8080` for the gateway application:

```
? Which *type* of application would you like to create? Microservice application
? What is the base name of your application? invoice
? As you are running in a microservice architecture, on which port would like your server to run? It should be unique to avoid port conflicts. (8081)
```

Then, we will select the default package name:

```
? Which *type* of application would you like to create? Microservice application
? What is the base name of your application? invoice
? As you are running in a microservice architecture, on which port would like your server to run? It should be unique to avoid port conflicts. 8081
? What is your default Java package name? (com.mycompany.store) com.mycompany.store
```

Since we have selected **JHipster Registry** for the gateway application, we will select the same here. Similarly, if we selected **Consul** for the gateway application, then we can select **Consul**. We can even choose to have no registry and then add any custom registry there:

```
? Which *type* of application would you like to create? Microservice application
? What is the base name of your application? invoice
? As you are running in a microservice architecture, on which port would like your server to run? It should be unique to avoid port conflicts. 8081
? What is your default Java package name? com.mycompany.store
? Which service discovery server do you want to use? (Use arrow keys)
> JHipster Registry (uses Eureka, provides Spring Cloud Config support and monitoring dashboards)
  Consul
  No service discovery
```

Then, JHipster asks for the type of authentication that we would like to use. We will select JWT authentication, the same as we have selected for the gateway application:

```
? Which *type* of application would you like to create? Microservice application
? What is the base name of your application? invoice
? As you are running in a microservice architecture, on which port would like your server to run? It should be unique to avoid port conflicts. 8081
? What is your default Java package name? com.mycompany.store
? Which service discovery server do you want to use? JHipster Registry (uses Eureka, provides Spring Cloud Config support and monitoring dashboards)
? Which *type* of authentication would you like to use? (Use arrow keys)
> JWT authentication (stateless, with a token)
  OAuth 2.0 / OIDC Authentication (stateful, works with Keycloak and Okta)
  Authentication with JHipster UAA server (the server must be generated separately)
```

Then, select the type of database that we need to have. As highlighted, the invoice service will have the SQL database. We will select the **SQL** option. JHipster provides an option to opt out of the database itself. When **No database** is selected, the application is generated with no database connection:

```
? Which *type* of application would you like to create? Microservice application
? What is the base name of your application? invoice
? As you are running in a microservice architecture, on which port would like your server to run? It should be unique to avoid port conflicts. 8081
? What is your default Java package name? com.mycompany.store
? Which service discovery server do you want to use? JHipster Registry (uses Eureka, provides Spring Cloud Config support and monitoring dashboards)
? Which *type* of authentication would you like to use? JWT authentication (stateless, with a token)
? Which *type* of database would you like to use? (Use arrow keys)
> SQL (H2, MySQL, MariaDB, PostgreSQL, Oracle, MSSQL)
  MongoDB
  Cassandra
  [BETA] Couchbase
  No database
```

We will select the production database as **MySQL**:

```
? Which *type* of application would you like to create? Microservice application
? What is the base name of your application? invoice
? As you are running in a microservice architecture, on which port would like your server to run? It should be unique to avoid port conflicts. 8081
? What is your default Java package name? com.mycompany.store
? Which service discovery server do you want to use? JHipster Registry (uses Eureka, provides Spring Cloud Config support and monitoring dashboards)
? Which *type* of authentication would you like to use? JWT authentication (stateless, with a token)
? Which *type* of database would you like to use? SQL (H2, MySQL, MariaDB, PostgreSQL, Oracle, MSSQL)
? Which *production* database would you like to use? (Use arrow keys)
> MySQL
  MariaDB
  PostgreSQL
  Oracle (Please follow our documentation to use the Oracle proprietary driver)
  Microsoft SQL Server
```

We will then select the development database as **H2 with disk-based persistence**:

```
? Which *type* of application would you like to create? Microservice application
? What is the base name of your application? invoice
? As you are running in a microservice architecture, on which port would like your server to run? It should be unique to avoid port conflicts. 8081
? What is your default Java package name? com.mycompany.store
? Which service discovery server do you want to use? JHipster Registry (uses Eureka, provides Spring Cloud Config support and monitoring dashboards)
? Which *type* of authentication would you like to use? JWT authentication (stateless, with a token)
? Which *type* of database would you like to use? SQL (H2, MySQL, MariaDB, PostgreSQL, Oracle, MSSQL)
? Which *production* database would you like to use? MySQL
? Which *development* database would you like to use? (Use arrow keys)
> H2 with disk-based persistence
  H2 with in-memory persistence
  MySQL
```

Then, we will select **HazelCast** cache as the Spring cache abstraction. Hazelcast provides a shared cache among all sessions. It is possible to hold the persistent data across the cluster or at the JVM level. We can have different modes available, with single or multiple nodes.

Ehcache is a local cache and it is useful for storing information in a single node. Infinispan and HazelCast are capable of creating a cluster and sharing information among multiple nodes, with HazelCast using a distributed cache, each of them connected together. On the other hand, Inifinispan is a hybrid cache:

```
? Which *type* of application would you like to create? Microservice application
? What is the base name of your application? invoice
? As you are running in a microservice architecture, on which port would like your server to run? It should be unique to avoid port conflicts. 8081
? What is your default Java package name? com.mycompany.store
? Which service discovery server do you want to use? JHipster Registry (uses Eureka, provides Spring Cloud Config support and monitoring dashboards)
? Which *type* of authentication would you like to use? JWT authentication (stateless, with a token)
? Which *type* of database would you like to use? SQL (H2, MySQL, MariaDB, PostgreSQL, Oracle, MSSQL)
? Which *production* database would you like to use? MySQL
? Which *development* database would you like to use? H2 with disk-based persistence
? Do you want to use the Spring cache abstraction? (Use arrow keys)
  Yes, with the Ehcache implementation (local cache, for a single node)
> Yes, with the Hazelcast implementation (distributed cache, for multiple nodes)
  [BETA] Yes, with the Infinispan (hybrid cache, for multiple nodes)
  No (when using an SQL database, this will also disable the Hibernate L2 cache)
```

Then, we will choose **Hibernate 2nd level cache**:

```
? Which *type* of application would you like to create? Microservice application
? What is the base name of your application? invoice
? As you are running in a microservice architecture, on which port would like your server to run? It should be unique to avoid port conflicts. 8081
? What is your default Java package name? com.mycompany.store
? Which service discovery server do you want to use? JHipster Registry (uses Eureka, provides Spring Cloud Config support and monitoring dashboards)
? Which *type* of authentication would you like to use? JWT authentication (stateless, with a token)
? Which *type* of database would you like to use? SQL (H2, MySQL, MariaDB, PostgreSQL, Oracle, MSSQL)
? Which *production* database would you like to use? MySQL
? Which *development* database would you like to use? H2 with disk-based persistence
? Do you want to use the Spring cache abstraction? Yes, with the Hazelcast implementation (distributed cache, for multiple nodes)
? Do you want to use Hibernate 2nd level cache? (Y/n)
```

We will select **Gradle** for the build tool:

```
? Which *type* of application would you like to create? Microservice application
? What is the base name of your application? invoice
? As you are running in a microservice architecture, on which port would like your server to run? It should be unique to avoid port conflicts. 8081
? What is your default Java package name? com.mycompany.store
? Which service discovery server do you want to use? JHipster Registry (uses Eureka, provides Spring Cloud Config support and monitoring dashboards)
? Which *type* of authentication would you like to use? JWT authentication (stateless, with a token)
? Which *type* of database would you like to use? SQL (H2, MySQL, MariaDB, PostgreSQL, Oracle, MSSQL)
? Which *production* database would you like to use? MySQL
? Which *development* database would you like to use? H2 with disk-based persistence
? Do you want to use the Spring cache abstraction? Yes, with the Hazelcast implementation (distributed cache, for multiple nodes)
? Do you want to use Hibernate 2nd level cache? Yes
? Would you like to use Maven or Gradle for building the backend?
  Maven
> Gradle
```

Then, JHipster asks whether we have any other technologies that we would like to add. We will not select anything here and go with the default option:

```
? Which *type* of application would you like to create? Microservice application
? What is the base name of your application? invoice
? As you are running in a microservice architecture, on which port would like your server to run? It should be unique to avoid port conflicts. 8081
? What is your default Java package name? com.mycompany.store
? Which service discovery server do you want to use? JHipster Registry (uses Eureka, provides Spring Cloud Config support and monitoring dashboards)
? Which *type* of authentication would you like to use? JWT authentication (stateless, with a token)
? Which *type* of database would you like to use? SQL (H2, MySQL, MariaDB, PostgreSQL, Oracle, MSSQL)
? Which *production* database would you like to use? MySQL
? Which *development* database would you like to use? H2 with disk-based persistence
? Do you want to use the Spring cache abstraction? Yes, with the Hazelcast implementation (distributed cache, for multiple nodes)
? Do you want to use Hibernate 2nd level cache? Yes
? Would you like to use Maven or Gradle for building the backend? Gradle
? Which other technologies would you like to use? (Press <space> to select, <a> to toggle all, <i> to inverse selection)
>o Search engine using Elasticsearch
 o API first development using swagger-codegen
 o Asynchronous messages using Apache Kafka
```

Then, we will opt to have **internationalization (i18n)**:

```
? Which *type* of application would you like to create? Microservice application
? What is the base name of your application? invoice
? As you are running in a microservice architecture, on which port would like your server to run? It should be unique to avoid port conflicts. 8081
? What is your default Java package name? com.mycompany.store
? Which service discovery server do you want to use? JHipster Registry (uses Eureka, provides Spring Cloud Config support and monitoring dashboards)
? Which *type* of authentication would you like to use? JWT authentication (stateless, with a token)
? Which *type* of database would you like to use? SQL (H2, MySQL, MariaDB, PostgreSQL, Oracle, MSSQL)
? Which *production* database would you like to use? MySQL
? Which *development* database would you like to use? H2 with disk-based persistence
? Do you want to use the Spring cache abstraction? Yes, with the Hazelcast implementation (distributed cache, for multiple nodes)
? Do you want to use Hibernate 2nd level cache? Yes
? Would you like to use Maven or Gradle for building the backend? Gradle
? Which other technologies would you like to use?
? Would you like to enable internationalization support? (Y/n)
```

And then, we will select **English** as the default option:

```
? Which *type* of application would you like to create? Microservice application
? What is the base name of your application? invoice
? As you are running in a microservice architecture, on which port would like your server to run? It should be unique to avoid port conflicts. 8081
? What is your default Java package name? com.mycompany.store
? Which service discovery server do you want to use? JHipster Registry (uses Eureka, provides Spring Cloud Config support and monitoring dashboards)
? Which *type* of authentication would you like to use? JWT authentication (stateless, with a token)
? Which *type* of database would you like to use? SQL (H2, MySQL, MariaDB, PostgreSQL, Oracle, MSSQL)
? Which *production* database would you like to use? MySQL
? Which *development* database would you like to use? H2 with disk-based persistence
? Do you want to use the Spring cache abstraction? Yes, with the Hazelcast implementation (distributed cache, for multiple nodes)
? Do you want to use Hibernate 2nd level cache? Yes
? Would you like to use Maven or Gradle for building the backend? Gradle
? Which other technologies would you like to use?
? Would you like to enable internationalization support? Yes
? Please choose the native language of the application (Use arrow keys)
> English
  Estonian
  Farsi
  French
  Galician
  German
  Greek
(Move up and down to reveal more choices)
```

And select the additional languages that we need:

```
? Which *type* of application would you like to create? Microservice application
? What is the base name of your application? invoice
? As you are running in a microservice architecture, on which port would like your server to run? It should be unique to avoid port conflicts. 8081
? What is your default Java package name? com.mycompany.store
? Which service discovery server do you want to use? JHipster Registry (uses Eureka, provides Spring Cloud Config support and monitoring dashboards)
? Which *type* of authentication would you like to use? JWT authentication (stateless, with a token)
? Which *type* of database would you like to use? SQL (H2, MySQL, MariaDB, PostgreSQL, Oracle, MSSQL)
? Which *production* database would you like to use? MySQL
? Which *development* database would you like to use? H2 with disk-based persistence
? Do you want to use the Spring cache abstraction? Yes, with the Hazelcast implementation (distributed cache, for multiple nodes)
? Do you want to use Hibernate 2nd level cache? Yes
? Would you like to use Maven or Gradle for building the backend? Gradle
? Which other technologies would you like to use?
? Would you like to enable internationalization support? Yes
? Please choose the native language of the application English
? Please choose additional languages to install
  o Armenian
  o Catalan
  o Chinese (Simplified)
 >* Chinese (Traditional)
  o Czech
  o Danish
  o Dutch
(Move up and down to reveal more choices)
```

Then, select any other testing frameworks that we would like to add to Gatling or
Cucumber. Note that since it will not generate a frontend application, options such as
Protractor are not listed:

```
? Which *type* of application would you like to create? Microservice application
? What is the base name of your application? invoice
? As you are running in a microservice architecture, on which port would like your server to run? It should be unique to avoid port conflicts. 8081
? What is your default Java package name? com.mycompany.store
? Which service discovery server do you want to use? JHipster Registry (uses Eureka, provides Spring Cloud Config support and monitoring dashboards)
? Which *type* of authentication would you like to use? JWT authentication (stateless, with a token)
? Which *type* of database would you like to use? SQL (H2, MySQL, MariaDB, PostgreSQL, Oracle, MSSQL)
? Which *production* database would you like to use? MySQL
? Which *development* database would you like to use? H2 with disk-based persistence
? Do you want to use the Spring cache abstraction? Yes, with the Hazelcast implementation (distributed cache, for multiple nodes)
? Do you want to use Hibernate 2nd level cache? Yes
? Would you like to use Maven or Gradle for building the backend? Gradle
? Which other technologies would you like to use?
? Would you like to enable internationalization support? Yes
? Please choose the native language of the application English
? Please choose additional languages to install Chinese (Traditional)
? Besides JUnit and Karma, which testing frameworks would you like to use? (Press <space> to select, <a> to toggle all, <i> to inverse selection)
 >o Gatling
  o Cucumber
```

Finally, we will select any other generators that we need to install from the JHipster marketplace. Currently, we will not select any other generators (default option):

```
? Which *type* of application would you like to create? Microservice application
? What is the base name of your application? invoice
? As you are running in a microservice architecture, on which port would like your server to run? It should be unique to avoid port conflicts. 8081
? What is your default Java package name? com.mycompany.store
? Which service discovery server do you want to use? JHipster Registry (uses Eureka, provides Spring Cloud Config support and monitoring dashboards)
? Which *type* of authentication would you like to use? JWT authentication (stateless, with a token)
? Which *type* of database would you like to use? SQL (H2, MySQL, MariaDB, PostgreSQL, Oracle, MSSQL)
? Which *production* database would you like to use? MySQL
? Which *development* database would you like to use? H2 with disk-based persistence
? Do you want to use the Spring cache abstraction? Yes, with the Hazelcast implementation (distributed cache, for multiple nodes)
? Do you want to use Hibernate 2nd level cache? Yes
? Would you like to use Maven or Gradle for building the backend? Gradle
? Which other technologies would you like to use?
? Would you like to enable internationalization support? Yes
? Please choose the native language of the application English
? Please choose additional languages to install Chinese (Traditional)
? Besides JUnit and Karma, which testing frameworks would you like to use?
? Would you like to install other generators from the JHipster Marketplace? (y/N) █
```

Then, the server application is generated:

```
Server application generated successfully.

Run your Spring Boot application:
 ./gradlew
Congratulations, JHipster execution is complete!
```

Our microservice application is generated. JHipster will automatically commit the generated files to Git. If you wish to do this step yourself, you can do so by passing the `skip-git` flag during execution, for example, `jhipster --skip-git`, and executing the steps manually as follows:

```
> git init
> git add --all
> git commit -am "generated invoice microservice application"
```

Microservice configuration

The application that is generated will not feature any frontend. Again, the invoice service is a Spring Boot-based application. The security features are configured in `MicroserviceSecurityConfiguration.java`.

Ignore all the frontend related requests, so whenever a user tries to reach any frontend-related resources such as HTML, CSS, and JS, the request will be ignored by the invoice service:

```
@Override
public void configure(WebSecurity web) throws Exception {
    web.ignoring()
            .antMatchers(HttpMethod.OPTIONS, "/**")
            .antMatchers("/app/**/*.{js,html}")
            .antMatchers("/bower_components/**")
            .antMatchers("/i18n/**")
            .antMatchers("/content/**")
            .antMatchers("/swagger-ui/index.html")
            .antMatchers("/test/**")
            .antMatchers("/h2-console/**");
}
```

Since the services are independent, they can be deployed and run on another server with a different IP address. This requires us to disable **CSRF** (**Cross Site Request Forgery**) by default. We will also enable the STATELESS session policy in session management. This makes our application unable to create or maintain any sessions. Every request is authenticated and authorized based on the token.

We will also use the STATELESS session policy in session management. This is the strictest session policy available. This will not allow our application to generate a session, and so our requests have to have the (time-bound) tokens attached to each and every request. This enhances the security of our services. Their stateless constraint is another advantage of using REST APIs.

 For more options and information on session policies, please look at the following documentation: `https://docs.spring.io/autorepo/docs/spring-security/4.2.3.RELEASE/apidocs/org/springframework/security/config/http/SessionCreationPolicy.html`.

Then, all API-related requests and Swagger resources should be allowed once the request is authorized (based on the JWT token):

```
@Override
protected void configure(HttpSecurity http) throws Exception {
    http
            .csrf()
            .disable()
            .headers()
            .frameOptions()
            .disable()
```

```
.and()
    .sessionManagement()
    .sessionCreationPolicy(SessionCreationPolicy.STATELESS)
.and()
    .authorizeRequests()
    .antMatchers("/api/**").authenticated()
    .antMatchers("/management/health").permitAll()
.antMatchers("/management/**").hasAuthority(AuthoritiesConstants.ADMIN)
    .antMatchers("/swagger-resources/configuration/ui").permitAll()
.and()
    .apply(securityConfigurerAdapter());
}
```

On the resource side, in `bootstrap.yml`, we have defined the registry-related information.

Our current microservice application uses the JHipster registry as the registry service in order to register and deregister their existence in a heartbeat. We need to provide the password of our registry service with which the application can connect to the registry service:

```
jhipster:
    registry:
        password: admin
```

Also, the name of the Spring Boot service and the default Spring Cloud Config parameters are enabled in the `bootstrap.yml`. We have also added the URI that we have to connect in order to fetch the configuration of the registry service:

```
spring:
    application:
        name: invoice
        ...
    cloud:
        config:
            fail-fast: false # if not in "prod" profile, do not force to
use Spring Cloud Config
            uri:
http://admin:${jhipster.registry.password}@localhost:8761/config
            # name of the config server's property source (file.yml) that
we want to use
            name: invoice
            ...
```

Similar to the gateway, the rest of the service-related configurations are done in the `application.yml` file.

The Eureka configuration is exactly the same as in the gateway application. All the generated applications will have a similar Eureka configuration:

```
eureka:
    client:
        enabled: true
        healthcheck:
            enabled: true
        fetch-registry: true
        register-with-eureka: true
        instance-info-replication-interval-seconds: 10
        registry-fetch-interval-seconds: 10
    instance:
        appname: invoice
        instanceId: invoice:${spring.application.instance-
id:${random.value}}
        lease-renewal-interval-in-seconds: 5
        lease-expiration-duration-in-seconds: 10
        status-page-url-path: ${management.context-path}/info
        health-check-url-path: ${management.context-path}/health
        metadata-map:
            zone: primary # This is needed for the load balancer
            profile: ${spring.profiles.active}
            version: ${info.project.version}
```

The database and JPA configurations are made:

```
spring:
    profiles:
        active: dev
    ...
    datasource:
        type: <connector jar>
        url: <db url>
        username: <username>
        password: <password>
    ...
    jpa:
        database-platform: <DB platform>
        database: <H2 or MySQL or any SQL database>
        show-sql: true
        properties:
            hibernate.id.new_generator_mappings: true
            hibernate.cache.use_second_level_cache: true
            hibernate.cache.use_query_cache: false
            hibernate.generate_statistics: true
            hibernate.cache.region.factory_class:
com.hazelcast.hibernate.HazelcastCacheRegionFactory
```

```
hibernate.cache.hazelcast.instance_name: invoice
hibernate.cache.use_minimal_puts: true
hibernate.cache.hazelcast.use_lite_member: true
```

The rest of the configurations remain similar to what was generated in the gateway application, and they can be tweaked or customized based on your requirements.

Now, we can boot up the application alongside the gateway application and registry service. Since the application tries to connect to the registry service first, if there is no registry service available at the specified location, then the application will not know where to connect and whom to respond to.

Thus, the invoice service is generated. Now, we can generate a notification service with NoSQL as the backend database.

Microservice application - notification service with NoSQL database

For an e-commerce website, it is really essential that orders are tracked and users are notified at the right moment. We will create a notification service which will notify users whenever their order status changes.

Application generation

Let's generate our second microservice application (notification service) in the e-commerce-app folder. Create a new folder where you will keep the microservices application. Let's name the folder notification. Go into the directory and start creating the application by running jhipster.

The first question we are asked is to select the type of application we would like to create. We have to choose **Microservice application** and then click *Enter*:

```
? Which *type* of application would you like to create?
  Monolithic application (recommended for simple projects)
> Microservice application
  Microservice gateway
  JHipster UAA server (for microservice OAuth2 authentication)
```

Then, we will select the default application name, `notification`:

```
? Which *type* of application would you like to create? Microservice application
? What is the base name of your application? (jhipster) notification
```

Then, we will select the port for the application. Since we have selected `8080` for the monolithic application and `8081` for the invoice service, we will use port `8082` for the notification service:

```
? Which *type* of application would you like to create? Microservice application
? What is the base name of your application? notification
? As you are running in a microservice architecture, on which port would like your server to run? It should be unique to avoid port conflicts. (8081) 8082
```

For the next three questions, we will use the same options as we did previously:

```
? Which *type* of application would you like to create? Microservice application
? What is the base name of your application? notification
? As you are running in a microservice architecture, on which port would like your server to run? It should be unique to avoid port conflicts. 8082
? What is your default Java package name? com.mycompany.store
? Which service discovery server do you want to use? JHipster Registry (uses Eureka, provides Spring Cloud Config support and monitoring dashboards)
? Which *type* of authentication would you like to use? (Use arrow keys)
> JWT authentication (stateless, with a token)
  OAuth 2.0 / OIDC Authentication (stateful, works with Keycloak and Okta)
  Authentication with JHipster UAA server (the server must be generated separately)
```

Then, we will select **MongoDB** as the database. After selecting **MongoDB**, JHipster will now ask for the different types of database you would like to use for the development and production servers. We will use MongoDB as both the development and production database:

```
? Which *type* of application would you like to create? Microservice application
? What is the base name of your application? notification
? As you are running in a microservice architecture, on which port would like your server to run? It should be unique to avoid port conflicts. 8082
? What is your default Java package name? com.mycompany.store
? Which service discovery server do you want to use? JHipster Registry (uses Eureka, provides Spring Cloud Config support and monitoring dashboards)
? Which *type* of authentication would you like to use? JWT authentication (stateless, with a token)
? Which *type* of database would you like to use?
  SQL (H2, MySQL, MariaDB, PostgreSQL, Oracle, MSSQL)
> MongoDB
  Cassandra
  [BETA] Couchbase
  No database
```

For the remaining questions, we will select options that are similar to what we chose for the invoice service:

```
? Which *type* of application would you like to create? Microservice application
? What is the base name of your application? notification
? As you are running in a microservice architecture, on which port would like your server to run? It should be unique to avoid port conflicts. 8082
? What is your default Java package name? com.mycompany.store
? Which service discovery server do you want to use? JHipster Registry (uses Eureka, provides Spring Cloud Config support and monitoring dashboards)
? Which *type* of authentication would you like to use? JWT authentication (stateless, with a token)
? Which *type* of database would you like to use? MongoDB
? Do you want to use the Spring cache abstraction? Yes, with the Hazelcast implementation (distributed cache, for multiple nodes)
? Would you like to use Maven or Gradle for building the backend? Gradle
? Which other technologies would you like to use?
? Would you like to enable internationalization support? Yes
? Please choose the native language of the application English
? Please choose additional languages to install Chinese (Traditional)
? Besides JUnit and Karma, which testing frameworks would you like to use?
? Would you like to install other generators from the JHipster Marketplace? No
```

The server is generated successfully:

```
Server application generated successfully.

Run your Spring Boot application:
 ./gradlew
Congratulations, JHipster execution is complete!
```

Our microservice application is generated. JHipster will automatically commit the generated files to Git. If you wish to do this step yourself, you can do so by passing the `skip-git` flag during execution, for example, `jhipster --skip-git`, and executing the steps manually as follows:

```
> git init
> git add --all
> git commit -am "generated notification microservice application"
```

Microservice configuration

The application is finally generated, since we have selected similar options for both microservices. The code generated will be similar, except for the database configuration:

```
data:
    mongodb:
        uri: mongodb://localhost:27017
        database: notification
```

Summary

Well, we have generated a gateway application and two microservice applications in this chapter. We have shown you how easy it is to generate a microservice bundle with JHipster. Now, before we run our application, we need to kick-start our registry server.

In the next chapter, we will kick-start the registry server, and we will also see how to add entities to our new services.

10
Working with Microservices

In the previous chapter, we created a gateway and two microservices using JHipster; now, let's see how we can further develop our microservices to include our domain model and additional business logic. Since we are converting our online shop monolith to a microservice architecture, we will see how the domain model we created using JDL can be converted into a microservice domain model. But before we can start, we need to set up some tools in order to work with microservices.

So in this chapter, we will see the following topics:

- How to set up JHipster Registry
- How to run the microservice setup locally
- Creating the domain model using JDL
- Generating the domain model in JHipster

Let's get started!

Setting up JHipster Registry locally

We have created our gateway and two microservice applications. The microservices have two different databases. So far, it has been easy and simple to create those with JHipster.

JHipster provides two different options we have previously seen, Consul and JHipster Registry. For our use case, let's go with JHipster Registry. We have already learned about JHipster Registry in Chapter 8, *Introduction to Microservice Server-Side Technologies*. Now, we will see how to set up and start it in our local development environment.

Now, these three services basically act as Eureka clients. We need a service registry that registers and deregisters the application as and when the application is started and stopped, respectively; this is JHipster Registry. The Eureka server (JHipster Registry server) acts as a master to all the Eureka clients.

Since JHipster Registry, as the name suggests, acts as a registry service, all microservice applications and the gateway will register/deregister themselves when the application starts and stops.

Let's recap a little bit of what we learned already. The JHipster Registry is made up of a Eureka server and Spring Cloud Config server and they help in the following

- **The Eureka server** helps in service discovery and load balancing the requests.
- **The Spring Cloud Config server** acts as a single place where we will manage the external properties of applications across environments. It also provides a dashboard for users. With this, users can manage and monitor the application.

This makes JHipster Registry an ideal choice for both monolithic and microservice architectures.

 If you are developing microservice applications where different services are written in different languages, and if you prefer consistency over availability of services, then you can choose Consul.

There are three ways in which we can set up JHipster Registry to run locally.

We can either download the WAR file (pre-packaged) and run it directly, or clone our GitHub repository and run from there. We can also use a Docker container to run it. We will see how to do each of these now.

 You can choose to use JHipster Registry while generating monolithic applications as well. Just select **yes** for the question **Do you want to use the JHipster Registry to configure, monitor and scale your application?** during generation.

Using a pre-packaged WAR file

Download the latest version of the pre-packaged executable WAR file from the registry releases page (`https://github.com/jhipster/jhipster-registry/releases`):

1. Open your terminal and then type the following command, replacing `<version>` with the latest one. If you are using Windows and do not have `curl` set up, you can also download the file by visiting the link in a browser:

   ```
   > curl
   https://github.com/jhipster/jhipster-
   registry/releases/download/v<version>/jhipster-registry-
   <version>.war
   ```

2. This will download the latest WAR file from the JHipster Registry project. Once downloaded, we can run JHipster Registry using the following command:

   ```
   > ./jhipster-registry-<version>.war --security.user.password=admin
   --jhipster.security.authentication.jwt.secret=secret-key --
   spring.cloud.config.server.native.search.locations=file:./central-
   config
   ```

Note that we pass a few values to our registry server; they are:

   `--security.user.password=admin`

Since JHipster Registry is built on top of the JHipster application, it will have the default admin user. For that admin user, we provide the password with the Spring property `security.user.password`:

   `--jhipster.security.authentication.jwt.secret=secret-key`

Then we define the JWT token for the application in two ways. We can either set the information in the environment variable and use that, or else add this key value when we define the secret. This also uses the `spring config` property to set the property:

   `--spring.cloud.config.server.native.search.locations`

3. Finally, we tell the JHipster Registry where to find the central configurations that are available for the Spring Cloud Config server.

Before we see what value to pass in here, we need to know about the Spring profiles in the context of `spring-cloud-config`. Spring Cloud Config supports `native` and `git` profiles by default.

In a `native` profile, the Cloud Config server expects its properties to be defined in a file, and we have to pass in the file location to the JHipster Registry. On the other hand, the `git` profile will expect `--spring.cloud.config.server.git.uri` to be set.

For example, the sample JHipster config file for the the registry is as follows:

```
configserver:
    name: JHipster Registry config server
    status: Connected to the JHipster Registry config server using ...
jhipster:
    security:
        authentication:
            jwt:
                secret: awesome-my-secret-token-to-change-in-production
```

This can be seen in the Spring Cloud Configuration page of the Registry as well:

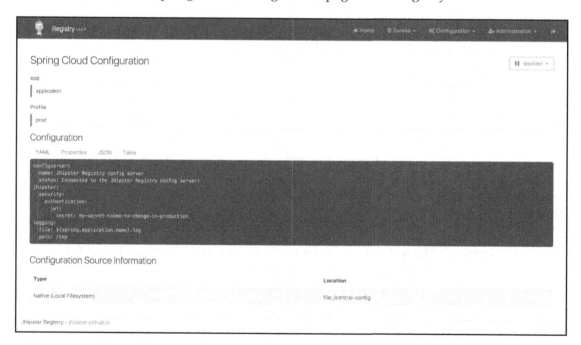

Just like the JHipster app provides `dev` and `prod` profiles, JHipster Registry also supports `dev` and `prod` profiles. By default, it will start in the `dev` profile when started, but we can make it run in a `prod` profile using `--spring.profiles.active=prod`, `git`, passing in the `git` URL, and then defining the configuration properties there. For production mode, `git` is the preferred profile to use on a Spring Cloud Server.

Building from source

If you want to work on leading-edge technology and are interested in exploring the latest features added to the JHipster Registry, then you can go a step further and clone the repository from GitHub:

1. Navigate to your preferred folder and run the following command:

    ```
    > git clone https://github.com/jhipster/jhipster-registry
    ```

2. Once cloned, navigate to the folder using the following command:

    ```
    > cd jhipster-registry
    ```

3. Run the application in dev mode as follows:

    ```
    > ./mvnw
    ```

    You can also run it in prod mode as follows:

    ```
    > ./mvnw -Pprod
    ```

4. You can also package and run the WAR file:

    ```
    > ./mvnw -Pprod package
    > target/jhipster-registry-<version>.war --
    spring.profiles.active=prod,git
    ```

Docker mode

You can also start JHipster Registry from the provided Docker image. The application that we generated already has the docker-compose file required.

For example, in the gateway application we created, look for the docker-compose file under src/main/docker/jhipster-registry.yml.

We can start the JHipster Registry by typing the following command in the terminal:

```
> cd gateway
> docker-compose -f src/main/docker/jhipster-registry.yml up
```

The `docker compose` file (`src/main/docker/jhipster-registry.yml`) contains:

```
version: 2
services:
    jhipster-registry:
        image: jhipster/jhipster-registry:v3.2.3
        volumes:
            - ./central-server-config:/central-config
        environment:
            - SPRING_PROFILES_ACTIVE=dev
            - SECURITY_USER_PASSWORD=admin
            - JHIPSTER_REGISTRY_PASSWORD=admin
            - SPRING_CLOUD_CONFIG_SERVER_NATIVE_SEARCH_LOCATION=
file:./central-config
        ports:
            -8761:8761
```

This defines the image as `jhipster-registry` with a version (the latest). It also defines a volume to mount the `central-config`, which is required by the Spring Cloud Config server to define the application properties for the microservice application and gateway. The environment variables such as the Spring profile, password for the admin, and cloud config search location are also defined here. The port in which it is exposed (`8761`) is also specified.

 Of course, this needs Docker to be installed and running on the machine.

In all preceding cases (when they are successful), it boots up JHipster Registry on port `8761` and uses native mode by default (unless otherwise changed explicitly). You can actually navigate to `http://localhost:8761` to access JHipster Registry and then log in to the application with the password that we used when we started the application.

Running a generated application locally

So we are all set now. We have generated a gateway application, we have a microservice with an SQL DB that runs with H2 in a dev profile and MySQL in a prod profile (invoice application), we have a microservice with MongoDB (notification application), and finally we just finished setting up our JHipster Registry locally. Now it is time to start everything locally and see how seamless our microservice setup works.

Gateway application pages

We head over to terminal now and then go to the `e-commerce-app` folder. Navigate to the `online-store` folder and start the gateway application in dev mode:

```
> cd online-store
> ./gradlew
```

This will start our **Gateway** application on port `8080`. Let's open `http://localhost:8080` in our favorite browser:

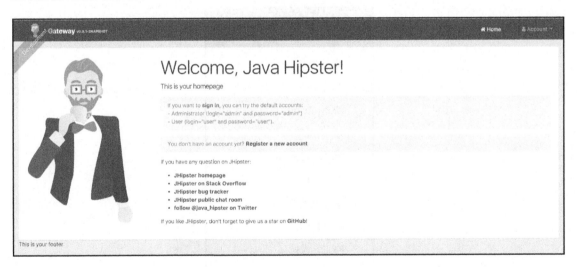

Then we can click on the **sign in** button on the home page or `Account/sign in` from the top menu, and then enter the username and password as `admin` and `admin` respectively.

Once logged in as an admin user, you can see the administration menu:

In the administration menu, you can find the following pages:

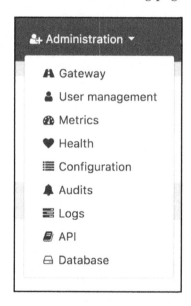

This includes the following:

Gateway: The Gateway page will show the list of microservice applications for which this application acts as a gateway. It will also show the routes and the services that handle the route, and the available servers for the route:

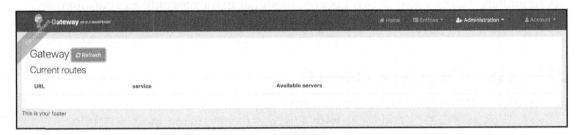

Currently, there is no microservice application booted up, so the page is empty. We will see how this page is changed once we start our notification and invoice services.

User management: This is similar to monolithic user management and holds the basic user information and management.

Metrics: The Metrics page holds the information about JVM metrics and service/DB statistics. This is, again, similar to the monolithic application. Added to that, this also shows the metric statistics for the microservice applications registered.

Health: The Health page shows the basic health information of the various services that we have in our application:

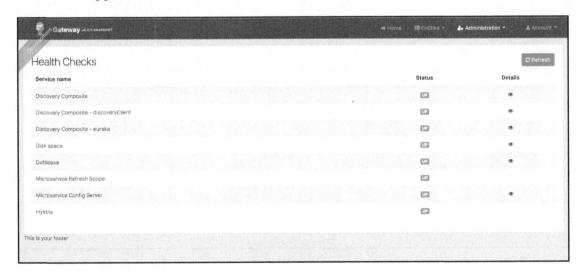

Similar to the monolithic application, it shows **Disk space** and **Database**. But added to that it also shows the health of the Discovery network (that is, the discoveryClient and the Eureka server). It also shows the microservice config server's health, which is `spring-cloud-config-server`, and then shows the health of the circuit breaker we use (Hystrix).

Configuration, Audits, Logs, and API pages are similar to the monolithic application we saw earlier.

JHipster Registry pages

Since we have started the registry server at port `8761`, we can visit `http://localhost:8761` and log in with `admin` as the username and `admin` (the password that we have provided when starting the application) as the password.

Upon logging in, JHipster Registry shows the following information in the form of a dashboard:

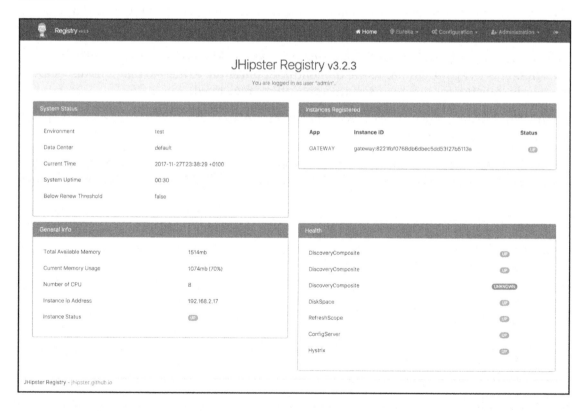

System status

This panel will show the environment in which the application is running and how long the application has been running (System uptime).

Below renew threshold

Our applications will have to send heartbeat signals to the registry service to notify the registry that the application is alive and running. The registry services rely on this heartbeat signal to register and deregister the application. That is, the existence of the application is determined with the help of this heartbeat ping. This is what will happen in the renew phase.

However, when the Eureka server is booting up, it will try to get all the information about instance registries from the nearby service. If the nearby service fails for any reason, then it will try to connect to all of its peers to fetch the information. If the Eureka server was able to fetch the information for all the servers, then it will set the renewal threshold based on the information received. Based on this information, JHipster Registry will hold the information on whether the current level is below the renewal threshold specified and notify users in the UI.

Instances registered

This will show basic information about the instances that have been registered with the registry. Since we have only booted up the gateway service, we will see only one instance here. Basically, this will list all the instances that are connected to this registry service.

It shows the status of the system, the name of the system, and then the instance ID. The instance ID is generated based on the configuration in the `application.yml` of JHipster Registry. It assigns a random value.

General info and health

It also shows general information about the JHipster Registry service and health information of the cluster of services, similar to the gateway health. The data here is fetched with the help of Spring Actuator health and metric endpoints.

Note the **UNKNOWN** in the **Health** section (refer to the preceding screenshot). It tells us that the Eureka server is not running in a highly available mode, or only one instance of JHipster Registry is running. When you boot another instance of the registry (that is, make the application highly available) it goes off.

Application listing page

This page lists the applications that are registered in the JHipster Registry service.

Navigate to **Administration** | **Gateway**:

It shows the following information:

- The current instance ID and its name
- The current status of the instance
- The version that is deployed
- The profile
- The zone in which it is deployed

The version number is fetched from the `build.gradle` or `pom.xml` for Gradle and Maven projects respectively.

The zone here normally refers to an Amazon zone. It is used by Ribbon to route the request to the nearest server. This configuration is useless if you don't use Amazon, and this is why we force it to *primary* (otherwise the load balancing algorithm would be wrong).

All the pages in the administration module will have a drop-down menu that lists the various instances that are registered, and we can select that instance to view its metrics, health, configuration, and other information depending on the page we are on.

Metrics page

By default, this will show Registry's JVM metrics and its service statistics:

We can select any instance from the drop-down menu provided and see its statistics, thus, making JHipster Registry a single point of information that provides all the necessary insight into your microservice architecture. For example, upon selecting the **Gateway** application instance, we will get gateway-related information:

Health page

The health page will list the health of the Registry itself and all the instances that are connected to it. For example, upon selecting the gateway application instance, we will get gateway-related information:

Configuration page

Similar to the health and metrics pages, JHipster Registry will provide detailed configuration of all the instances connected to it and we can choose the instances from the drop-down menu:

The following image shows configuration screen for the Gateway application

Logs page

Similar to the preceding pages, the log page will also show the real-time logs of the application. This is really useful for debugging and getting more information when there is a failure:

 The logs are formatted at the application level. The console here shows `tail -f` for consolidating logs.

The following image shows logs from the Gateway application:

Swagger API endpoints

The microservice architecture relies heavily on API calls between gateway and services, services and registry, and gateway and registries. So it is essential for developers and users to get to know the API endpoints that they can access, as well as the information required to access those endpoints.

This can be a lot of work. Fortunately, libraries such as Swagger come to the rescue. We just have to add the standard comments to the methods, and then the Swagger API will do the necessary work to extract information from them and convert them into a beautiful user interface:

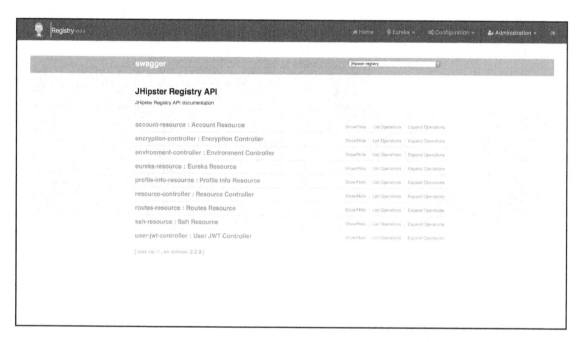

The preceding image shows the default generated Swagger UI page. It lists all the endpoints available, and then provides the list of operations that it provides. It shows the playground where we can frame requests and test them for output.

> Normally, the Swagger API docs are available only in development mode. If you are developing an API service and if there is a need to expose this to end users or external developers using your service, you can enable it in production by setting the **swagger** profile, along with `prod`, by setting `spring.profiles.active=prod, swagger`.

Similar to the other pages, this also lists the various instances that are connected to this registry service and we can select them from the drop-down menu (upper-right corner) to see what APIs are provided by various applications:

The listed operations in the gateway API will provide the following information:

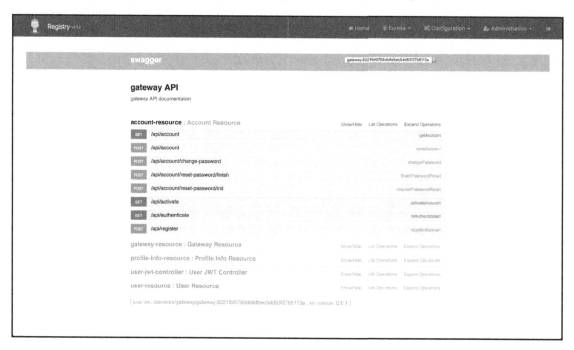

It lists all the operations that are available in the `AccountResource` file. It shows the method type (GET / POST / PUT / DELETE), and then the endpoint and the method name that is present in the `AccountResource` file:

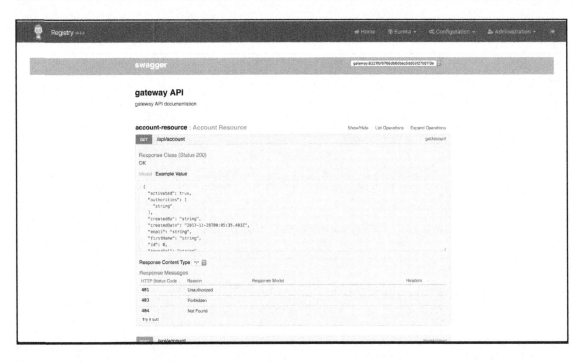

Upon clicking any one of the endpoints, it shows detailed information about the response classes, response errors, response content type, and also how the response object is structured. In addition to this, it also shows how the model object is constructed. These are particularly helpful for end users who want to access these APIs:

```
UserDTO {
    activated (boolean, optional),
    authorities (Array[string], optional),
    createdBy (string, optional),
    createdDate (string, optional),
    email (string, optional),
    firstName (string, optional),
    id (integer, optional),
    imageUrl (string, optional),
    langKey (string, optional),
    lastModifiedDate (string, optional),
    lastModifiedBy (string optional),
    lastName (string, optional),
    login (string)
}
```

Next, there is an option to try out the endpoint upon clicking the button:

Response Messages

HTTP Status Code	Reason	Response Model	Headers
401	Unauthorized		
403	Forbidden		
404	Not Found		

Try it out! Hide Response

Curl

```
curl -X GET --header 'Accept: application/json' --header 'Authorization: Bearer eyJhbGciOiJIUzUxMiJ9.eyJzdWIiOiJhZG1pbi
```

Request URL

```
http://localhost:9061/services/gateway/gateway:8221fbf0768db6dbec5dd53f27b5113a/api/account
```

Response Body

```
{
  "id": 3,
  "login": "admin",
  "firstName": "Administrator",
  "lastName": "Administrator",
  "email": "admin@localhost",
  "imageUrl": "",
  "activated": true,
  "langKey": "en",
  "createdBy": "system",
  "createdDate": "2017-11-27T22:22:02.410Z",
  "lastModifiedBy": "system",
  "lastModifiedDate": null,
  "authorities": [
    "ROLE_USER",
    "ROLE_ADMIN"
  ]
}
```

Response Code

It shows the request and its response. It also shows how to frame the request, along with the authentication token. It provides the response code and the response header information that is returned by the server, which is also extremely useful for API programmers:

```
Response Code

  200

Response Headers

  {
    "pragma": "no-cache",
    "content-type": "application/json;charset=UTF-8",
    "cache-control": "no-cache, no-store, max-age=0, must-revalidate",
    "expires": "0"
  }
```

Running invoice and notification applications locally

We have started the gateway and the registry services. We can then go to our invoice and notification application folders and then run them locally:

```
> cd invoice
> ./gradlew
```

Open another terminal and run the following command:

```
> cd notification
> ./gradlew
```

This will run them in 8081 and 8082 ports respectively:

```
----------------------------------------------------------------------
          Config Server:  Connected to the JHipster Registry config server!
----------------------------------------------------------------------
```

Upon starting the application, it will also try to connect to JHipster Registry and register itself. You can watch for the preceding message once your server has started, to make sure that it is connected to JHipster Registry.

You can alternatively test this via your **Gateway** application. Log in to your **Gateway** application and then navigate to **Administration | Gateway**:

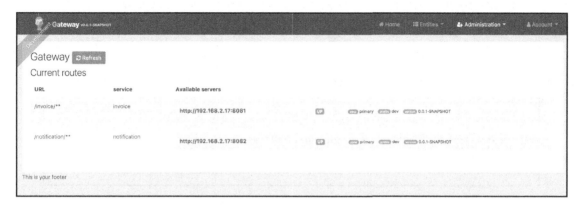

Here, you can see the two microservice applications, **invoice** and **notification**, are booted up and they are available at their respective URLs.

You can also check the JHipster Registry service to list the registered instances:

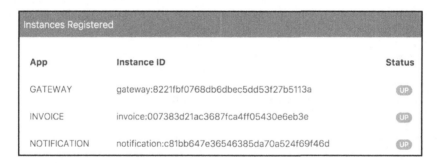

Similarly, all the other pages in JHipster Registry will start to show the invoice and notification as one of the instances, and we can get their health, configuration, logs, and metrics right from JHipster Registry.

If you have followed along with the book, this will be the directory structure you will have:

```
↑    ~/Book     find . -type d -depth 1
./notification
./jhipster-registry
./gateway
./invoice
↑    ~/Book
```

Modeling entities in JDL

Since we have already used the JDL studio when we were setting up our monolithic application, it's time to update it.

As discussed in the previous chapter, we will move the entities from a monolithic application to a gateway application, then, remove the invoice-related entities from the monolithic application, use them in our invoice microservice, and then update the related invoice references in that. Finally, we create entities for the notification microservice.

The following diagram shows our new JDL entity model:

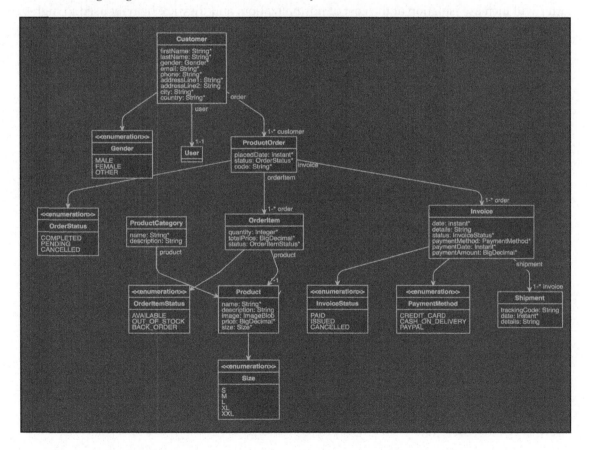

The invoice is a perfect candidate to move out into a separate service. We can completely decouple invoice and its dependencies, but this will cause one problem in our current application—the `ProductOrder` entity is related to the `Invoice` table and we have to remove this dependency while keeping the relationship (but not as a foreign key) as an indirect key in `ProductOrder` that connects with the `Invoice` entity.

This can be achieved in two ways. We can change the foreign key into just another column in the `ProductOrder` entity, or create another entity called `InvoiceOrder` that just holds InvoiceIDs and `ProductOrder` IDs and map it to the `ProductOrder` entity.

The former keeps the table structure more or less the same and allows easier migration. The latter will increase isolation at the cost of normalization, and they are heavily used in high-performance applications. As you see, both have their own merits and demerits. The approach you should take depends purely on your requirement. We will consider the first approach.

As a first step, we will remove the relationship from Product owner in JDL defined in `online-store.jh` as shown for:

```
relationship OneToMany {
    . . .
    ProductOrder{invoice} to Invoice{order},
    . . .
}
```

Remove the highlighted line and move all the invoice-related entities to the `invoice-jdl.jh` file.

Then, go to the Product Order entity, add an `invoiceId` field, and mark it as the `Long` type. It is an optional field and hence doesn't need the required keyword:

```
entity ProductOrder {
    placedDate Instant required
    status OrderStatus required
    invoiceId Long
    code String required
}
```

Entities for microservices can be tagged using the microservice keyword supported by JDL. This helps JHipster to identify entities that belong to a specific microservice. It follows the same JDL options syntax that we saw earlier:

```
<OPTION> <ENTITIES | * | all> [with <VALUE>] [except <ENTITIES>]
```

- microservice keyword
- Followed by the names of the entity, comma separated if multiple
- Followed by the with keyword
- Followed by the name of the microservice

 We should use different files for microservices' entities, so that we create two files, invoice-jdl.jh and notification-jdl.jh, that contain the entities related to invoice and notification respectively, along with the original.

Then, we map the existing Invoice entity to the microservice in our JDL:

```
microservice Invoice, Shipment with Invoice
entity Invoice {
    date Instant required
    details String
    status InvoiceStatus required
    paymentMethod PaymentMethod required
    paymentDate Instant required
    paymentAmount BigDecimal required
}

enum InvoiceStatus {
    PAID, ISSUED, CANCELLED
}

entity Shipment {
    trackingCode String
    date Instant required
    details String
}

enum PaymentMethod {
    CREDIT_CARD, CASH_ON_DELIVERY, PAYPAL
}

relationship OneToMany {
    Invoice{shipment} to Shipment{invoice}
}
```

```
service * with serviceClass
paginate Invoice, Shipment with pagination
microservice * with invoice
```

Then, it is time to create another JDL file to hold the notification service details. Create a file called **notification-jdl.jh** and add the entities for notifications into it:

```
entity Notification {
    date Instant required
    details String
    sentDate Instant required
    format NotificationType required
    userId Long required
    productId Long required
}

enum NotificationType {
    EMAIL, SMS, PARCEL
}
```

Then, we bind these entities to the `Notification` microservice, with the following:

```
microservice * with notification
```

That is it. We have defined the domain model for our microservices.

Entity generation on microservices

Our JDL is ready to use now. The next step will be generating the entities in the gateway and the services. To start with, we will download our JDL files from the JDL studio. Once downloaded, we will move the files into our gateway and microservice applications respectively.

Once moved, run the following command after navigating into the gateway application folder. This will create the entities for the gateway and also create the UI for the microservice entities in the gateway:

```
> cd e-commerce-app/online-store
> jhipster import-jdl online-store.jh
> jhipster import-jdl ../notification/notification-jdl.jh --skip-ui-
  grouping
> jhipster import-jdl ../invoice/invoice-jdl.jh --skip-ui-grouping
```

The `--skip-ui-grouping` flag disables the client-side entity component grouping behavior for microservices introduced in JHipster 5.x. This helps us to cherry-pick our changes from the monolithic application without many conflicts. This grouping behavior is useful when you have entities with the same name in different services.

Run the following command for the notification service so that the backend for the entities are created there:

```
> cd e-commerce-app/notification
> jhipster import-jdl notification-jdl.jh
```

Run the following command for the invoice service so that the backends for the entities are created there:

```
> cd e-commerce-app/invoice
> jhipster import-jdl invoice-jdl.jh
```

JHipster will ask about overwriting the modified files; please select the applicable ones. We will use "a" ->, which means that it will overwrite everything.

Don't forget to cherry-pick any changes we made to entities originally in the monolith back to our gateway and microservices.

Don't forget to commit the changes in each of the services and gateway. You could also init the entire `e-commerce-app` folder as a `git` source if you like, by running `git init`:

```
> cd e-commerce-app
> git init
> git add --all
> git commit -am "entities generated using JDL"
```

Explaining the generated code

In the notification service, once we have generated the application, the following files were created:

```
Using JHipster version installed locally in current project's node_modules
Executing jhipster:import-jdl jhipster-jdl.jh
Options:
The jdl is being parsed.
Writing entity JSON files.
Updated entities are: Notification
Generating entities.

Found the .jhipster/Notification.json configuration file, entity can be automatically generated!

The entity Notification is being updated.

    create src/main/java/com/mycompany/myapp/domain/Notification.java
    create src/main/java/com/mycompany/myapp/repository/NotificationRepository.java
    create src/main/java/com/mycompany/myapp/web/rest/NotificationResource.java
    create src/test/java/com/mycompany/myapp/web/rest/NotificationResourceIntTest.java
    create src/main/java/com/mycompany/myapp/domain/enumeration/NotificationType.java
Entity generation completed
Congratulations, JHipster execution is complete!
```

As you can see, this will only generate the backend files and not the frontend files, since they are already generated in the gateway service.

Similarly, running the `jhipster import-jdl` command in the invoice application will generate similar Java files:

```
Using JHipster version installed locally in current project's node_modules
Executing jhipster:import-jdl jhipster-jdl.jh
Options:
The jdl is being parsed.
Writing entity JSON files.
Updated entities are: Invoice,Shipment
Generating entities.

Found the .jhipster/Invoice.json configuration file, entity can be automatically generated!


The entity Invoice is being updated.


Found the .jhipster/Shipment.json configuration file, entity can be automatically generated!


The entity Shipment is being updated.

    create src/main/resources/config/liquibase/changelog/20171212194917_added_entity_Invoice.xml
    create src/main/java/com/mycompany/myapp/domain/Invoice.java
    create src/main/java/com/mycompany/myapp/repository/InvoiceRepository.java
    create src/main/java/com/mycompany/myapp/web/rest/InvoiceResource.java
    create src/main/java/com/mycompany/myapp/service/InvoiceService.java
    create src/test/java/com/mycompany/myapp/web/rest/InvoiceResourceIntTest.java
  conflict src/main/resources/config/liquibase/master.xml
? Overwrite src/main/resources/config/liquibase/master.xml? overwrite this and all others
     force src/main/resources/config/liquibase/master.xml
    create src/main/java/com/mycompany/myapp/domain/enumeration/InvoiceStatus.java
    create src/main/java/com/mycompany/myapp/domain/enumeration/PaymentMethod.java
    create src/main/resources/config/liquibase/changelog/20171212194918_added_entity_Shipment.xml
    create src/main/resources/config/liquibase/changelog/20171212194918_added_entity_constraints_Shipment.xml
    create src/main/java/com/mycompany/myapp/domain/Shipment.java
    create src/main/java/com/mycompany/myapp/repository/ShipmentRepository.java
    create src/main/java/com/mycompany/myapp/web/rest/ShipmentResource.java
    create src/main/java/com/mycompany/myapp/service/ShipmentService.java
    create src/test/java/com/mycompany/myapp/web/rest/ShipmentResourceIntTest.java
Entity generation completed
Entity generation completed
Congratulations, JHipster execution is complete!
```

Gateway application

In the Gateway application, the entire frontend (including the entities in microservices) will be generated. Since JHipster produces proxy-based microservices, all the frontend code will live in the Gateway application:

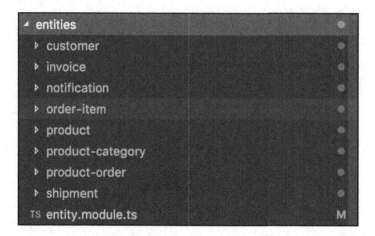

`ProductOrder.Java` will remove the `Invoice` as a foreign key and then use the long value that we passed in here:

```
/**
 * A Product Owner
 */
...
public class ProductOrder implements Serializable {
...
@Column(name = "invoice_id")
private Long invoiceId;
...
}
```

So, the application is generated completely. Now, it is time to run it.

Fire up three consoles (since we need to run three applications). If we have the applications running already, then we just need to compile them and Spring devtools will auto reload the applications. Make sure the registry is already running as well:

- In console 1, navigate to the gateway and then start the server with `./gradlew` if it is not already running, otherwise compile with `./gradlew compileJava`

- In console 2, navigate to the invoice and then start the server with `./gradlew` if it is not already running, otherwise compile with `./gradlew compileJava`
- In console 3, navigate to the notification and then start the server with `./gradlew` if it is not already running, otherwise compile with `./gradlew compileJava`

Explaining the generated pages

Once the application has started successfully, it is time to spin up your favorite browser and navigate to the gateway server at `http://localhost:8080`.

Once logged in, you can see that the entities are generated in the gateway application and they are available under the entity **nav** menu.

It includes all the gateway entities and also the microservice entities:

This is the invoice screen created in the gateway application:

Try to create a few entities to verify that everything is working fine.

Summary

Since we have done a lot of things in this chapter, let's recap what we have done so far.

We have successfully generated a gateway and two microservices. We have downloaded JHipster Registry and then started it locally. We have successfully segregated and generated the entity files for a notification and invoice service. We have finally booted up all our applications and saw how things are generated, and were able to create the microservice application. Last but not least, we have also committed all our changes to Git (in other words, reached a checkpoint).

11
Deploying with Docker Compose

We have generated the application and it is ready for production. In this chapter, we will focus on how to deploy the application using Docker Compose. We will also see the various options that JHipster provides for deployment, followed by how to deploy our registry and console alongside the application.

In this chapter, we will look into:

- A short introduction to Docker Compose
- Kickstarting Kubernetes
- Introducing OpenShift
- Explaining Rancher

Then we will discuss locally with JHipster Registry and JHipster Console

Introducing microservice deployment options

The success of an application not only depends on how well we design it. It depends on how well we implement (deploy and maintain) it.

A well-designed microservice application in a low-availability environment is useless. So it is equally important to decide on a deployment strategy that increases its chances to succeed. When it comes to deployment, there is a plethora of tools available. Each one of them has its pros and cons, and we have to choose one that is suitable for our needs. JHipster currently provides sub-generators to create configuration files to containerize, deploy, and manage the microservices via the following:

- Docker
- Kubernetes (also helps to orchestrate your deployment)
- OpenShift (also provides private cloud deployment)
- Rancher (also provides complete container management)

We will see them in detail in the following sections.

A short introduction to Docker Compose

Shipping code to the server is always difficult, especially when you want to scale it. This is mainly because we have to manually create the same environment and make sure the application has all the necessary connectivity (to other services) that is needed. This was a major pain point for teams when shipping and scaling their code.

> *Shipping code to the server is difficult.*

Containers were the game-changer in this field. They helped to bundle the entire application along with dependencies in a shippable container, and all we need is to provide an environment in which these containers can run. This simplified the process of shipping code to the server and also among the development teams. This also reduced the amount of time a team spent making sure that the application ran seamlessly across the environment.

Containers solve the application deployment problem, but how do we scale them?

The Docker Compose tool comes to the rescue here. First, let's see what Docker Compose is, and then see what problems it solves.

Docker Compose is a tool that helps to define and run multi-container Docker applications with a single file. That is, we use a `.yaml` file to define the requirements and/or dependencies of the application. Then, with `docker-compose`, we can create newer deployments and start our applications as defined in the `docker-compose` file.

So, what is required in a `docker-compose` file?

The following code segment is a sample `docker-compose` file that will start a Redis database on port `5000`:

```
version: '3'
services:
  web:
    build: .
    ports:
      - "5000:5000"
  redis:
    image: "redis:alpine"
```

The first line of the `docker-compose` file should be the version of the `docker-compose` tool.

Then we need to specify all the necessary services that we need for our application to run. They should be defined in the `services:` section.

We can also define multiple services inside here, giving a name to each (`web` and `redis`).

This is followed by how to build the `service` (either via a command to build or referring a Dockerfile).

If the application needs any port access, we can configure it using `5000:5000` (that is internal port: external port).

Then, we have to specify the volume information. This basically tells `docker-compose` to serve the files from the location specified.

Once we have specified the services required for our application, then we can start the application via `docker-compose`. This will start your entire application along with the services, and expose the `services` on the port specified.

With `docker-compose`, we can perform the following operations:

- **Start**: `docker-compose -f <docker_file> up`
- **Stop**: `docker-compose -f <docker_file> down`

We can also perform the following operations:

- **List the running services and their status**: `docker ps`
- **Logs**: `docker log <container_id>`

In the compose file, we can add the project name, as follows:

```
version: '3'
COMPOSE_PROJECT_NAME: "myapp"
services:
  web:
    build: .
    ports:
      - "5000:5000"
  redis:
    image: "redis:alpine"
```

This can be used for identifying multiple environments. With the help of this, we can isolate multiple environments. This helps us to handle multiple instances across various `dev`, `QA`, and `prod` environments.

`Docker-compose` is itself a great tool for deploying your application along with all the services it needs. It provides infrastructure as a code. It is an excellent choice for development, QA, and other environments except for production. But why?

`Docker-compose` is really good for creating and starting your application. However, when you want to update an existing container there will be a definite downtime, since `docker-compose` will recreate the entire container (there are few workarounds to make this happen but still, `docker-compose` needs some improvement in this space.)

Kickstarting Kubernetes

According to the Kubernetes website:

> *"Kubernetes is an open-source system for automating deployment, scaling, and management of containerized applications."*

It is a simple and powerful tool for automatic deployment, scaling, and managing containerized applications. It provides zero downtime when you roll out a newer application or update an existing application. You can automate it to scale in and out based on certain factors. It also provides self-healing, such that Kubernetes automatically detects the failing application and spins up a new instance. We can also define secrets and configuration that can be used across instances.

Kubernetes primarily focuses on zero downtime production applications upgrades, and also scales them as required.

A single deployable component is called a **pod** in Kubernetes. This can be as simple as a running process in the container. A group of pods can be combined together to form a **deployment**.

Similar to `docker-compose`, we can define the applications and their required services in a single YAML file or multiple files (as per our convenience).

Here also, we start with an `apiVersion` in a Kubernetes deployment file.

The following code is a sample Kubernetes file that will start a Nginx server:

```yaml
apiVersion: v1
kind: Service
metadata:
  name: nginxsvc
  labels:
    app: nginx
spec:
  type: NodePort
  ports:
  - port: 80
    protocol: TCP
    name: http
  - port: 443
    protocol: TCP
    name: https
  selector:
    app: nginx
```

Followed by the type, which takes either a pod, deployment, namespace, ingress (load balancing the pods), role, and many more.

Ingress forms a layer between the services and the internet so that all the inbound connections are controlled or configured with the ingress controller before sending them to Kubernetes services on the cluster. On the other hand, the egress controller controls or configures services going out of the Kubernetes cluster.

This is followed by the metadata information, such as the type of environments, the application name (nginxsvc), and labels (Kubernetes uses this information to identify and segregate the pods). Kubernetes uses this metadata information to identify the particular pods or a group of pods, and we can manage the instances with this metadata. This is one of the key differences with `docker-compose`, where `docker-compose` doesn't have the flexibility of defining the metadata about the containers.

This is followed by the spec, where we define the specification of the images or our application. We can also define the pull strategy for our images as well as define the environment variables along with the exposed ports. We can define the resource limitations on the machine (or VM) for a particular service. They provide health checks, that is, each service is monitored for the health and when some services fail, they are immediately replaced by newer ones. They also provide service discovery out of the box, by assigning each pod an IP, which makes it easier for the services to identify and interact with them. They also provide a better dashboard, to visualize your architecture and the status of the application. You can do most of the management via this dashboard, such as checking the status, logs, scale up, or down the services, and so on.

Since Kubernetes provide a complete orchestration of our services with configurable options, it makes it really hard to set up initially, and this means it is not ideal for a development environment. We also need the **kubectl** CLI tool for management. Despite the fact that we use Docker images inside, the Docker CLI can't be used.

There is also **Minikube** (minified Kubernetes), which is used for developing and testing applications locally.

Kubernetes not only takes care of containerizing your application, it also helps to scale, manage, and deploy your application. It orchestrates your entire application deployment. Additionally, it also provides service discovery and automated health checks.

We will focus more on the Kubernetes sub-generator in the following chapter.

Introducing OpenShift

OpenShift is a multi-cloud, open source container application platform. It is based on Kubernetes and used for developing, deploying, and managing applications. It is a common platform for developers and operations. It helps them to build, deploy, and manage applications consistently across hybrid cloud and multi-cloud infrastructures.

For developers, it provides a self-service platform in which they can provision, build, and deploy applications and their components. With automated workflows for converting your source to the image, it helps developers go from source to ready-to-run, dockerized images.

For operations, it provides a secure, enterprise-grade Kubernetes for policy-based controls and automation for application management, such as cluster services, scheduling, and orchestration with load balancing and auto-scaling capabilities.

JHipster also provides OpenShift deployment files as a separate sub-generator. We can generate them by running `jhipster openshift` and answering the questions as needed. This will generate OpenShift related deployment files.

Explaining Rancher

Rancher is a container management platform. It is also open source. It helps to deploy and maintain containers for any organization. Rancher is merely a deployment server that is installed on any Linux machine or cluster. So to use Rancher, we should first start the Rancher container, and this requires Docker to be available.

Once started, we can log in to Rancher and start deploying our applications. It also has role management. Rancher provides an option to choose between Swarm, Kubernetes, or Cattle (and other cluster deployment options). It also provides details about the infrastructure and applications that are deployed. It shows detailed information about the containers, registries, data pools, and other information (related to the container and infrastructure).

It also provides options to tweak the Kubernetes or Swarm settings as needed, so it makes it much easier to scale up and down. It also provides options to launch the entire application stack via its UI or using `docker-compose.yml` and `rancher-compose.yml`. It also has the capability to load the external services and use them (such as a load balancer).

JHipster also provides Rancher deployment files as a separate sub-generator. We can generate them by running `jhipster rancher` and answering the questions as needed. This will generate the Rancher configuration files.

Generated Docker Compose files

By default, JHipster will generate Docker Compose files that enable us to run the application completely in the containerized environment, irrespective of the options chosen. For example, in the gateway application that we have generated, the following files are generated by default under `src/main/docker`:

- `sonar.yml`: This file creates and starts a SonarQube server
- `mysql.yml`: This file creates and starts a MySQL database server and creates a user and schema
- `jhipster-registry.yml`: This file creates and starts a JHipster Registry service
- `app.yml`: This is the main file that creates and starts the application along with services such as JHipster registry and the database

In addition to this, JHipster also creates a Dockerfile, which helps you to containerize the application alone.

Then we can see a folder called `central-server-config`. This will be used as a central configuration server for the JHipster Registry.

When the registry and the application are running in Docker, it uses `application.yml` from the `docker-config` folder as the central configuration server.

On the other hand, when running only the registry in Docker mode, the application, not in Docker, will use `application.yml` from the `localhost-config` folder. The key difference is that the URL defining the Eureka client varies.

Let's see the Docker files that have been generated.

Walking through the generated files

Let's start with the `app.yml` file under `src/main/docker` inside your gateway application.

As we saw at the beginning of the chapter, the file starts with the Docker version that it supports:

```
version: '2'
```

This is followed by the services section where we define the various services, applications, or components that we will kick start with this Docker file.

Under services section, we will define a name for the service, in our case we have used `gateway-app`, followed by the image that we want to use as a container. This image is generated with the help of the Docker file that we have in that folder.

This is followed by the series of environment variables that our application will depend on, they include:

- `SPRING_PROFILES_ACTIVE`: Tells the application to run in production mode and expose Swagger endpoints.
- `EUREKA_CLIENT_SERVICE_URL_DEFAULTZONE`: Tells the application where to check for the JHipster Registry (which is the Eureka client that we are using. If we have chosen Consul here, then the application will point to the Consul URL)
- `SPRING_CLOUD_CONFIG_URI`: Tells the application where to look for the `config` service for the application.
- `SPRING_DATASOURCE_URL`: Tells the application where to look for the data source.
- `JHIPSTER_SLEEP`: This is a custom property that we have used to make sure that the JHipster Registry starts before the application starts up.

Finally, we specify on which port the application should run and be exposed:

```
services:
    gateway-app:
        image: 'gateway'
        environment:
            - SPRING_PROFILES_ACTIVE=prod,swagger
            -
EUREKA_CLIENT_SERVICE_URL_DEFAULTZONE=http://admin:$${jhipster.regi
stry.password}@jhipster-registry:8761/eureka
            -
SPRING_CLOUD_CONFIG_URI=http://admin:$${jhipster.registry.password}
@jhipster-registry:8761/config
            - SPRING_DATASOURCE_URL=jdbc:mysql://gateway-
mysql:3306/gateway?.....
            - JHIPSTER_SLEEP=30
        ports:
            8080:8080
```

We have just defined the service with the `docker-compose` file; now we have to specify two other services that are needed for our application to run. They are the database and JHipster Registry.

So, we register another service called `gateway-mysql`, which creates and starts the MySQL server. We can define MySQL as a separate Docker Compose file and link them in here. So, we put an `extends` keyword followed by the `docker-compose` file and the service that we have to start from the specified `docker-compose` file:

```
gateway-mysql:
    extends:
        file: mysql.yml
        service: gateway-mysql.yml
```

Then we input the following code for the `mysql.yml` file, shown as follows:

```
version: '2'
services:
    gateway-mysql:
        image: mysql:5.7.20
        # volumes:
        # - ~/volumes/jhipster/gateway/mysql/:/var/lib/mysql/
        environment:
            - MYSQL_USER=root
            - MYSQL_ALLOW_EMPTY_PASSWORD=yes
            - MYSQL_DATABASE=gateway
        ports:
            - 3306:3306
        command: mysqld --lower_case_table_names=1 --skip-ssl --
character_set_server=utf8 --explicit_defaults_for_timestamp
```

We have again started with the version that it supports followed by the `services` keyword and then specify the `service` name, `gateway-mysql` that is used in the `app.yml` file. If you want to specify a volume for the persistent data storage you can uncomment the commented volumes segment. This basically maps the local file location to Docker's internal location so that the data is persistent even if the Docker image itself is replaced or updated.

This is followed by a set of environment variables, such as the username and the password (we have set it to empty here, but for a real production application it is recommended to set it to a more complex password), and then the database schema name.

We have also specified the command that we need to run to start the MySQL server.

Then we go back to the `app.yml` file and we then define the JHipster Registry service. This will again extend the `jhipster-registry.yml` and `docker-compose` file. One more thing to note here is, even though we extend the services from another Docker file, we can override the environment variables that we have specified in the original `docker-compose` file. This comes in handy in certain cases where we have to kickstart our application with different or customized values. In our case, we have overridden the location of the Spring Cloud Config server file location from that of the original:

```
jhipster-registry:
    extends:
        file: jhipster-registry.yml
        service: jhipster-registry
    environment:
        -
SPRING_CLOUD_CONFIG_SERVER_NATIVE_SEARCH_LOCATIONS=file:./central-
config/docker-config/
```

The `Jhipster-registry.yml` file:

```
version: '2'
services:
    jhipster-registry:
        image: jhipster/jhipster-registry:v3.2.3
        volumes:
            - ./central-server-config:/central-config
        # When run with the "dev" Spring profile, the JHipster Registry
will
        # read the config from the local filesystem (central-server-
config directory)
        # When run with the "prod" Spring profile, it will read the
configuration from a Git                    repository
            # See
http://www.jhipster.tech/microservices-architecture/#registry_app_c
onfiguration
        environment:
            - SPRING_PROFILES_ACTIVE=dev
            - SECURITY_USER_PASSWORD=admin
            - JHIPSTER_REGISTRY_PASSWORD=admin
            -
SPRING_CLOUD_CONFIG_SERVER_NATIVE_SEARCH_LOCATIONS=file:./central-
config/localhost-config/
            # - GIT_URI=https://github.com/jhipster/jhipster-registry/
            # - GIT_SEARCH_PATHS=central-config
        ports:
            - 8761:8761
```

We have defined the central-config for JHipster Registry as follows. We have configured the secret for the JWT and the Eureka client's URL. The JWT token specified is used for services to authorize and communicate between them and the registry:

```
# Common configuration shared between all applications
configserver:
    name: Docker JHipster Registry
    status: Connected to the JHipster Registry running in Docker
jhipster:
    security:
        authentication:
            jwt:
                secret: my-secret-token-to-change-in-production
eureka:
    client:
        service-url:
            defaultZone:
http://admin:${jhipster.registry.password}@localhost:8761/eureka/
```

Added to these, we also generate a `sonar.yml`, (this file is not important for deploying your application):

```
version: '2'
services:
    gateway-sonar:
        image: sonarqube:6.5-alpine
        ports:
            - 9000:9000
            - 9092:9092
```

Similarly, in the microservices, that is, in our invoice and the notification applications, we will have similar files generated. They are the same except for the change in the service name.

Unlike MySQL, MongoDB is also capable of running as a cluster with different nodes and configuration. We need to specify them differently here. So we will create have two docker-compose files. `mongodb.yml` is for starting the MongoDB with a single node, and the `mongodb-cluster.yml` to start the MongoDB as the cluster.

Please check the database port number between the gateway and the microservice application. If they use the same database, there may be a clash in the port number since JHipster generates the same port number for both. Change it to any other unused port, or Docker Compose will show an error. In our case, I have changed it to 3307.

Building and deploying everything to Docker locally

There are multiple ways in which we can use the `docker-compose` files based on our needs.

In general, when we are developing the application, we can run the application with the general Maven or Gradle command so that we can debug the application and also reload the changes faster, and start the database and JHipster registry with Docker.

Otherwise, you can start the entire application from the `app.yml` file, which will kickstart the database, JHipster Registry, and then the application itself. To do that, open your terminal or Command Prompt, go to the application folder, and then run the following command:

```
> cd gateway
```

Then we have to first Dockerize the application by taking a production build of our application with the following command:

```
> ./gradlew bootRepackage -Pprod buildDocker
```

Once done, we can start the app via the `docker-compose` command:

```
> docker-compose -f src/main/docker/app.yml up -d
```

`-f` specifies the file with which `docker-compose` should start the server. The `-d` flag tells `docker-compose` to run everything in detached mode. This will start the application in Docker and expose the application on port 8080, the registry server on port 8761, and the database on port 3306.

Then we can go to the respective microservices folder and do the same, create a docker image with the following command:

```
> ./gradlew bootRepackage -Pprod buildDocker
```

Then we can start the application via `docker-compose` with the following command:

```
> docker-compose -f <filename> -d
```

We can check the running Docker containers with the following command:

> **docker ps -a**

It should list all seven containers:

As you can see, there are three app containers (gateway/notification, and invoice), and then a JHipster-Registry, followed by three database containers (two MySQL and one MongoDB). The order may vary).

If you are using JHipster Version 5 or above use `bootWar` instead of the `bootRepackage` command in Gradle.

Generating docker-compose files for microservices

There are many `docker-compose` files and maintaining them is hard. Thankfully, JHipster has a `docker-compose` sub generator bundled with it. The `Docker-compose` sub generator helps you to organize all your application's Dockerfiles together. It creates a single Dockerfile that refers to the application's Dockerfiles.

Let's go to the base folder and create a folder and name it `docker-compose`:

> **mkdir docker-compose && cd docker-compose**

Once inside the `docker-compose` folder, we can run the following command:

> **jhipster docker-compose**

This will generate the Dockerfiles.

As usual, it will ask us a series of questions, before generating the files:

```
Using JHipster version installed globally
Executing jhipster:docker-compose
Options:
 Welcome to the JHipster Docker Compose Sub-Generator
Files will be generated in folder: /Users/sendilkumar/Dev/Book/docker-compose
? Which *type* of application would you like to deploy?
   Monolithic application
 > Microservice application
```

At first, it asks which type of application we would like to deploy. We will select the microservice application as an option.

This is followed by choosing the type of gateway that we would like to use; there are two options available, a JHipster-gateway with Zuul proxy, and the more exciting, Traefik gateway with Consul

Let us choose JHipster-gateway with Zuul proxy:

```
Using JHipster version installed globally
Executing jhipster:docker-compose
Options:
 Welcome to the JHipster Docker Compose Sub-Generator
Files will be generated in folder: /Users/sendilkumar/Dev/Book/docker-compose
? Which *type* of application would you like to deploy? Microservice application
? Which *type* of gateway would you like to use? (Use arrow keys)
 > JHipster gateway based on Netflix Zuul
   [BETA] Traefik gateway (only works with Consul)
```

Then, we have to select the location of the microservices gateway and applications. This is the main reason why we have generated the applications inside a single parent folder. This will help plugins and sub-generators to easily find the docker configuration files created. We will select the default option (**../**)

```
Using JHipster version installed globally
Executing jhipster:docker-compose
Options:
 Welcome to the JHipster Docker Compose Sub-Generator
Files will be generated in folder: /Users/sendilkumar/Dev/Book/docker-compose
? Which *type* of application would you like to deploy? Microservice application
? Which *type* of gateway would you like to use? JHipster gateway based on Netflix Zuul
? Enter the root directory where your gateway(s) and microservices are located (../)
```

After selecting the location, JHipster will search inside the given folder for any JHipster generated the application and list them in the next question.

In our case, it lists **notification**, **invoice**, and **gateway**. We can choose all of them and hit *Enter*:

```
Using JHipster version installed globally
Executing jhipster:docker-compose
Options:
  Welcome to the JHipster Docker Compose Sub-Generator
Files will be generated in folder: /Users/sendilkumar/Dev/Book/docker-compose
? Which *type* of application would you like to deploy? Microservice application
? Which *type* of gateway would you like to use? JHipster gateway based on Netflix Zuul
? Enter the root directory where your gateway(s) and microservices are located ../
3 applications found at /Users/sendilkumar/Dev/Book/

? Which applications do you want to include in your configuration?
 ⊙ gateway
 ⊙ invoice
)⊙ notification
```

It automatically detects that we have used MongoDB and asks us the next question; whether we would like to have MongoDB as a cluster. We will not choose anything here:

```
Using JHipster version installed globally
Executing jhipster:docker-compose
Options:
  Welcome to the JHipster Docker Compose Sub-Generator
Files will be generated in folder: /Users/sendilkumar/Dev/Book/docker-compose
? Which *type* of application would you like to deploy? Microservice application
? Which *type* of gateway would you like to use? JHipster gateway based on Netflix Zuul
? Enter the root directory where your gateway(s) and microservices are located ../
3 applications found at /Users/sendilkumar/Dev/Book/

? Which applications do you want to include in your configuration? gateway, invoice, notification
? Which applications do you want to use with clustered databases (only available with MongoDB and Couchbase)?
)⊙ notification
```

Then it asks about the console; whether we need to set up any consoles for the application. We will choose logs and metrics with the JHipster Console (based on ELK and Zipkin):

```
      /Dev/Book/docker compose     jhipster docker compose
Using JHipster version installed globally
Executing jhipster:docker-compose
Options:
Welcome to the JHipster Docker Compose Sub-Generator
Files will be generated in folder: /Users/sendilkumar/Dev/Book/docker-compose
? Which *type* of application would you like to deploy? Microservice application
? Which *type* of gateway would you like to use? JHipster gateway based on Netflix Zuul
? Enter the root directory where your gateway(s) and microservices are located ../
3 applications found at /Users/sendilkumar/Dev/Book/

? Which applications do you want to include in your configuration? gateway, invoice, notification
? Which applications do you want to use with clustered databases (only available with MongoDB and Couchbase)?
? Do you want to setup monitoring for your applications ?
  No
> Yes, for logs and metrics with the JHipster Console (based on ELK and Zipkin)
  Yes, for metrics only with Prometheus (only compatible with JHipster >= v3.12)
```

We can either opt out from the monitoring option or choose Prometheus. That connects with Prometheus and shows metrics only.

Then JHipster asks whether you need Curator or Zipkin:

- Curator will help you to curate and manage the indices created by Elasticsearch
- Zipkin (as discussed in the previous chapter)

```
Using JHipster version installed globally
Executing jhipster:docker-compose
Options:
Welcome to the JHipster Docker Compose Sub-Generator
Files will be generated in folder: /Users/sendilkumar/Dev/Book/docker-compose
? Which *type* of application would you like to deploy? Microservice application
? Which *type* of gateway would you like to use? JHipster gateway based on Netflix Zuul
? Enter the root directory where your gateway(s) and microservices are located ../
3 applications found at /Users/sendilkumar/Dev/Book/

? Which applications do you want to include in your configuration? gateway, invoice, notification
? Which applications do you want to use with clustered databases (only available with MongoDB and Couchbase)?
? Do you want to setup monitoring for your applications ? Yes, for logs and metrics with the JHipster Console (based on ELK and Zipkin)
? You have selected the JHipster Console which is based on the ELK stack and additional technologies, which one do you want to use ?
  o Curator, to help you curate and manage your Elasticsearch indices
  )  Zipkin, for distributed tracing (only compatible with JHipster >= v4.2.0)
```

Since the JHipster console is chosen, it will ask for additional pieces of information supported by the console. They include Zipkin and Curator. We have already seen Zipkin. Curator, on the other hand, will help us to manage and curate the indices in Elasticsearch.

We will choose only Zipkin here.

```
Using JHipster version installed globally
Executing jhipster:docker-compose
Options:
 Welcome to the JHipster Docker Compose Sub-Generator 
Files will be generated in folder: /Users/sendilkumar/Dev/Book/docker-compose
? Which *type* of application would you like to deploy? Microservice application
? Which *type* of gateway would you like to use? JHipster gateway based on Netflix Zuul
? Enter the root directory where your gateway(s) and microservices are located ../
3 applications found at /Users/sendilkumar/Dev/Book/

? Which applications do you want to include in your configuration? gateway, invoice, notification
? Which applications do you want to use with clustered databases (only available with MongoDB and Couchbase)?
? Do you want to setup monitoring for your applications ? Yes, for logs and metrics with the JHipster Console (based on ELK and Zipkin)
? You have selected the JHipster Console which is based on the ELK stack and additional technologies, which one do you want to use ? Zipkin, for distributed tracing (only compatible with JHipster >= v4.2.0)
JHipster registry detected as the service discovery and configuration provider used by your apps
? Enter the admin password used to secure the JHipster Registry [admin]
```

 We can also choose nothing here and go with the default option.

Finally, it asks for the password for the JHipster Registry; we will go with the default here:

```
Using JHipster version installed globally
Executing jhipster:docker-compose
Options:
 Welcome to the JHipster Docker Compose Sub-Generator 
Files will be generated in folder: /Users/sendilkumar/Dev/Book/docker-compose
? Which *type* of application would you like to deploy? Microservice application
? Which *type* of gateway would you like to use? JHipster gateway based on Netflix Zuul
? Enter the root directory where your gateway(s) and microservices are located ../
3 applications found at /Users/sendilkumar/Dev/Book/

? Which applications do you want to include in your configuration? gateway, invoice, notification
? Which applications do you want to use with clustered databases (only available with MongoDB and Couchbase)?
? Do you want to setup monitoring for your applications ? Yes, for logs and metrics with the JHipster Console (based on ELK and Zipkin)
? You have selected the JHipster Console which is based on the ELK stack and additional technologies, which one do you want to use ? Zipkin, for distributed tracing (only compatible with JHipster >= v4.2.0)
JHipster registry detected as the service discovery and configuration provider used by your apps
? Enter the admin password used to secure the JHipster Registry admin

Checking Docker images in applications' directories...
   create docker-compose.yml
   create README-DOCKER-COMPOSE.md
   create jhipster-registry.yml
   create central-server-config/application.yml
   create jhipster-console.yml
   create log-conf/logstash.conf
   create log-data/.gitignore

Docker Compose configuration successfully generated!
You can launch all your infrastructure by running : docker-compose up -d
Congratulations, JHipster execution is complete!
```

That is it; we have just created a higher-level Dockerfile that has information about all the services that we need to run the application successfully.

Now we can just run the entire suite with the following command:

```
> docker-compose up -d
```

This will start the gateway, notification, invoice, and the registry, along with the console and all other required services.

Features of the deployed application

Thus, the deployed applications are ready to be launched. We can launch the JHipster Registry at `http://localhost:8761`; it will list all the registered applications:

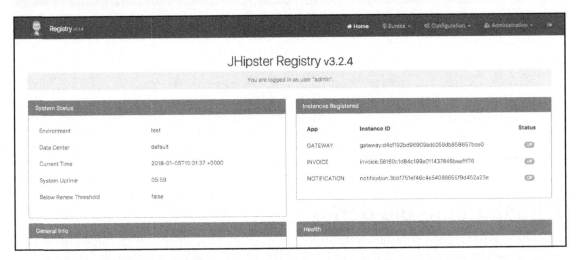

Added to that, the registry also tells us the number of instances that are registered. Navigate to **Eureka | Instances** to check that. Currently, we have one of each instance registered:

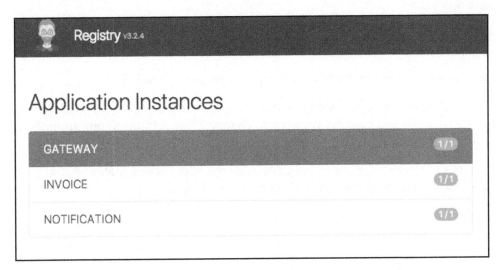

Similarly, the Gateway application will list down the microservices that are connected to it. Go to `http://localhost:8080`.

Navigate to **Administration** | **Gateway** to see the microservices applications that are connected to this Gateway application:

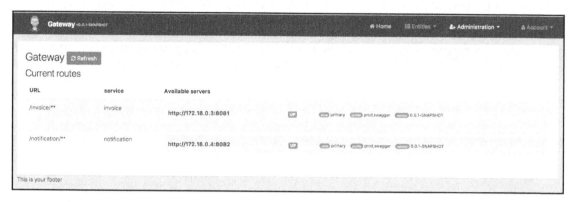

JHipster console demo

JHipster also provides a console application based on the ELK stack, which can be used for logs and metrics monitoring of the application. JHipster Console is another open source application. It is really useful and provides some nice dashboards to visualize the application. As with other JHipster products, it is much easier to get started with the JHipster Console.

Let's go back to our book folder, and then clone the JHipster console project from GitHub (https://github.com/jhipster/jhipster-console):

```
> git clone https://github.com/jhipster/jhipster-console
```

Before we start our console, we need to make our applications log the metrics and log into the console. To make that happen, we need to change a few settings in our applications and then restart them.

Let's go to our `application-prod.yml` file in all the applications (gateway and microservices application) and enable the logstash and logs:

```
metrics: # DropWizard Metrics configuration, used by MetricsConfiguration
    ...
    logs: # Reports Dropwizard metrics in the logs
        enabled: true
        report-frequency: 60 # in seconds
logging:
    logstash: # Forward logs to logstash over a socket, used by
```

```
LoggingConfiguration
        enabled: true
        host: localhost
        port: 5000
        queue-size: 512
```

Set enabled to true in `metrics.logs.enabled` and also `logging.logstash.enabled`. This will push the logs to the console application. JHipster Console will collect this information and show it in nice-looking dashboards with the help of Kibana.

Once cloned, we can go into this folder and then start the `jhipster-console` with the help of `docker-compose`:

```
> cd jhipster-console
> docker-compose up -d
```

That is it. Your console is running on `http://localhost:5601`.

Kibana provides the following (customizable) dashboards:

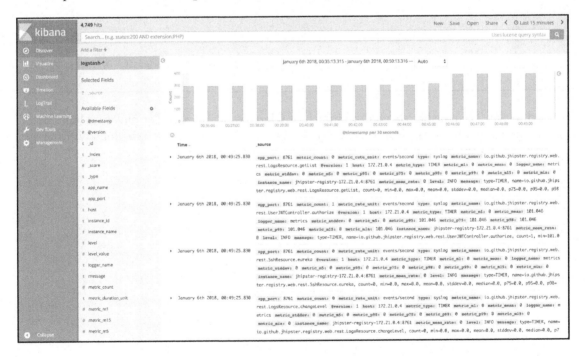

Kibana also provides application-level metrics, such as JVM threads metrics and other details:

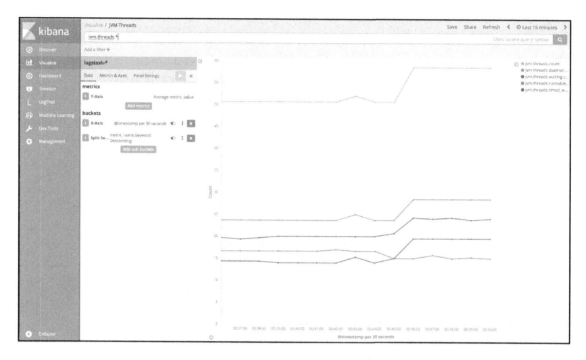

Added to this, the console also has an interface where we can see the application logs. It shows the log of all the applications deployed. We can filter and search the logs with respect to the application:

Jan 06 00:50:25 jhipster-registry jhipsterRegistry:1c6ecec271be0ace5a86ec37a9c027b0: INFO - metrics : type=GAUGE, name=jvm.threads.runnable.count, value=11
Jan 06 00:50:25 jhipster-registry jhipsterRegistry:1c6ecec271be0ace5a86ec37a9c027b0: INFO - metrics : type=GAUGE, name=jvm.threads.timed_waiting.count, value=36
Jan 06 00:50:25 jhipster-registry jhipsterRegistry:1c6ecec271be0ace5a86ec37a9c027b0: INFO - metrics : type=METER, name=com.codahale.metrics.servlet.InstrumentedFilter.responseCodes.ok, count=167, mean_
rate=0.07434354752815567, m1=0.0166198917401331083, m5=0.014972736588488742, m15=0.078973160782722619, rate_unit=events/second
Jan 06 00:50:25 jhipster-registry jhipsterRegistry:1c6ecec271be0ace5a86ec37a9c027b0: INFO - metrics : type=METER, name=com.codahale.metrics.servlet.InstrumentedFilter.responseCodes.notFound, count=0, m
ean_rate=0.0, m1=0.0, m5=0.0, m15=0.0, rate_unit=events/second
Jan 06 00:50:25 jhipster-registry jhipsterRegistry:1c6ecec271be0ace5a86ec37a9c027b0: INFO - metrics : type=COUNTER, name=com.codahale.metrics.servlet.InstrumentedFilter.activeRequests, count=0
Jan 06 00:50:25 jhipster-registry jhipsterRegistry:1c6ecec271be0ace5a86ec37a9c027b0: INFO - metrics : type=METER, name=com.codahale.metrics.servlet.InstrumentedFilter.errors, count=0, mean_rate=0.0, m1
=0.0, m5=0.0, m15=0.0, rate_unit=events/second
Jan 06 00:50:25 jhipster-registry jhipsterRegistry:1c6ecec271be0ace5a86ec37a9c027b0: INFO - metrics : type=METER, name=com.codahale.metrics.servlet.InstrumentedFilter.responseCodes.other, count=0, mean
_rate=0.0, m1=0.0, m5=0.0, m15=0.0, rate_unit=events/second
Jan 06 00:50:25 jhipster-registry jhipsterRegistry:1c6ecec271be0ace5a86ec37a9c027b0: INFO - metrics : type=METER, name=com.codahale.metrics.servlet.InstrumentedFilter.responseCodes.noContent, count=0,
mean_rate=0.0, m1=0.0, m5=0.0, m15=0.0, rate_unit=events/second
Jan 06 00:50:25 jhipster-registry jhipsterRegistry:1c6ecec271be0ace5a86ec37a9c027b0: INFO - metrics : type=METER, name=com.codahale.metrics.servlet.InstrumentedFilter.responseCodes.created, count=0, me
an_rate=0.0, m1=0.0, m5=0.0, m15=0.0, rate_unit=events/second
Jan 06 00:50:25 jhipster-registry jhipsterRegistry:1c6ecec271be0ace5a86ec37a9c027b0: INFO - metrics : type=GAUGE, name=jvm.threads.waiting.count, value=35
Jan 06 00:50:25 jhipster-registry jhipsterRegistry:1c6ecec271be0ace5a86ec37a9c027b0: INFO - metrics : type=METER, name=com.codahale.metrics.servlet.InstrumentedFilter.timeouts, count=0, mean_rate=0.0,
m1=0.0, m5=0.0, m15=0.0, rate_unit=events/second
Jan 06 00:50:25 jhipster-registry jhipsterRegistry:1c6ecec271be0ace5a86ec37a9c027b0: INFO - metrics : type=METER, name=com.codahale.metrics.servlet.InstrumentedFilter.responseCodes.badRequest, count=0,
mean_rate=0.0, m1=0.0, m5=0.0, m15=0.0, rate_unit=events/second
Jan 06 00:50:25 jhipster-registry jhipsterRegistry:1c6ecec271be0ace5a86ec37a9c027b0: INFO - metrics : type=METER, name=com.codahale.metrics.servlet.InstrumentedFilter.responseCodes.serverError, count=
0, mean_rate=0.0, m1=0.0, m5=0.0, m15=0.0, rate_unit=events/second
Jan 06 00:50:25 jhipster-registry jhipsterRegistry:1c6ecec271be0ace5a86ec37a9c027b0: INFO - metrics : type=TIMER, name=io.github.jhipster.registry.web.rest.EurekaResource.eureka, count=9, min=0.1238, m
ax=24.8306, mean=0.289032498403221776, stddev=0.9136504409448479, median=0.1814, p75=0.5463, p98=3.2806, p99=24.8306, p999=24.8306, mean_rate=0.0039669634566215205, m1=8.06499471968017E-15, m
5=4.7200528439382226E-5, m15=0.0011439732965072222, rate_unit=events/second, duration_unit=milliseconds
Jan 06 00:50:25 jhipster-registry jhipsterRegistry:1c6ecec271be0ace5a86ec37a9c027b0: INFO - metrics : type=TIMER, name=com.codahale.metrics.servlet.InstrumentedFilter.requests, count=167, min=1.5781, m
ax=1474.1219, mean=248.0257140750610202, stddev=50.68559718083201, median=271.8671, p75=294.5749, p95=294.5749, p98=294.5749, p99=294.5749, p999=294.5749, mean_rate=0.07434389235267787, m1=0.016619891740
13107, m5=0.014972285096673268, m15=0.07897246144133883, rate_unit=events/second, duration_unit=milliseconds
Jan 06 00:50:25 jhipster-registry jhipsterRegistry:1c6ecec271be0ace5a86ec37a9c027b0: INFO - metrics : type=TIMER, name=io.github.jhipster.registry.web.rest.EurekaResource.replicas, count=0, min=0.
0, max=0.0, mean=0.0, stddev=0.0, median=0.0, p75=0.0, p95=0.0, p98=0.0, p99=0.0, p999=0.0, mean_rate=0.0, m1=0.0, m5=0.0, m15=0.0, rate_unit=events/second, duration_unit=milliseconds
Jan 06 00:50:25 jhipster-registry jhipsterRegistry:1c6ecec271be0ace5a86ec37a9c027b0: INFO - metrics : type=TIMER, name=io.github.jhipster.registry.web.rest.LogsResource.changeLevel, count=0, min=0.0, m
ax=0.0, mean=0.0, stddev=0.0, median=0.0, p75=0.0, p95=0.0, p98=0.0, p99=0.0, p999=0.0, mean_rate=0.0, m1=0.0, m5=0.0, m15=0.0, rate_unit=events/second, duration_unit=milliseconds
Jan 06 00:50:25 jhipster-registry jhipsterRegistry:1c6ecec271be0ace5a86ec37a9c027b0: INFO - metrics : type=TIMER, name=io.github.jhipster.registry.web.rest.EurekaResource.lastn, count=0, min=0.0, max=
0.0, mean=0.0, stddev=0.0, median=0.0, p75=0.0, p98=0.0, p99=0.0, p999=0.0, mean_rate=0.0, m1=0.0, m5=0.0, m15=0.0, rate_unit=events/second, duration_unit=milliseconds
Jan 06 00:50:25 jhipster-registry jhipsterRegistry:1c6ecec271be0ace5a86ec37a9c027b0: INFO - metrics : type=TIMER, name=io.github.jhipster.registry.web.rest.AccountResource.isAuthenticated, count=0, min
=0.0, max=0.0, mean=0.0, stddev=0.0, median=0.0, p75=0.0, p95=0.0, p98=0.0, p99=0.0, p999=0.0, mean_rate=0.0, m1=0.0, m5=0.0, m15=0.0, rate_unit=events/second, duration_unit=milliseconds
Jan 06 00:50:25 jhipster-registry jhipsterRegistry:1c6ecec271be0ace5a86ec37a9c027b0: INFO - metrics : type=TIMER, name=io.github.jhipster.registry.web.rest.LogsResource.getList, count=0, min=0.0, max=
0.0, mean=0.0, stddev=0.0, median=0.0, p75=0.0, p98=0.0, p99=0.0, p999=0.0, mean_rate=0.0, m1=0.0, m5=0.0, m15=0.0, rate_unit=events/second, duration_unit=milliseconds
Jan 06 00:50:25 jhipster-registry jhipsterRegistry:1c6ecec271be0ace5a86ec37a9c027b0: INFO - metrics : type=TIMER, name=io.github.jhipster.registry.web.rest.AccountResource.getAccount, count=9, min=0.08
3, max=13.8581, mean=0.1101395240741859, stddev=0.446131233056011565, median=0.083, p75=0.083, p95=0.1918, p98=0.2156, p99=0.3844, p999=13.8581, mean_rate=0.003975041098019476, m1=8.06499471968017E-15,
m5=4.7200528439382226E-5, m15=0.0011439732965072222, rate_unit=events/second, duration_unit=milliseconds
Jan 06 00:50:25 jhipster-registry jhipsterRegistry:1c6ecec271be0ace5a86ec37a9c027b0: INFO - metrics : type=TIMER, name=io.github.jhipster.registry.web.rest.UserJWTController.authorize, count=1, min=10
1.0463, max=101.0463, mean=101.0463, stddev=0.0, median=101.0463, p75=101.0463, p95=101.0463, p98=101.0463, p99=101.0463, p999=101.0463, mean_rate=4.41656292862948886E-4, m1=4.38187382478323BE-1B, m5=2.
5516489930957726-6, m15=1.816413473009020116E-4, rate_unit=events/second, duration_unit=milliseconds
Jan 06 00:50:25 jhipster-registry jhipsterRegistry:1c6ecec271be0ace5a86ec37a9c027b0: INFO - metrics : type=TIMER, name=io.github.jhipster.registry.web.rest.RoutesResource.getRoutes, count=0, min=0.0, m
ax=0.0, mean=0.0, stddev=0.0, median=0.0, p75=0.0, p98=0.0, p99=0.0, p999=0.0, mean_rate=0.0, m1=0.0, m5=0.0, m15=0.0, rate_unit=events/second, duration_unit=milliseconds
Jan 06 00:50:25 jhipster-registry jhipsterRegistry:1c6ecec271be0ace5a86ec37a9c027b0: INFO - metrics : type=TIMER, name=io.github.jhipster.registry.web.rest.SshResource.eureka, count=0, min=0.0, max=0.
0, mean=0.0, stddev=0.0, median=0.0, p75=0.0, p95=0.0, p98=0.0, p99=0.0, p999=0.0, mean_rate=0.0, m1=0.0, m5=0.0, m15=0.0, rate_unit=events/second, duration_unit=milliseconds

Kibana also provides a machine-learning tab where we can create a job to track the data and then choose any metric available to track it as a sum, count, high count, and so on.

Scaling up with Docker Swarm

Docker Swarm is Docker's orchestrating layer to manage the containers. It is a cluster management tool that focuses on creating replicas of your services, networks, as well as storage resources available to it and managing them.

The Docker Swarm is nothing more than a cluster of Docker nodes. They act as a manager or worker. One interesting feature to note is that a Docker container inside the Swarm can either be a manager or worker or both. This helps the swarm to allocate a new manager when the manager nodes go down.

At a high level, the manager nodes are responsible for cluster management tasks and execute containers. The workers are responsible for executing the containers only.

JHipster applications give us the flexibility to scale our entire application with a single command, with JHipster's `docker-compose sub-generator`:

```
> docker-compose scale <app-name>=<scale to>
```

Now we can scale the instances, using the following command:

```
> docker-compose scale invoice-app=2
```

The preceding command will spin another invoice instance and we can see it on the dashboard, as follows:

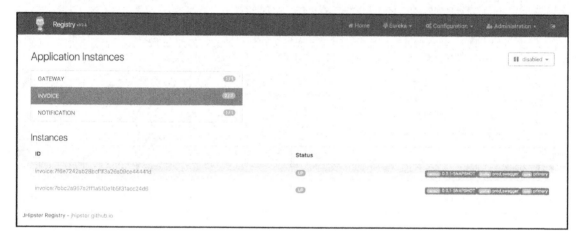

Summary

So far, we have seen how to generate, set up, and start JHipster Registry and console, and, we have looked at their features. This was followed by how to scale the application with `docker-swarm`.

In the next chapter, we will see how to deploy the application to the Google Cloud using Kubernetes.

12
Deploying to the Cloud with Kubernetes

Kubernetes, also known as the container orchestration tool. As we have seen in the previous chapter, it comes with many additional features and is much easier to configure and manage. This makes Kubernetes a default choice for any container orchestration. The ability to mask the lower-level details and provide out-of-the-box service discovery, self-healing, and health checks attracted many companies and organizations to switch to Kubernetes. Aside from that, Kubernetes is the evolution of Google's internal orchestration tool.

In this chapter, we will cover the following topics:

- Generating Kubernetes configuration files with JHipster
- Walking through the generated files
- Deploying the application to Google Cloud with Kubernetes

Generating Kubernetes configuration files with JHipster

Knowing the components of Kubernetes and how it works is beyond the scope of this book. However, we will look at how JHipster simplifies microservices deployment with Kubernetes. Let's go ahead and generate the Kubernetes configuration file.

Similar to the `docker-compose` sub-generator, JHipster also comes bundled with a Kubernetes sub-generator. In order to use it, just like with `docker-compose`, we will create a new folder and name it Kubernetes. Then, we will go inside the folder to create the configuration files.

We can create Kubernetes configuration files with the following command and then answer the questions that the sub-generator asks us:

```
> mkdir kubernetes && cd kubernetes
```

To install kubectl, please follow the instructions at Kubernetes' website (`https://kubernetes.io/docs/tasks/tools/install-kubectl/`).

 Kubernetes sub-generator needs kubectl (v1.2 or later) to be installed on your computer. kubectl is the command line interface for Kubernetes.

We can also install Cloud SDK from Google Cloud, which will also install kubectl. To set up gcloud:

1. Download the binary (based on your operating system) from `https://cloud.google.com/sdk/`.
2. Then, install the application by following the steps given on the website (make sure that you have python installed).
3. Once installed, set up Google Cloud. In order to set up Google Cloud, run `gcloud init`.
4. This will then ask you to log in to your Google account:

```
> jhipster kubernetes
```

 As we have seen already, Kubernetes needs separate tools for running locally (that is for development purposes). Therefore, if you need to do things locally, please install minikube from Kubernetes.

The first question the sub-generator asks is which type of application we'd like to deploy. It provides two options, which are monolithic and microservices. We will choose the microservices option:

```
? Which *type* of application would you like to deploy? (Use arrow keys)
> Monolithic application
  Microservice application
```

Then, it asks us to enter the root directory. We will select the default option since our directories are present as the siblings of the Kubernetes folder:

```
? Which *type* of application would you like to deploy? Microservice application
? Enter the root directory where your gateway(s) and microservices are located (../)
```

Then, the sub-generator will list all the folders with our JHipster generated application. Here, it will list all three applications that we need—**gateway**, **invoice**, and **notification**. Select all three applications and hit enter:

```
? Which *type* of application would you like to deploy? Microservice application
? Enter the root directory where your gateway(s) and microservices are located ../
3 applications found at /Users/sendilkumar/Dev/Book/

? Which applications do you want to include in your configuration? (Press <space> to select, <a> to toggle all, <i> to inverse selection)
>o gateway
 o invoice
 o notification
```

Then, it will ask us to provide the password for the registry service. In our case, it is JHipster Registry. We will select the default one for now, but it is generally advisable to use a strong password here:

```
? Which *type* of application would you like to deploy? Microservice application
? Enter the root directory where your gateway(s) and microservices are located ../
3 applications found at /Users/sendilkumar/Dev/Book/

? Which applications do you want to include in your configuration? gateway, invoice, notification
JHipster registry detected as the service discovery and configuration provider used by your apps
? Enter the admin password used to secure the JHipster Registry (admin)
```

Afterward, it will ask us for the namespace that we need to use in Kubernetes. So, what is a namespace?

We can consider namespaces as a group within which resources should be named uniquely. When the cluster is shared between different users or teams, namespaces can provide resource quotas for them. Ideally, namespaces should be used only for a larger team. For smaller teams, it is better to go with default options. Kubernetes, by default, provides three namespaces, which are as follows:

- `Default`: When you start a container or pod without providing any namespaces, they will end up in the default namespace
- `Kube-system`: This namespace contains Kubernetes system-based objects
- `Kube-admin`: This is a public namespace, which will be shown to all the users publically without any authentication

We will select the default namespace here:

```
? Which *type* of application would you like to deploy? Microservice application
? Enter the root directory where your gateway(s) and microservices are located ../
3 applications found at /Users/sendilkumar/Dev/Book/

? Which applications do you want to include in your configuration? gateway, invoice, notification
JHipster registry detected as the service discovery and configuration provider used by your apps
? Enter the admin password used to secure the JHipster Registry admin
? What should we use for the Kubernetes namespace? (default)
```

Then, the sub-generator will ask for our Docker repository name so that Kubernetes can use this Docker repository to pull the images (the login username of the Docker repository):

```
? Which *type* of application would you like to deploy? Microservice application
? Enter the root directory where your gateway(s) and microservices are located ../
3 applications found at /Users/sendilkumar/Dev/Book/

? Which applications do you want to include in your configuration? gateway, invoice, notification
JHipster registry detected as the service discovery and configuration provider used by your apps
? Enter the admin password used to secure the JHipster Registry admin
? What should we use for the Kubernetes namespace? default
? What should we use for the base Docker repository name?
```

Then, the sub-generator will ask for our command so that we can push the image to the Docker repository. We will select the default command here:

```
? Which *type* of application would you like to deploy? Microservice application
? Enter the root directory where your gateway(s) and microservices are located ../
3 applications found at /Users/sendilkumar/Dev/Book/

? Which applications do you want to include in your configuration? gateway, invoice, notification
JHipster registry detected as the service discovery and configuration provider used by your apps
? Enter the admin password used to secure the JHipster Registry admin
? What should we use for the Kubernetes namespace? default
? What should we use for the base Docker repository name? sendilkumarn
? What command should we use for push Docker image to repository? (docker push)
```

Then, it will ask whether we need the JHipster-console for log aggregation, and we will select **Yes**:

```
? Which *type* of application would you like to deploy? Microservice application
? Enter the root directory where your gateway(s) and microservices are located ../
3 applications found at /Users/sendilkumar/Dev/Book/

? Which applications do you want to include in your configuration? gateway, invoice, notification
JHipster registry detected as the service discovery and configuration provider used by your apps
? Enter the admin password used to secure the JHipster Registry admin
? What should we use for the Kubernetes namespace? default
? What should we use for the base Docker repository name? sendilkumarn
? What command should we use for push Docker image to repository? docker push
? Do you want to use JHipster Console for log aggregation (ELK)? (Y/n)
```

JHipster also comes with Prometheus integration, so the next question will be whether we would like to export our services to Prometheus. It needs a Prometheus operator in general to work. We will select **No** for this:

```
? Which *type* of application would you like to deploy? Microservice application
? Enter the root directory where your gateway(s) and microservices are located ../
3 applications found at /Users/sendilkumar/Dev/Book/

? Which applications do you want to include in your configuration? gateway, invoice, notification
JHipster registry detected as the service discovery and configuration provider used by your apps
? Enter the admin password used to secure the JHipster Registry admin
? What should we use for the Kubernetes namespace? default
? What should we use for the base Docker repository name? sendilkumarn
? What command should we use for push Docker image to repository? docker push
? Do you want to use JHipster Console for log aggregation (ELK)? Yes
? Do you want to export your services for Prometheus (needs a running prometheus operator)? (Y/n)
```

Then, the generator will ask us to choose the Kubernetes service type. So, what is the service type?

In Kubernetes, everything that we deploy is a pod. These pods are managed by replication controllers, which can create and destroy any pods. Each pod needs an identifier, so they are tagged with an IP address. This dynamic nature of pods will lead to a lot of problems for other pods that depend on them. To come up with a solution for this problem, Kubernetes introduced services. Services are nothing but a logical grouping of unique pods which have policies attached to them. These policies are applicable for all the pods inside the services, but we need to publish these services to the external world to access them.

 One of the most powerful features of Kubernetes is that they help to maintain the number of replicas of pods consistently. The replication controller helps to maintain the pods count by automatically shutting down and booting up the pods.

Kubernetes gives us four different service types, as follows:

- `Cluster IP`: This is the default type. This will assign the cluster's internal IP and make it visible within the cluster itself.
- `NodePort`: This will expose the service to a static port in the Node's IP. The port will be random and will be chosen between `30000-32767`.
- `LoadBalancer`: This will expose the service externally. Kubernetes will assign an IP automatically. This will create a route to the NodePort and Cluster IP internally.
- `Ingress`: An Ingress is a special option that Kubernetes provides. This will provide load-balancing, SSL termination, and name-based virtual hosting to the services.

We will select the `LoadBalancer` option:

```
? Which *type* of application would you like to deploy? Microservice application
? Enter the root directory where your gateway(s) and microservices are located ../
3 applications found at /Users/sendilkumar/Dev/Book/

? Which applications do you want to include in your configuration? gateway, invoice, notification
JHipster registry detected as the service discovery and configuration provider used by your apps
? Enter the admin password used to secure the JHipster Registry admin
? What should we use for the Kubernetes namespace? default
? What should we use for the base Docker repository name? sendilkumar
? What command should we use for push Docker image to repository? docker push
? Do you want to use JHipster Console for log aggregation (ELK)? Yes
? Do you want to export your services for Prometheus (needs a running prometheus operator)? No
? Choose the kubernetes service type for your edge services LoadBalancer - Let a kubernetes cloud provider automatically assign an IP
```

That's it. This will generate the necessary configuration files for us to deploy the application with Kubernetes. Next up, we will check the files that have been generated.

Walking through the generated files

The files generated by JHipster are in the following structure. That is, each application will have its own folder and the files related to that service will be present inside it.

We will start with the gateway application. There will be three generated files, which will be the `gateway-service`, `gateway-mysql`, and `gateway-deployment.yml` files.

The following is the `gateway-service.yml` file:

```
apiVersion: v1
kind: Service
metadata:
    name: gateway
    namespace: default
    labels:
        app: gateway
spec:
    selector:
        app: gateway
    type: LoadBalancer
ports:
 - name: web
    port: 8080
```

The first line defines the API version of Kubernetes, followed by the kind of template or object that this template carries. This template will have a service inside of it.

Then, we will have the metadata information. Kubernetes uses this metadata information to group certain services together. In the metadata, we can define:

- The service name
- The namespace it belongs to
- The labels, which are key and value pairs

Then, we will define the spec. The spec in the Kubernetes object will provide the state of the service. In the spec, we can define the number of replicas we need. We can also define the selector, within which we can specify the service with identifiers. We can also specify the type of the service. Kubernetes will take the information from this spec and then maintain the application in the state provided (we will have a look at the spec gateway in a while), followed by the ports in which port the application should run. This is similar to the Dockerfile, so we are exposing the 8080 port for the gateway service.

Then, we have the gateway-mysql.yml file, where we have defined our MySQL server for the gateway application. The difference here is that the spec points to gateway-mysql, which is defined in the same file and is exposed on port 3306:

```
apiVersion: v1
kind: Service
metadata:
    name: gateway-mysql
    namespace: default
spec:
    selector:
        app: gateway-mysql
ports:
    - port: 3306
```

In the gateway-mysql app declaration, we have specified the database and environment properties that are needed for our application to run. Here, the kind is mentioned as **deployment**. The job of the deployment object is to change the state of the services to the state that is defined in the deployment object.

Here, we have defined a single replica of the MySQL server, followed by the spec, where we have mentioned the version of MySQL that we need (the container). This is then followed by the username, password, and then the database schema. We can also specify the volume information with volume mounts for persistent storage:

Note: we can also define a spec inside a spec object (as shown in the following code):

```
apiVersion: extensions/v1beta1
kind: Deployment
metadata:
    ... // metadata
spec:
    replicas: 1
```

```
... // metadata related information
spec:
    ... //volumes and other information
    containers:
     - name: mysql
       image: mysql:5.7.20
      env:
         ...  // environment details
      ports:
         ... // port
      volumeMounts:
         ... //Mapping the volume to the external persistent location
```

Similarly, we have `gateway-deployment.yml`, in which we have defined the gateway application and its environment properties along with the other details like ports, probes and so on.

A similar approach is done for both the invoice and notification services. You can find them in their respective folders.

In `JHipster-registry`, alongside `Service` and `Deployment`, we have defined Secret and StatefulSet.

The secret is used to handle passwords. It will be an opaque type and the password is base64 encoded.

Then, we have the StatefulSet, which are similar to pod except they have a sticky identity. Pods are dynamic in nature. These pods have a persistent identifier that is maintained throughout. It makes sense for a registry server to be defined as a StatefulSet, since it is essential that the registry server should be identified by a persistent identifier. This enables all services to connect to that single endpoint and get the necessary information. If the registry server is down, then communication between the services will also have problems, since the services connect to other services via the registry server.

There are various options that are available to set the controller, which are as follows:

- **Replica Set**: Provides a replica of pods at any time with selectors
- **Replica Controller**: Provides a replica of pods without any selectors
- **StatefulSet**: Makes the pod unique by providing it with a persistent identifier
- **DaemonSet**: Provides a copy of the pod which is going to be run

The JHipster Registry is configured in a cluster and with high availability. The UI access to the JHipster Registry is also restricted to the cluster for better security.

Similarly, configuration files are generated for the JHipster Console, and they are placed in a console folder, which is `jhipster-console.yml`, where the JHipster Console is also defined.

The JHipster Console runs on an ELK stack, so we need Elasticsearch, which is defined in `jhipster-elasticsearch.yml`, followed by Logstash in the `jhipster-logstash.yml` file.

Deploying the application to Google Cloud with Kubernetes

We have created Kubernetes configuration files with the `jhipster kubernetes` command. The next step is to build the artifacts and deploy them into Google Cloud.

Kubernetes will use the image from the Docker Registry. We configured the Docker username when we generated the application, so the first step will be to tag those images and then push them to our Docker repository.

To do so, we will do the following:

We will open the terminal and go to the Kubernetes folder that we have generated:

```
> docker image tag gateway sendilkumarn/gateway
```

And we will push this image into the Docker repository:

```
> docker push sendilkumarn/gateway
```

 Note: you have to log in to the Docker Hub before pushing the image. You can login to Docker using the `docker login` command followed by your username and password. If you don't have an account, you can create one at the following link: `https://cloud.docker.com/`.

Similarly, push the invoice application to the Docker repository:

```
> docker image tag invoice sendilkumarn/invoice
> docker push sendilkumarn/invoice
```

Do the same for notification:

```
> docker image tag notification sendilkumarn/notification
> docker push sendilkumarn/notification
```

This will push gateway, invoice, and notification to the Docker repository. We can check this in the Docker console:

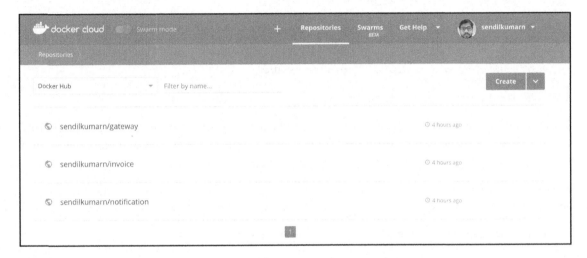

Now, we can connect to gcloud and deploy our containers with Kubernetes.

This assumes that you have set up gcloud SDK and kubectl on your machine.

First, we will log in to the gcloud via the Terminal. In order to do that, open your Terminal:

```
> gcloud init  // if this is the first time you are using gcloud (Ignore
this step if you logged in already)
```

Then, gcloud will ask you to log in to your google account. Once validated, this will list the projects that you might already have.

Here, we can choose **[31] Create a new project** by entering the number before creating a new project. Then, press enter. It will ask you to enter the project information and then configure a few Google services for that project. Then, gcloud will list all the available regions and you can choose a region that suits you.

If you have already logged in to the console and used it for other projects, then you can switch projects using the following command:

```
> gcloud config set project <project-name>
```

This will set the project, region, and the setting chosen as the default.

Then, you have to enable Kubernetes in our application. We can do this by logging in to our Google Cloud console via the browser. Then, select the project that we have just created and go to https://console.cloud.google.com/kubernetes/list.

This will create a cluster for your project. Instead, you can create a cluster using the `gcloud` command:

```
> gcloud container clusters create online-store
```

The following is the output of the preceding command:

```
gcloud container clusters create --help
✗ ↑ ➤╼   gcloud container clusters create online-store
Creating cluster online-store...done.
Created [https://container.googleapis.com/v1/projects/online-store-191519/zones/europe-west3-a/clusters/online-store].
kubeconfig entry generated for online-store.
NAME          LOCATION       MASTER_VERSION  MASTER_IP       MACHINE_TYPE   NODE_VERSION  NUM_NODES  STATUS
online-store  europe-west3-a  1.7.11-gke.1    35.198.128.163  n1-standard-1  1.7.11-gke.1  3          RUNNING
```

Thus, the cluster is created with 3 nodes.

Then, we can go to our Kubernetes folder and start deploying the services using kubectl:

```
> kubectl apply -f <project-name>
```

The output will be as follows:

```
†  dev/Book/kubernetes    kubectl apply -f console
deployment "jhipster-console" created
service "jhipster-console" created
deployment "jhipster-elasticsearch" created
service "jhipster-elasticsearch" created
deployment "jhipster-logstash" created
service "jhipster-logstash" created
configmap "logstash-config" created
†  dev/Book/kubernetes    kubectl apply -f registry
configmap "application-config" created
secret "registry-secret" created
service "jhipster-registry" created
statefulset "jhipster-registry" created
†  dev/Book/kubernetes    kubectl apply -f gateway
deployment "gateway" created
deployment "gateway-mysql" created
service "gateway-mysql" created
service "gateway" created
†  dev/Book/kubernetes    kubectl apply -f invoice
deployment "invoice" created
deployment "invoice-mysql" created
service "invoice-mysql" created
service "invoice" created
†  dev/Book/kubernetes    kubectl apply -f notification
deployment "notification" created
deployment "notification-mongodb" created
service "notification-mongodb" created
service "notification" created
```

This will create all the applications in the Google Cloud environment, under your project.

You can check the pods deployment process using the following command:

```
> kubectl get pods --watch
```

This will list down the `pods` that are spinning up and shutting down:

NAME	READY	STATUS	RESTARTS	AGE
gateway-1784569679-2hkbr	0/1	Pending	0	7m
gateway-mysql-1968103184-cxz53	1/1	Running	0	7m
invoice-2850039085-wstm2	0/1	Running	1	7m
invoice-mysql-2912488894-k0gpg	1/1	Running	0	7m
jhipster-console-454754796-mpbpq	1/1	Running	0	7m
jhipster-logstash-991753751-qkrjz	1/1	Running	0	7m
jhipster-registry-0	1/1	Running	0	7m
jhipster-registry-1	1/1	Running	0	7m
notification-2844814829-wvk9m	0/1	Pending	0	7m
notification-mongodb-41817184-r8b99	1/1	Running	0	7m

You can also get the logs of the application using the following command:

```
> kubectl logs <name as shown above>
```

The following is the output:

You can get the application's external IP using this piece of code:

```
> kubectl get svc gateway
```

This will list the application's name, type, IP address, external address, ports, and uptime:

NAME	TYPE	CLUSTER-IP	EXTERNAL-IP	PORT(S)	AGE
gateway	LoadBalancer	10.39.246.178	35.198.80.78	8080:31770/TCP	14m

We can find the same information on the Google Cloud console:

The application can be accessed at the preceding **External-IP**:

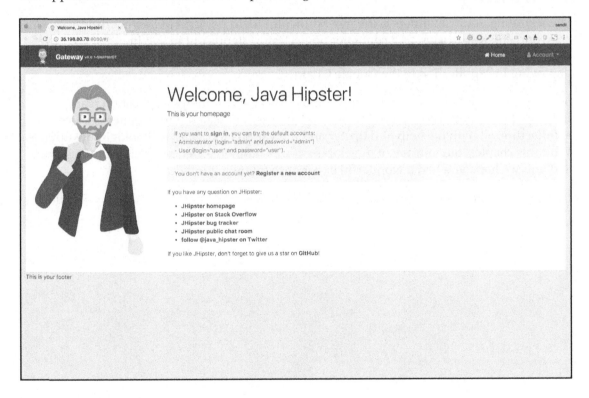

You can also scale the application by using the following command:

```
> kubectl scale deployment <app-name> --replicas <number-of-replicas>
```

 The JHipster-registry is deployed in headless mode. In order to check the JHipster registry, we can explicitly expose the service by using this command—**kubectl expose service jhipster-registry --type=NodePort --name=exposed-registry**—and then we can access the application via `exposed-registry`.

Summary

Orchestrating your containers is the most difficult task to perform in the microservices environment. Kubernetes, as a container orchestrator, stands out in solving this. We have seen how to generate the configuration file for Kubernetes with JHipster, followed by deploying the application to the Google Cloud.

So far, we've seen how we can develop and deploy an e-commerce application using JHipster. We started with a monolith and we successfully scaled it into a microservice architecture, all with the help of JHipster and the various tools and technologies it supports. With this chapter, our journey of developing the e-commerce web application comes to an end and we hope you had a wonderful experience following it though.

In the next chapter, we will see how you can use JHipster further to create an application with a React client-side application, so stay tuned.

13
Using React for the Client-Side

So far, we have seen how to build web applications and microservices with Angular as the client-side framework. AngularJS was the most popular client-side framework until the new Angular 2 framework was released. Angular 2 caused a major disruption due to its backward incompatible architecture and gave way to more people migrating to React. Hence, the tides have shifted and now React is the most popular and sought-after client-side framework, followed by Angular. JHipster added experimental support for React with version 4.11 and with JHipster Version 5.0; React support will become BETA and ready for mainstream use.

In this chapter, we will cover the following topics:

- Generating an application with React client-side
- Technical stack and source code
- Generating an entity with React client side

Generating an application with React client side

Let's dive in straight away and create a React application with JHipster. You will need to open a Terminal to run the commands:

1. Create a new folder and navigate to it by running `mkdir jhipster-react && cd jhipster-react`.
2. Now run the `jhipster` command in the Terminal. If you are running JHipster version 4.x instead of 5.x, then you will have to pass the experimental flag by running `jhipster --experimental`.

3. JHipster will start with prompts; let's select default options for everything except for the question **Which *Framework* would you like to use for the client?** For this question, choose **[BETA] React** and proceed.

4. Once all the prompts are completed, JHipster will generate the application and start installing dependencies before formatting the code using Prettier (`https://prettier.io/`) and starting the webpack build.

> You can run `yarn prettier:format` to format the client-side code anytime. It will also be automatically run whenever you commit something with a git pre-commit hook.

Our selected options will look as follows:

```
? Which *type* of application would you like to create? Monolithic
application (recommended for simple projects)
? What is the base name of your application? jhreact
? What is your default Java package name? com.jhipsterbook.demo
? Do you want to use the JHipster Registry to configure, monitor and scale
your application? No
? Which *type* of authentication would you like to use? JWT authentication
(stateless, with a token)
? Which *type* of database would you like to use? SQL (H2, MySQL, MariaDB,
PostgreSQL, Oracle, MSSQL)
? Which *production* database would you like to use? MySQL
? Which *development* database would you like to use? H2 with disk-based
persistence
? Do you want to use the Spring cache abstraction? Yes, with the Ehcache
implementation (local cache, for a single node)
? Do you want to use Hibernate 2nd level cache? Yes
? Would you like to use Maven or Gradle for building the backend? Maven
? Which other technologies would you like to use?
? Which *Framework* would you like to use for the client? [BETA] React
? Would you like to enable *SASS* support using the LibSass stylesheet
preprocessor? No
? Would you like to enable internationalization support? Yes
? Please choose the native language of the application English
? Please choose additional languages to install Chinese (Simplified)
? Besides JUnit and Karma, which testing frameworks would you like to use?
? Would you like to install other generators from the JHipster Marketplace?
No
```

That's it; we are done. Our first JHipster React application was created successfully. Now let's start the application to play around.

We will choose the default Maven build option which JHipster created a wrapper for already, so let's start our server by running . /mvnw in a Terminal.

Maven will download the necessary dependencies and will start the Spring Boot application using the embedded Undertow container. You could choose Gradle instead of Maven if you prefer. Once the application successfully starts, we will see the following in the console:

```
2018-03-04 16:37:48.096 INFO 4730 --- [ restartedMain]
com.jhipsterbook.demo.JhreactApp :
----------------------------------------------------------
  Application 'jhreact' is running! Access URLs:
  Local: http://localhost:8080
  External: http://192.168.2.7:8080
  Profile(s): [swagger, dev]
----------------------------------------------------------
```

Visit the URL(http://localhost:8080) in your favorite browser to see the application in action:

You will see the home screen with the hipster dude looking back at you. Notice the React tattoo on his neck.

Go ahead and log in using the default admin user and play around.

The application looks exactly same as the Angular application we built earlier, except for the image, of course, and has all the same account and administration modules. This will make it more interesting for us to see the technical stack and source code.

Technical stack and source code

Before we dive into the generated code, let's talk about the technical stack. We already looked at React in Chapter 2, *Getting Started with JHipster*, but let's recap.

React is a view rendering library created by Jordan Walke in 2011, and was open sourced in May 2013. It is maintained and backed by Facebook and has a huge community behind it. React follows the JS approach for HTML, where the markup code is written using JavaScript. To reduce verbosity, React uses a syntax sugar for Javascript called JSX (https:/ /reactjs.org/docs/introducing-jsx.html) to describe view elements. It looks similar to HTML, but it is not exactly HTML as some of the standard HTML attributes such as class, for example, is renamed to className, and attribute names are written using camelCase rather than dash-case.

For example, the following is a JSX snippet. You always need to have to use React in context for JSX to work:

```
const element = <div><strong>Hello there</strong></div>
```

When it comes to TypeScript, the JSX extension becomes TSX.

React uses a concept called Virtual DOM to improve the rendering efficiency. Virtual DOM is a lightweight copy of the actual DOM, and by comparing the virtual DOM after an update against the virtual DOM snapshot before the update, React can decide what exactly changed and render only that on to the actual DOM, hence making render cycles efficient and fast.

React components can have their own state and you can pass properties to a component, which are available to the component as props.

Unlike Angular, React is not a full-fledged MVVM framework. It is just a view rendering library and hence when building React applications, we would always have to add a few more libraries for things like state management, routing, and so on.

Technical stacks

The following are the technical stacks used by JHipster when React is chosen as the client side framework:

- **Rendering**: React written using TypeScript
- **State management**: Redux + React Redux + Redux Promise Middleware + Redux Thunk
- **Routing**: React router
- **HTTP**: Axios
- **Responsive design**: Bootstrap 4 + Reactstrap
- **Linting**: Tslint
- **Utilities**: Lodash
- **Unit testing**: Karma + Mocha + Chai + Enzyme
- **Build**: Webpack

Let's look at some of the most important components of the stack.

Using TypeScript

The client side is built using React, but instead of going with the traditional Javascript ES6, we are using TypeScript as the language of choice. This gives you the flexibility to use some of the concepts that you may be already familiar with if you come from a server-side background. It also provides static type checking, which makes development more efficient and less error-prone.

 Visit `https://github.com/piotrwitek/react-redux-typescript-guide` to learn about how to make the most out of Typescript + React.

State management with Redux and friends

React provides basic state management within React components, but sometimes it is not sufficient, especially when your application needs to share state between multiple components. State management solutions like Flux, Redux, and MobX and quite popular in the React world and JHipster uses Redux as the state management layer.

When should you use the React component state?

- **If the variable can always be calculated using a prop**: Don't use component state, calculate the variable during rendering
- **If the variable is not used in rendering but to hold data**: Don't use component state, use private class fields
- **If the variable is obtained from an API and is required by more than one component**: Don't use component state, use Redux global state and pass the variable as a prop

Redux (`https://redux.js.org/`) is a predictable state management solution for JavaScript, evolved from the Flux concept (`https://facebook.github.io/flux/`). Redux provides a global immutable store which can only be updated by emitting or dispatching actions. An action is an object which describes what changed, and it uses a pure reducer function to transform the state. A reducer is a pure function which takes in the current state and action and returns a new state.

React Redux is a binding for Redux that provides a higher order component called `connect` for React, which is used to connect React components to the Redux store. Let's take a look at `src/main/webapp/app/modules/home/home.tsx`, for example:

```
export class Home extends React.Component<IHomeProp, IHomeState> {
  ...
}

const mapStateToProps = storeState => ({
  account: storeState.authentication.account,
  isAuthenticated: storeState.authentication.isAuthenticated
});
const mapDispatchToProps = { getSession };

export default connect(mapStateToProps, mapDispatchToProps)(Home);
```

The `mapStateToProps` function is used to map properties from the global Redux store to the components props. The `mapDispatchToProps` function is used to wrap the given functions with the Redux dispatch call.

Redux Promise Middleware (`https://github.com/pburtchaell/redux-promise-middleware`) is used to handle asynchronous action payloads. It accepts a Promise and dispatches pending, fulfilled, and rejected actions based on the Promise state. It is useful when Redux actions are making HTTP requests or performing async operations.

Redux Thunk (`https://github.com/gaearon/redux-thunk`) is another middleware used to chain actions. It is useful when an action has to call another action based on certain conditions or in general to handle side effects.

Routing with React Router

React Router (`https://reacttraining.com/react-router/web/guides/philosophy`) is used for client-side routing. The default setup with JHipster is to use Hash History-based routing. It provides a simple component-based routing along with a flexible API for advanced routing setups. Routes can be defined anywhere in the application alongside the normal React rendering code. JHipster provides some custom wrappers such as `PrivateRoute` to enable authorization-based routing.

Let's take a look at `src/main/webapp/app/routes.tsx`, for example:

```
const Routes = () => (
  <div className="view-routes">
    <Route exact path="/" component={Home} />
    <Route path="/login" component={Login} />
    <Route path="/logout" component={Logout} />
    <Route path="/register" component={Register} />
    <Route path="/activate/:key?" component={Activate} />
    <Route path="/reset/request" component={PasswordResetInit} />
    <Route path="/reset/finish/:key?" component={PasswordResetFinish} />
    <PrivateRoute path="/admin" component={Admin} />
    <PrivateRoute path="/account" component={Account} />
    <Route path="**" component={Entities} />
  </div>
);

export default Routes;
```

HTTP requests using Axios

Axios (`https://github.com/axios/axios`) is a Promise-based HTTP client. It is a powerful and flexible library with a very straightforward API. It is used to fetch data from the JHipster application's server-side REST endpoints from Redux actions. The resulting Promise is resolved by the Redux Promise Middleware to provide data to the reducer.

The following shows a Redux action with an asynchronous payload:

```
export const getRoles = () => ({
  type: ACTION_TYPES.FETCH_ROLES,
  payload: axios.get(`${apiUrl}/authorities`)
});
```

Bootstrap components using Reactstrap

JHipster uses Bootstrap 4 as its UI framework and since we are building a React application, it makes sense to use a Native React binding instead of Bootstrap's JQuery-based components. Reactstrap (`https://reactstrap.github.io/`) provides pure React components for Bootstrap 4. We also make use of the Availity reactstrap Validation (`https://availity.github.io/availity-reactstrap-validation/`) library, which provides form validation support for Reactstrap form elements.

Let's take a look at `src/main/webapp/app/modules/login/login-modal.tsx`, for example:

```
<Modal isOpen={this.props.showModal} toggle={handleClose} backdrop="static"
id="login-page">
  <AvForm onSubmit={this.handleSubmit}>
    <ModalHeader toggle={handleClose} id="login-title">
      ...
    </ModalHeader>
    <ModalBody>
      <div className="row">
        ...
        <div className="col-md-12">
          <AvField
            name="username"
            label={...}
            placeholder={...}
            required
            errorMessage="Username cannot be empty!"
          />
          ...
        </div>
```

```
      </div>
      <Alert color="warning">
        ...
      </Alert>
      ...
    </ModalBody>
    <ModalFooter>
      ...
    </ModalFooter>
  </AvForm>
</Modal>
```

Unit testing setup

JHipster uses a combination of Karma, Mocha, Chai, and Enzyme to unit test the client-side components.

Karma (https://karma-runner.github.io/2.0/index.html) is used as the test runner and Mocha (https://mochajs.org/) is used as the testing framework. Chai (http://chaijs.com/) is an assertion library with great plugin support. We use its BDD (Behavior-driven development) style assertions. Enzyme (http://airbnb.io/enzyme/) is a testing utility for React which makes it easy to unit test React components. In combination, these libraries provide a rich and intuitive testing environment for React.

Let's run the generated unit tests. Run `yarn test` in a Terminal.

Generating source code

Let's take a look at the generated code. Since we already saw the server-side code in previous chapters, we will only look at the client-side code here:

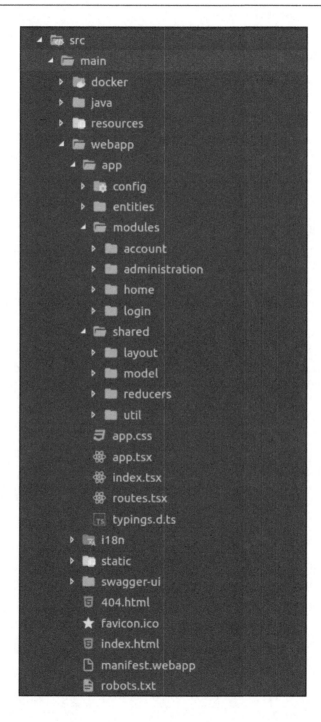

The structure is quite similar to what we saw for Angular, but the React code is organized slightly differently. We are concerned only about the code inside `src/main/webapp/app` as everything else is exactly the same as what we saw for the Angular application.

Let's take a look at some of the important parts of the code:

- `index.tsx`: This is the entry point of our application. This is where we bootstrap React to the `root div` and initialize the Redux store:

```
...
const devTools = process.env.NODE_ENV === 'development' ? <DevTools
/> : null;
const store = initStore();
registerLocales(store);

const actions = bindActionCreators({ clearAuthentication },
store.dispatch);
setupAxiosInterceptors(
  () => actions.clearAuthentication('login.error.unauthorized')
);

const rootEl = document.getElementById('root');
const render = Component =>
  ReactDOM.render(
    <AppContainer>
      <Provider store={store}>
        <div>
          ...
          {devTools}
          <Component />
        </div>
      </Provider>
    </AppContainer>,
    rootEl
  );

render(AppComponent);
...
```

- `app.tsx`: This is our main application component. We declare the React router and the main application UI structure here:

```
...
export class App extends React.Component<IAppProps> {
  componentDidMount() {
    this.props.getSession();
  }

  handleLogout = () => {
    this.props.logout();
  };

  render() {
    const paddingTop = '60px';
    return (
      <Router>
        <div className="app-container" style={{ paddingTop }}>
          <Header
            ...
          />
          <div className="container-fluid view-container" id="app-
view-container">
            <Card className="jh-card">
              <AppRoutes />
            </Card>
            <Footer />
          </div>
          <ModalContainer />
        </div>
      </Router>
    );
  }
}
...
```

- `routes.tsx`: The application's main parent routes are defined here and they are imported in the `app.tsx` from here.

- `config`: This is where framework level configurations are done:
    - `axios-interceptor.ts`: HTTP interceptors are configured here. This is where the JWT tokens are set to requests and errors are handled.
    - `constants.ts`: Application constants.
    - `*-middleware.ts`: Error, Notification, and Logging middleware for Redux are configured here.
    - `store.ts`: Redux store configuration is done here. Middlewares are registered during this stage.

The order of the middlewares in the array is important as they act like a pipeline, passing actions from one middleware to another as shown here:

```
const defaultMiddlewares = [
  thunkMiddleware,
  errorMiddleware,
  notificationMiddleware,
  promiseMiddleware(),
  loadingBarMiddleware(),
  loggerMiddleware
];
```

    - `translation.ts`: i18n-related configurations are done here.
- `entities`: The entity modules are present here.
- `modules`: Application UI modules are here:
    - `account`: Account pages like settings, password reset, and so on are here
    - `administration`: The admin screens like metric, health, user-management, and so on are here
    - `home`: Home screen of the application
    - `login`: Login and logout components
- `shared`: Shared components and reducers:
    - `layout`: Layout related components like header, footer, and so on
    - `model`: Typescript model for entities

- reducers: shared reducers used by the application:
    - authentication.ts: This is for authentication-related actions and reducers. Let's use the LOGIN action. The action accepts username, password, and rememberMe and dispatches the ACTION_TYPES.LOGIN with an asynchronous payload from an HTTP call to authenticate our credentials. We use the **async/await** feature from ES7 to avoid complex callbacks here. The result from the dispatch is obtained from when we extract the JWT bearerToken and store it in the local or session storage of the browser based on the remember me setting passed. The dispatch of ACTION_TYPES.LOGIN will trigger the appropriate case in the reducer based on the status of the promise:

```
...

export const ACTION_TYPES = {
  LOGIN: 'authentication/LOGIN',
  ...
};

const initialState = {
  ...
};

// Reducer
export default (state = initialState, action) => {
  switch (action.type) {
    case REQUEST(ACTION_TYPES.LOGIN):
    case REQUEST(ACTION_TYPES.GET_SESSION):
      return {
        ...state,
        loading: true
      };
    case FAILURE(ACTION_TYPES.LOGIN):
      return {
        ...initialState,
        errorMessage: action.payload,
        showModalLogin: true,
        loginError: true
      };
```

```
    ...
    case SUCCESS(ACTION_TYPES.LOGIN):
      return {
        ...state,
        loading: false,
        loginError: false,
        showModalLogin: false,
        loginSuccess: true
      };
    ...
    default:
      return state;
  }
};
...
export const login =
  (username, password, rememberMe = false) => async
(dispatch, getState) => {
  const result = await dispatch({
    type: ACTION_TYPES.LOGIN,
    payload: axios.post('/api/authenticate', {
username, password, rememberMe })
  });
  const bearerToken =
result.value.headers.authorization;
  if (bearerToken && bearerToken.slice(0, 7) ===
'Bearer ') {
    const jwt = bearerToken.slice(7,
bearerToken.length);
    if (rememberMe) {
      Storage.local.set('jhi-authenticationToken',
jwt);
    } else {
      Storage.session.set('jhi-authenticationToken',
jwt);
    }
  }
  dispatch(getSession());
};
...
```

- `util`: Utility functions.

The folder structure of the unit test code is also quite similar:

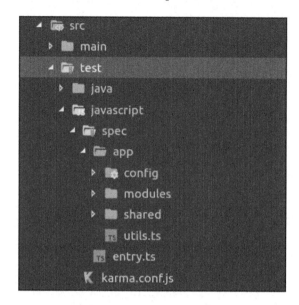

Generating an entity with React client side

Let's see how we can create an entity using the JHipster entity generator with a React client side. We will create a simple Employee entity with the name, age, and date of birth fields:

1. Open a Terminal and navigate to the folder of the React app and run `jhipster entity employee`.
2. Create the fields one by one, select yes for the question **Do you want to add a field to your entity?,** and start filling in the field name for the next question, **What is the name of your field?**
3. Select **String** as the field type for the next question, **What is the type of your field?**
4. For the question **Which validation rules do you want to add?,** choose **Required** for name field and proceed.
5. Continue the process for the following fields. `age` and `dob`. `age` are of type Integer and `dob` is of type Instant.
6. When asked again, **Do you want to add a field to your entity?,** choose no.
7. For the next question, **Do you want to add a relationship to another entity?,** choose yes.

8. Provide `user` as the name of the other entity and as the name of the relationship for the following questions.
9. For the next question, **What is the type of the relationship?,** let's create a one-to-one relationship with the user.
10. Choose no for the next question and no again when asked to add another relationship.
11. For the following questions, select the default options and proceed.

The command will produce the following console output:

```
Using JHipster version installed globally
Executing jhipster:entity employee
Options:

The entity employee is being created.

...

================== Employee ==================
Fields
name (String) required
age (Integer)
dob (Instant)

Relationships
user (User) one-to-one

? Do you want to use separate service class for your business
logic? No, the REST controller should use the repository directly
? Do you want pagination on your entity? No
```

JHipster will generate the entity and run Prettier and the webpack build.

12. If your server is not running, start it in a Terminal by running `./mvnw`. If it is already running, then just compile the new code by running `./mvnw compile`, and Spring DevTools will restart the app automatically.

13. Start BrowserSync in another Terminal by running `yarn start` and check the employee entity we just created:

14. Create an entity to check everything works fine:

For the entity we created, JHipster generated/updated the following files:

```
Everything is configured, generating the entity...

   create .jhipster/Employee.json
   create src/main/resources/config/liquibase/changelog/20180304193534_added_entity_Employee.xml
   create src/main/resources/config/liquibase/changelog/20180304193534_added_entity_constraints_Employee.xml
   create src/main/java/com/jhipsterbook/demo/domain/Employee.java
   create src/main/java/com/jhipsterbook/demo/repository/EmployeeRepository.java
   create src/main/java/com/jhipsterbook/demo/web/rest/EmployeeResource.java
   create src/test/java/com/jhipsterbook/demo/web/rest/EmployeeResourceIntTest.java
 conflict src/main/resources/config/liquibase/master.xml
? Overwrite src/main/resources/config/liquibase/master.xml? overwrite this and all others
    force src/main/resources/config/liquibase/master.xml
    force src/main/java/com/jhipsterbook/demo/config/CacheConfiguration.java
   create src/main/webapp/app/entities/employee/employee-delete-dialog.tsx
   create src/main/webapp/app/entities/employee/employee-detail.tsx
   create src/main/webapp/app/entities/employee/employee-dialog.tsx
   create src/main/webapp/app/entities/employee/employee.tsx
   create src/main/webapp/app/entities/employee/employee.reducer.ts
   create src/main/webapp/app/shared/model/employee.model.ts
   create src/main/webapp/app/entities/employee/index.tsx
    force src/main/webapp/app/entities/index.tsx
    force src/main/webapp/app/shared/reducers/index.ts
    force src/main/webapp/app/shared/layout/header/header.tsx
   create src/main/webapp/i18n/en/employee.json
    force src/main/webapp/i18n/en/global.json
   create src/main/webapp/i18n/zh-cn/employee.json
    force src/main/webapp/i18n/zh-cn/global.json
```

On the React client side, we have the following files:

```
src/main/webapp/app/entities/employee/employee-delete-dialog.tsx
src/main/webapp/app/entities/employee/employee-detail.tsx
src/main/webapp/app/entities/employee/employee-dialog.tsx
src/main/webapp/app/entities/employee/employee.tsx
src/main/webapp/app/entities/employee/employee.reducer.ts
src/main/webapp/app/shared/model/employee.model.ts
src/main/webapp/app/entities/employee/index.tsx
```

The `index.ts` file declares the routes for the entity:

```
    <Switch>
      <Route exact path={match.url} component={Employee} />
      <ModalRoute exact parentPath={match.url} path={`${match.url}/new`}
        component={EmployeeDialog} />
      <ModalRoute exact parentPath={match.url}
  path={`${match.url}/:id/delete`}
        component={EmployeeDeleteDialog} />
      <ModalRoute exact parentPath={match.url}
```

```
path={`${match.url}/:id/edit`}
        component={EmployeeDialog} />
      <Route exact path={`${match.url}/:id`} component={EmployeeDetail} />
    </Switch>
```

employee.reducer.ts declares the actions and reducer for the entity, for example, let's use the action and reducer to create an entity. The createEntity action dispatches the ACTION_TYPES.CREATE_EMPLOYEE with the HTTP payload and metadata for notifications. Once the HTTP request resolves, we dispatch the getEntities action to fetch the updated entity list.

The reducer is common for create and update actions. Let's take a look at the create action and reducer:

```
...
export const ACTION_TYPES = {
  ...
  CREATE_EMPLOYEE: 'employee/CREATE_EMPLOYEE',
  ...
};

const initialState = {
  ...
};

// Reducer
export default (state = initialState, action) => {
  switch (action.type) {
    ...
    case REQUEST(ACTION_TYPES.CREATE_EMPLOYEE):
    ...
      return {
        ...
      };
    ...
    case FAILURE(ACTION_TYPES.CREATE_EMPLOYEE):
    ...
      return {
        ...
      };
    ...
    case SUCCESS(ACTION_TYPES.CREATE_EMPLOYEE):
    case SUCCESS(ACTION_TYPES.UPDATE_EMPLOYEE):
      return {
        ...
      };
    ...
```

```
      default:
        return state;
    }
};

const apiUrl = SERVER_API_URL + '/api/employees';
...

export const createEntity: ICrudPutAction = entity => async dispatch => {
  const result = await dispatch({
    type: ACTION_TYPES.CREATE_EMPLOYEE,
    meta: {
      successMessage: messages.DATA_CREATE_SUCCESS_ALERT,
      errorMessage: messages.DATA_UPDATE_ERROR_ALERT
    },
    payload: axios.post(apiUrl, entity)
  });
  dispatch(getEntities());
  return result;
};
...
```

employee.tsx, employee-dialog.tsx, employee-detail.tsx, and employee-delete-dialog.tsx declare the entity listing, entity model dialog, entity detail, and entity delete dialog respectively. Let's look at employee.tsx, for example. We define the type for the props using a TypeScript interface, IEmployeeProps, which is passed as the generic for the React.Component type. We trigger the actions to fetch entities and users when our component mounts using the componentDidMount lifecycle method. The render method returns the JSX for the UI.

The component is connected to the Redux store using the higher-order component. Let's take a look:

```
...
export interface IEmployeeProps {
  getEntities: ICrudGetAllAction;
  employees: any[];
  getusers: ICrudGetAllAction;
  match: any;
}

export class Employee extends React.Component<IEmployeeProps> {
  componentDidMount() {
    this.props.getEntities();
    this.props.getusers();
  }
```

```
  render() {
    ...
  }
}

const mapStateToProps = storeState => ({
  employees: storeState.employee.entities
});

const mapDispatchToProps = { getusers, getEntities };

export default connect(mapStateToProps, mapDispatchToProps)(Employee);
```

The other components also follow a similar approach. Codewise React code has much less boilerplate and is more concise compared to Angular.

Summary

In this chapter, we learned general concepts about React, Redux, and other libraries on the React ecosystem. We also learned how to create a React app using JHipster and generated entities for it. We saw how we can make use of TypeScript with React and also walked through the generated code. We also ran and tested our created application. In the next chapter, we will conclude the book with best practices from the JHipster community and next steps to make use of what you've learned so far.

14
Best Practices with JHipster

In the previous chapters of the book, we learned about JHipster and the various tools and technologies it supports in detail. These are the things we have learned so far:

- We learned to develop monolithic and microservice applications. We also learned about differences in the architecture and reasons to choose one over the other.
- We created entities using JDL, and we customized the generated applications for our business needs.
- We created a CI-CD setup using Jenkins.
- We deployed the monolith application to the Heroku cloud
- We deployed the microservice architecture to the Google cloud using Kubernetes and Docker.
- We learned about Spring Framework, Spring Boot, Angular, React, Docker, and much more.

In this chapter, we will see what steps to take next and use what you have learned from this book, and we will also talk about some of the best practices, tips, tricks, and suggestions from the JHipster community. As core contributors of JHipster, we will also provide some insights and lessons learned by us in this chapter. The following are some of the topics that we will touch upon:

- The next steps to pursue
- The best practices to keep in mind
- Using JHipster modules

The next steps to pursue

JHipster supports a lot of technologies and learning about all of them would require an insane amount of time and effort; it cannot be done in a single book. Each technology supported would require a book on its own to learn and master it. If you are already familiar with the core concepts of web development, you will have a fairly good idea how a JHipster application works by now. We hope this book gave you a good introduction to the technologies and JHipster itself. But this in itself isn't sufficient; you will have to keep learning more to become a master. The following are some of the tasks that you can pursue to hone your skills in web development using JHipster further. But, before that, we would recommend that you learn more about Spring Framework and the Angular/React ecosystem to complement what you have learned in this book.

Adding a shopping cart for the application

In `Chapter 5`, *Customization and Further Development*, we saw how the generated application can be customized to make it look and behave like an e-commerce website. As mentioned there, it is not enough to make the application truly usable. The following are some of the features that you can try to implement to make the application more feature complete:

1. Add a simple shopping cart feature on the client-side:
    1. Create a `ProductOrder` object to hold the `OrderItems`. The `ProductOrder` is related to the Customer so tag it to the customer using details of the currently logged-in user.
    2. Add an **add to cart** button to the product items in the list. On clicking the button, create a new `OrderItem` for the Product and add the `OrderItem` to the `ProductOrder`'s `OrderItems` array. If the same product is clicked more than once, increase the quantity attribute of the existing `OrderItem`. Add a shopping cart dialog to list down all the `OrderItems` added to the `ProductOrder`. It can use a similar listing UI to the products, or a simple table to show the product, total price, and quantity.
    3. Add a `view cart` button to the product list page to view the shopping cart dialog.

2. Add an order now feature:
    1. Add an order now button to the product list page.
    2. On clicking the button, send the `ProductOrder` to the REST API to create a new `ProductOrder`, use the `product-order.service.ts` for this.
    3. At the backend, modify the save method of `ProductOrderService.java` to create an Invoice and Shipment for the `ProductOrder` and save them all.
    4. Let us assume that we accept cash on delivery so let us skip integrating with a payment gateway for now.

3. Send an order confirmation to the customer:
    1. JHipster comes with mail configuration and templates out of the box. You can configure your own SMTP server details in `src/main/resources/config/application-*.yml`. Refer to `http://www.jhipster.tech/tips/011_tip_configuring_email_in_jhipster.html` for instructions on how to configure popular SMTP services.
    2. Create a new email template in `src/main/resources/mails` for order confirmation. Provide the details of products, total price, and quantity in the email.
    3. Use the provided `sendEmailFromTemplate` method in `MailService.java` to send the email when an Invoice is successfully created.

4. Create a customer profile when registering a new user:
    1. Add fields to the registration page and create customer entity for every user from the details automatically.

Try to apply the changes to the microservice application as well.

Improving end-to-end tests

In Chapter 6, *Testing and Continuous Integration*, we saw that some of the e2e tests were commented out due to the difficulty in generating tests for an entity with a required relationship. Try to fix the tests with the following approach:

1. Add a method to delete entities after creation, similar to what we saw in Chapter 6, *Testing and Continuous Integration*, for the customer entity spec.

2. Uncomment the commented out e2e tests in the files under `src/test/javascript/e2e/entities`.

3. Navigate the protractor to the related entity page and create a new item. If the related entity has required relationships then follow the same approach and nest them until all the required entities are in place. This can be done in a `beforeAll` method of the test as well.

4. Now go back to the entity under test and see whether the test works fine.

5. Once the test is complete, delete the created entities in the `afterAll` method of the test.

6. Explore whether you can automate the creation of an entity item on the page object of the entity and use it when needed.

Improving the CI/CD pipeline

In `Chapter 6`, *Testing and Continuous Integration*, when we created the `Jenkinsfile` using the CI/CD sub-generator, we commented out the deployment stage. Re-enable it and check whether the application is deployed to Heroku when you make new commits:

- See if you can add e2e tests to the pipeline.
- If your application is on GitHub, try to add Travis to the project using the ci-cd sub-generator.

Building a JHipster module

JHipster has two mechanisms to extend its features:

- A modules system, which lets users build their own Yeoman generators (`http://www.jhipster.tech/modules/creating-a-module/`) to complement JHipster
- A new blueprint mechanism introduced with JHipster 5 to customize required parts of the code generated by JHipster

The difference between a **module** and a **blueprint** is that a blueprint lets you override certain parts of the generated application while JHipster scaffolds the remaining parts. For example, a blueprint can override the client-side code alone, while the server side is generated by JHipster. A module, on the other hand, can only change what is generated by JHipster and hence is more suitable for adding complementing features on top of the ones created by JHipster.

Try to build a module to add a simple page to your application.

You can use the JHipster module generator (`https://github.com/jhipster/generator-jhipster-module`) to scaffold a new module.

Best practices to keep in mind

Over the years, the JHipster community has identified and adopted a lot of best practices from the technologies and tools it supports and from the general technical community. While JHipster has tried to follow these best practices in the code it creates, the following are some best practices, tips, and tricks that you as a user should follow.

Choosing a client-side framework

When using JHipster you have an option to choose between Angular and React as the client-side framework. Do not choose something just for its hype, choose based on your requirement, team composition, and familiarity:

- If you come from a heavy Java/Spring background, then Angular will be much easier to follow and work with
- If your application requires heavy state management and shared state, then React would be a more natural fit
- If you are planning to build a native mobile client for your application then the more mature React is a good choice for this space, with React Native allowing you to reuse a lot of code between your web and mobile application
- If your application depends heavily on HTML pages produced by a design team or a third-party, then Angular will be much easier to integrate than React

If you need a lot of widgets that are not part of standard Bootstrap, then use an existing widget library, such as PrimeNG or VMware Clarity, rather than assembling widgets from different origins. However, if you need only a few more widgets on top of Bootstrap, then stick to Bootstrap and use a Bootstrap compatible widget for Angular or React.

Regardless of what you choose, follow the guidelines and best practices from that project's community.

Choosing a database option

JHipster provides support for many kinds of databases, ranging from SQL to NoSQL. The following are some considerations when choosing a DB:

- For most cases, a SQL DB would be more than sufficient, hence if you do not see any reason to go with other NoSQL solutions, stick to SQL and choose from MySQL, Postgres, Oracle, MariaDB, and MS SQL:
    - If you are on an enterprise with Oracle or MS SQL subscriptions, then it would make sense to choose them as you would benefit from the support and enterprise features provided
    - If you need to store and query a lot of JSON data, then Postgres offers the best JSON support with full-text search capabilities
    - For most simple use cases, MySQL or MariaDB will suffice
    - Always choose a second-level Hibernate cache when working with a SQL DB
    - When choosing a development database for SQL:
        - Choose an H2 file DB if you want a simple development setup with persistent data.
        - Choose the same DB as the production DB if you want faster restarts and your persistent data doesn't need to be wiped every now and then. If you are using the provided Docker images, then wiping data will not be an issue.
        - Choose an H2 in-memory DB if you do not want any persistent data during development and would like a clean state on each restart

- If your use case requires a lot of heavy data reads/writes, and if the data is not very relational, then Cassandra would be a perfect fit, as it is distributed and can work under extremely heavy loads.
- For a normal, non-relational data structure, MongoDB may be sufficient. You could also use Postgres as a NoSQL JSON store if needed.
- If you need enterprise support for NoSQL, CouchBase is a good option.
- Use Elasticsearch along with the primary DB for full-text search. If you only need simple filtering, use the JPA filtering option provided. Refer to: `http://www.jhipster.tech/entities-filtering/`.

Architecture considerations

We have already discussed choosing a microservice or monolithic architecture in `Chapter 1`, *Introduction to Modern Web Application Development*. Here are some more points when it comes to architecture:

- Don't use a microservice architecture if you're a small team. Microservices are about scaling teams more than anything. It's often easier to break up your monolith than start with microservices.
- Use asynchronous messaging in your monolith if you think you may need to refactor to microservices in the future. JHipster provides support for Apache Kafka, which is a good solution for asynchronous messaging.

   Asynchronous messaging is the best way of building stateless systems. It is important in a microservice architecture as you might often want communications to be stateless and non-blocking. Some of the popular solutions for this are Apache Kafka (`http://kafka.apache.org/`), RabbitMQ (`https://www.rabbitmq.com/`), and gRPC (`https://grpc.io`). ReactiveX (`http://reactivex.io/`) and Spring Reactor (`http://projectreactor.io/`) are popular abstractions for working with asynchronous systems. Asynchronous messaging also makes the systems loosely coupled.

- If you intend to expose an API to a third party, do *API first* development. We now have a good workflow to do it with Swagger Codegen. Refer to `http://www.jhipster.tech/doing-api-first-development/` for more info.

- When doing communication between microservices with REST, don't put interface code in a shared package; it would tightly couple APIs to their clients, thus arriving at a distributed monolith.
- With JHipster, it is possible to split the client and server. Refer to `http://www.jhipster.tech/separating-front-end-and-api/`. However, think twice before separating them, as it will require you to open up CORS, which makes the security more vulnerable, and such architecture brings its own issues. So do this only if you have a good reason to do so.
- Use DTOs at the service layer so that you can aggregate entities and define a better API without exposing entities to the client. You will have to enable the service layer for your entities to use this with JHipster.
- Learn the technology stack of your application before you start development.
- Make yourself familiar with the provided toolbelt, such as build tools (Maven/Gradle/Webpack), BrowserSync, and so on.

Security considerations

Security is one of the most important aspects of any application, and you should consider the following when choosing a security mechanism:

- For most use cases JWT authentication will be sufficient, so stick to that if you are not sure
- If you want single-sign-on in your application, use OAuth 2.0 / OIDC rather than trying to make JWT or session authentication work as an SSO solution
- If you already have Keycloak or Okta set up in your company, choose OAuth 2.0/OIDC and connect to them
- Choose session-based authentication only if you want a stateful authentication

Deployment and maintenance

There are a lot of good practices here; some of the important ones are:

- Docker is a must-have for integration testing of microservices, but going into production with Docker is not easy so use an orchestration tool, such as Kubernetes, for that.

- Run a prod build immediately after the application is generated and deploy to prod immediately while your app is still very simple. This will help ease any deployment issues, as you will be sure that the app works fine out of the box.
- The prod build is quite different from the dev build when it comes to the client side, as the resources are minified and optimized. When adding any frontend code, libraries always verify the prod build as well.
- Always run end-to-end protractor tests with the prod profile.
- Embrace the embedded servlet engine and forget about deploying to a JEE server such as WebLogic, WebSphere, JBoss, and so on. The artifacts produced are executable and have an embedded Undertow server.

 Did you know that Java EE is being renamed to Jakarta EE? Refer to `https://www.infoq.com/news/2018/03/java-ee-becomes-jakarta-ee` for more info.

- Upgrade often using the JHipster upgrade sub-generator. This will ensure the tools and technologies you use are up to date and secure.
- Remove all secrets from `application-prod.yml` and use placeholders to inject values from the command line or environment variables. Never put any secrets or passwords in code or config files.

General best practices

In general, these are some best practices you should consider:

- If you start creating entities using the entity sub-generator, then use `export-jdl` and switch to JDL once you have more than a handful of entities.
- Generate your application without any modules first and add required modules only when the need arises.
- Evaluate a module carefully before adding it. Make sure it supports the stack you have chosen.
- Follow each underlying technology's *best practices*. Angular best practices, Spring best practices, and so on. Change something only if there is a good reason to do so.

- Use the provided library versions on the client side and server side. It's hard work to have them all working together, so stick to them. Update them when JHipster updates them or only if you really need to fix a bug or a security issue.
- Follow the workflows provided by JHipster. They are here to help you. There is usually a very good reason to use them in the recommended way. Read the JHipster documentation before looking for help outside.
- You have a great working environment out of the box; don't break it.
    - Frontend and backend updates are automatic and fast using live reload. Make use of them.
    - Production deployment is easy using the provided sub-generators.
- Use the provided sub-generators for the cloud platform you are deploying to.
- Git is your friend. Commit each time you add a module or an entity, or when using a sub-generator. Every mistake (including in the database) should be easy to rollback with Git.

Using JHipster modules

JHipster modules and blueprints are a great way to add more features and functionality to your generated code. There are many modules (55 at the time of writing) available to choose from in the JHipster marketplace (`http://www.jhipster.tech/modules/marketplace`), and you can also build your own modules to suit your needs. Some of the modules worth noticing are as follows:

- **Ignite JHipster**: This provides a React Native boilerplate for JHipster apps. An ideal way to kickstart your React Native application using JHipster as the backend.
- **Entity Audit**: This module enables entity audits. It uses Hibernate audit hooks to create a custom audit for entity CRUD operations. It also provides Javers as the auditing mechanism instead of the custom Hibernate auditing. It also provides a nice UI to view the audits in an Angular application. It will enable auditing for new entities as well as existing entities.
- **Ionic**: This provides an Ionic client for JHipster apps. It is an ideal solution if you want to create mobile applications with a JHipster backend and Angular frontend with Ionic.
- **Swagger CLI**: Module provides support for generating Swagger clients for a JHipster application.

- **gRPC**: This module generates gRPC reactive endpoints for a JHipster application. It supports entities as well, and is an ideal choice if you want a non-blocking reactive API for your JHipster application.
- **VueJS**: This module provides VueJS support for JHipster applications. It creates minimal boilerplate to start client-side development for JHipster apps using VueJS.

Take a look at the following steps:

1. To use a JHipster module first install it using `npm i -g generator-<module-name>` or `yarn add global generator-<module-name>`.
2. Once installed, go into the JHipster application directory and execute `yo <module-name>` to initiate the module and follow the prompts.

Contributing to JHipster

One of the best ways to learn JHipster and the technologies it supports is by contributing to JHipster directly. Refer to the contribution guide (`https://github.com/jhipster/generator-jhipster/blob/master/CONTRIBUTING.md`) for details about setting up JHipster for development.

You can contribute to the project in many ways; some of them are as follows:

- If you find a bug, enter an issue in the GitHub project (`https://github.com/jhipster/generator-jhipster`), follow the guidelines in the issue template, run `jhipster info`, and provide steps to reproduce. You can also try to fix the issue yourself and submit a PR if you're successful.
- Work on open issues and feature requests. This way you will learn the internals of JHipster and the technologies used along the way.
- Answer JHipster related questions on Stack Overflow (`https://stackoverflow.com/questions/tagged/jhipster`).

Summary

Our journey together through JHipster and full stack development has come to an end. In this chapter, we learned about many best practices identified by the JHipster community. Try to complete the assignments in the *Next steps to pursue* section, as it will help you to apply what you have learned and will help you understand the concepts better.

We hope you have had a fabulous learning experience, and hope what you have learned from the book about JHipster will help you with your next project.

Follow @java_hipster on Twitter so you can see when new releases come out and security vulnerabilities are revealed.

If you have questions or issues regarding JHipster, post your questions to Stack Overflow (https://stackoverflow.com/questions/tagged/jhipster) and add the jhipster tag. The team will be notified and will be happy to help!

Other Books You May Enjoy

If you enjoyed this book, you may be interested in these other books by Packt:

Java EE 8 and Angular
Prashant Padmanabhan

ISBN: 978-1-78829-120-0

- Write CDI-based code in Java EE 8 applications
- Build an understanding of Microservices and what they mean in Java EE context
- Use Docker to build and run a microservice application
- Use configuration options to work effectively with JSON documents
- Understand asynchronous task handling and writing REST API clients
- Explore the fundamentals of TypeScript, which sets the foundation for working on Angular projects
- Use Angular CLI to add and manage new features
- Use JSON Web tokens to secure Angular applications against malicious attacks

Hands-On Full Stack Development with Angular 5 and Firebase
Uttam Agarwal

ISBN: 978-1-78829-873-5

- Understand the core concepts of Angular framework
- Create web pages with Angular as front end and Firebase as back end
- Develop a real-time social networking application
- Make your application live with Firebase hosting
- Engage your user using Firebase cloud messaging
- Grow your application with Google analytics
- Learn about Progressive Web App

Leave a review - let other readers know what you think

Please share your thoughts on this book with others by leaving a review on the site that you bought it from. If you purchased the book from Amazon, please leave us an honest review on this book's Amazon page. This is vital so that other potential readers can see and use your unbiased opinion to make purchasing decisions, we can understand what our customers think about our products, and our authors can see your feedback on the title that they have worked with Packt to create. It will only take a few minutes of your time, but is valuable to other potential customers, our authors, and Packt. Thank you!

Index

Made in the USA
Monee, IL
31 October 2020